Luminos is the Open Access monograph publishing program from UC Press. Luminos provides a framework for preserving and reinvigorating monograph publishing for the future and increases the reach and visibility of important scholarly work. Titles published in the UC Press Luminos model are published with the same high standards for selection, peer review, production, and marketing as those in our traditional program. www.luminosoa.org

The Endurance of Palestinian Political Factions

The Endurance of Palestinian Political Factions

An Everyday Perspective from Nahr el-Bared Camp

Perla Issa

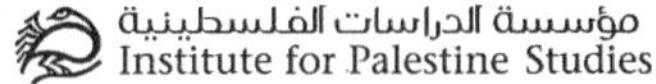

UNIVERSITY OF CALIFORNIA PRESS

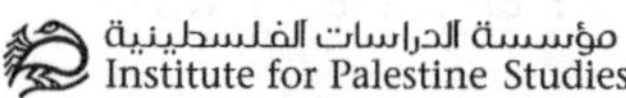

Institute for Palestine Studies

The Institute for Palestine Studies is the oldest institute in the world
devoted exclusively to documentation, research, analysis, and publication
on Palestinian affairs and the Arab-Israeli conflict. It was established in
1963 as an independent, nonprofit Arab institute unaffiliated with any
political organization or government.

This work expresses its authors' opinions, which do not necessarily reflect
the views or positions of the Institute.

University of California Press
Oakland, California

Suggested citation: Issa, P. *The Endurance of Palestinian Political Factions:
An Everyday Perspective from Nahr el-Bared Camp*. Oakland: University of
California Press, 2021. DOI: https://doi.org/10.1525/luminos.107

Library of Congress Cataloging-in-Publication Data
Names: Issa, Perla, author.
Title: The endurance of Palestinian political factions : an everyday
    perspective from Nahr el-Bared camp / Perla Issa.
Description: Oakland, California : University of California Press, [2021] |
    Series: New directions in palestinian studies; 3 | Includes
    bibliographical references and index.
Identifiers: LCCN 2020057476 (print) | LCCN 2020057477 (ebook) |
    ISBN 9780520380592 (paperback) | ISBN 9780520380608 (ebook)
Subjects: LCSH: Nahr al-Bārid (Refugee camp) | Refugees, Palestinian
    Arab—Social aspects—Lebanon.
Classification: LCC HV640.5.P36 I87 2021 (print) | LCC HV640.5.P36
    (ebook) | DDC 325/.21095692—dc23
LC record available at https://lccn.loc.gov/2020057476
LC ebook record available at https://lccn.loc.gov/2020057477

Manufactured in the United States of America

29 28 27 26 25 24 23 22 21
10 9 8 7 6 5 4 3 2 1

CONTENTS

From the Series Editor

There was a time when the political imagination of Palestinians revolved tightly around "factions" such as Fateh, PFLP, and DFLP. So much so, that it was impossible to disentangle the personal from the political. Relationships—familial, local, economic, romantic, and so on—always mediated politics and the politics of factions coursed through these relationships like an electrical current. I recall as a faculty member at Birzeit University in the early 1980s that almost every student, staff, teacher, or administrator—whether they wanted to or not, or whether it was true or not—was identified as affiliated (*maḥsūb*), formally or informally, to one faction or another. Far more often than not, these markers were based not on activism or ideological position, but on that person's interactions with family, friends, colleagues, lovers, and enemies. Inversely, factions were incubators for the production and reproduction of social relations that formed them in the first place; or so it seemed at that time.

Among the population of the Palestinian territories conquered by Israel in 1967 (West Bank, East Jerusalem, and Gaza), this hyper-political condition deepened and culminated in the first Intifada (1987–1993), then was almost immediately eviscerated by the imposition of a new political order based on the Oslo Accords. In Lebanon, the fall of the factions came a decade earlier with the 1982 Israeli invasion, which expelled the PLO and destroyed most of its political, social, economic, and cultural institutions. Young men with Kalashnikovs who had long dominated public spaces in the refugee camps faded away and the organizations they belonged to turned into pitiful shadows of their former selves. The end of the armed struggle (*thawra*) phase of the Palestinian national movement also meant, or so it seemed at that time, the end of the PLO factions that embodied it. Henceforth, nary a kind word could be heard about the factions in the Palestinian refugee camps of Lebanon.

Yet, almost four decades later, the monopoly of factions over political representation in the camps continues to endure even though they have little or no political legitimacy. How is this possible? Explaining continuity is a much harder analytical nut to crack than accounting for change. Through microstudies of family home life in Nahr al-Bared refugee camp in Lebanon, Perla Issa argues that this continuity is due to the double nature of factions. They are embedded social networks, but their daily practices create the effect of a separate bounded entity. In this intimate and long-term ethnographic study of quotidian acts, such as how people join factions and how aid is distributed, Issa maps out the ways power relations are produced in the process of demarcating a line between inside an organization and outside of it. Like a chameleon, the social relations are camouflaged and give the appearance of power, thus allowing discredited factions to remain central to political and social life.

The implications of Issa's theoretical frame, methodological approach, and empirical findings are significant for Palestinian studies. The past generation has witnessed a major expansion of what qualifies as "political" in narrating the history of Palestine and the Palestinians so as to include subaltern actors and the minutia of everyday life. Rosemary Sayigh—and the many excellent anthropologists of camp life in Lebanon, Syria, Jordan, West Bank, and Gaza that built on her work—have cleared a wide path for this expansion. Issa's is the first granular study of how political factions are produced and one of the rare few on Nahr al-Bared camp, which was viciously destroyed in 2007 then partially rebuilt.

The intellectual and political implications of Issa's study are also relevant to those seeking to understand the internal impasse of Palestinian politics in certain periods, such as the centrality of discredited political formations during the Mandate period and, once again, in the post-Oslo era. How is it, for example, that the Ramallah-based Palestinian Authority has still been able to dominate political life in the West Bank over the past generation even though it enjoys little popular support? The endurance of what appears to be discrete political structures located outside society long after their shelf life has expired is, moreover, a global phenomenon. As Issa poignantly relates, a particularly relevant example is the factional sectarian system in Lebanon, which has survived one of the most massive uprisings in the country's history in 2019, even though it has been publicly discredited and hated since the outbreak of the civil war in 1975.

The New Directions in Palestinian Studies (NDPS) book series centers "ordinary" Palestinians in knowledge production projects that engage the Palestinian condition as a site for the production of theory. Issa's book joins the two previous books in the NDPS series—*Palestinian Chicago*, a study of diaspora activism by Loren Lybarger, and *Al-Haq*, a global history by Lynn Welchman about Palestine's pioneering and internationally influential human rights organization—in exploring how the Palestinian experience can help us understand, mobilize, and effect change in a world still struggling to find a decolonial political compass long after the demise of the third world project of the Bandung era.

ACKNOWLEDGMENTS

My biggest fortune in life has always been the people I have met. The writing of this book is no exception. I would like to thank first and foremost the people of Nahr el-Bared camp, and my host family in particular. While they remain anonymous, they have been my best and most patient teachers. I was humbled by their strength, inspired by their laughter, and made a better person by their example. I hope one day I can be a positive force in their lives the way they have strengthened mine. This book is dedicated to them.

Furthermore, I feel a profound sense of gratitude towards my mentors, whose encouragement and faith in my abilities were instrumental throughout this project. Michael Dumper helped me through the early stages of my research. He patiently provided the freedom to probe many avenues of inquiry. Daniel Neep taught me what it means to stay with a problem, to push against my own limitations, and to savor the slow, and at times unexpected, rewards. He extended to me his intellect, labour, and time; I can never hope to repay the debt.

Friends and colleagues were instrumental in keeping me sane and providing me with much needed support to keep going forward when everything seemed to be going backwards. I would like to especially thank Ismael Sheikh Hassan, Hala Abou-Zaki, Rosemary Sayigh, Rochelle Davis, Nadya Hajj, Mariam Balhas, Hana Sleiman, Farah Salka, Polly Withers, Leen al-Habash, and Brown Carson. I would also like to acknowledge Ali Alloush, who graciously allowed me to use his photographs.

This project started as a PhD thesis and was funded by a Studentship from the Politics Department at Exeter University. I am grateful for this financial support. I am also thankful for the support that the Institute for Palestine Studies offered me as a Resident Researcher, which allowed me to dedicate time to turn my thesis into a book. Thanks go to Maher Charif, Muhammad Ali-Khalidi, Camille Mansour, and Khaled Farraj for their support. Furthermore this manuscript benefited from the Project on Middle East Political Science (POMEPS) book development workshop, which provided me with critical and helpful feedback that made a real difference in how I thought and wrote about my research. Parts of chapters 1, 3, and 4 previously appeared in "Rethinking Palestinian Political Factions," *Middle East Critique* 27, no. 3 (2018): 261–274, and are republished with permission of the journal. Parts of chapter 5 previously appeared in "Fracturing Communities: Aid Distribution in a Palestinian Refugee Camp," *Journal for Palestine Studies* 48, no. 3 (2019): 7–20, and are republished with the permission of the Institute for Palestine Studies. I would also like to thank the editors of the University of California Press's New Directions in Palestinian Studies series—Beshara Doumani, Samera Esmier, Rema Hammami, Rashid Khalidi, and Sherene Seikaly—for embracing the project. Thank you as well as to Executive Editor Niels Hooper, Project Editor Francisco Reinking, and Editorial Assistants Robin Manley and Madison Wetzell, and a special thanks to copyeditor Catherine Osborne, who helped in more than one way.

I would also like to acknowledge my family: my parents and sister. It is hard to truly assess the extent of their influence, as their contribution to my life goes well beyond what is possible for me to comprehend. Finally, I would like to thank my daughters Yasmina and Nai, who graciously endured while the making of this book took me away from them time and again.

NOTE ON TRANSLITERATION

I adopt the system of Arabic transliteration from the *International Journal of Middle East Studies.*

FIGURE 1. Boy in wheelbarrow, Nahr el-Bared camp. Photograph: Ali Alloush.

1

———

Introduction

"Empty Buildings"

After the departure of the PLO [in 1982] factions became empty buildings.

A Fatah veteran told me this once: if there was a building that was a charitable organization and used to help people a lot, or if it was for a good man, and this person died, [. . .] this doesn't mean that the building was still good, because there was a good man in it. So yes. This was how he explained it.

Palestinian refugees in Lebanon often referred to Palestinian political factions as buildings. For example, Palestinians talked of "entering a faction" (*dakhalit tanẓīm*) as if they were entering an edifice. Palestinians also referred to factionalized Palestinians as having a "back" (*ḍahir*). This expression was meant to indicate that factions provided a sort of protection to their members. This image of having something behind you, protecting you, was reminiscent of the walls of a building. Finally, they talked of a "political ceiling" (*sa'af siyāsī*) to indicate the hierarchy, or the vertical limitations within the factions. The notion of "entering," of a "back" and a "ceiling," pointed to an imagination where factions appeared as edifices. Visualizing factions as building-like structures is indeed appealing: it draws boundaries that separate faction members from non-members; it represents the hierarchy inside factions, with the rank and file at the bottom and the leadership at the top; it demarcates the faction from other factions, other buildings; and it helps explain how the faction exists even when the people "inside" change. In other words, the metaphor of a building-like structure illustrates how factions seem to exist separately from the people "inside" them.

This image of the faction as an entity with a life of its own is also evident in the academic literature on Palestinian politics. Factions are mostly viewed as autonomous bodies, studied as a whole and spoken of in the singular ("Fatah did this" or "Hamas declared that"). Factions are mostly examined through an analysis of party literature, the writings of party founders, and interviews with the leadership (e.g., Abu-Amr 1994; Broning 2013; Y. Sayigh 1997). In other words, they focus on the intentions, actions and words of the leadership and chart the founding, histories, ideologies, regional and international alliances, funding sources, and evolution of the factions throughout the years (Baumgarten 2005; Brynen 1990b; Cobban 1984; Cubert 1997; Gunning 2008; Hroub 2006; R. Khalidi 2006; Knudsen 2005; Milton-Edwards and Farrell 2010; Y. Sayigh 1997; Usher 2006). As such, the literature implies that it is possible to study factions without examining the practices of those who form their very core. With the exception of the leadership, studies of factions rarely examine the lives, ideas, actions, and desires of faction members; instead, they study factions as if they were shells, existing separately and independently from the people they are supposed to encompass. Very little ethnographic evidence documents how the abstract notion of factions takes concrete shape in the daily lives of Palestinian refugees in Lebanon, how Palestinians encounter factions, and whether factions retain their unitary appearance or disintegrate. As such, research on Palestinian political factions has failed to illuminate the quotidian practices of Palestinian refugees that tell us about the production and reproduction of factions in everyday life.

This lack of attention to the everyday interactions between Palestinian political factions and Palestinian refugees is even more puzzling when we realize how unpopular the factions are and how well-documented this unpopularity is. Indeed, numerous studies highlight the general dissatisfaction of Palestinian refugees towards Palestinian political factions (Frisch 2009; Khalili 2005; Kortam 2011; Peteet 1995; R. Sayigh 2001, 96; 2011; 2012; Suleiman 1999). They have been accused of factionalism (R. Sayigh 2012, 22), of corruption (Brynen 1995b, 25; R. Sayigh 2012, 22), and betrayal (Allan 2014; Khalili 2004; Peteet 1995). Some voice concern for the future of Palestinian factions in light of their inability to establish an independent Palestinian state (Broning 2013, 5), others call for new Palestinian political parties to form (Kuttab 2011), while others refer to them as failed national movements (Ghanem 2010). Despite such attention to the current dismal state of Palestinian political factions, the actual process through which discredited factions are produced and re-produced in everyday life remains largely unexplored.

This book is an ethnographic study of Palestinian political factions through an immersion in daily home life, carried out in Nahr el-Bared camp in the north of Lebanon. It probes two interrelated sets of questions. Firstly, it asks how unpopular and discredited factions are reproduced on a day-to-day basis. How do they remain the center of political life in the face of widespread condemnation? Suleiman (1999, 76) states that "one of the main challenges facing Palestinian society in the refugee camps of Lebanon is the lack of a political and social authority that is regarded by the Palestinians themselves, as well as by others, as their legitimate representative." The lack of meaningful representation not only affects the conduct in and future of peace negotiations, but also the daily lives of Palestinians world-wide; it compounds their existing problems. Even the simplest task of replacing a broken electrical generator in a refugee camp becomes complicated (Kortam 2011), not to mention finding solutions to major crises such as the destruction of Nahr el-Bared camp (Knudsen 2011). My research aims to understand the dynamics at play. How are factions maintaining a monopoly over political representation and camp organization even when they are delegitimized in refugees' eyes? Officially, the different political factions in the camps are divided along broad political stances vis-à-vis the "peace process," whether they support the Oslo accords or not, and whether they are Islamic or secular in nature. Are these broad political and ideological differences more important to the refugees than the resolution of their daily problems of water, electricity, education, and health?

Secondly, this work inquires into the ontological nature of factions. It asks how Palestinian political factions, which are clearly made of people, came to be imagined both in the academic literature and in everyday speech as "entities" or "buildings" with lives of their own, existing separately from the very people and practices they contain. Scholars routinely use a multitude of metaphors to refer to factions: they are called "actors," "players," "political bodies," or "political structures," and these in turn are ascribed actions, aspirations, intentions and identities. All of these metaphors point to an imagination where factions form particular "entities" that "exist" in their own right. These "actors" or "structures" are then studied through an examination of their ideologies, regional and international alliances, and sources of funding without examining the daily practices of those who form their very core—their members. For example, a study of seven major political factions in Palestine that aims to introduce the different parties to the readers does so by providing an overview of key historical developments to trace the ideological foundations of each faction, followed by biographies of key personalities, interviews with persons in positions of authority, excerpts from election programs and party communiqués, and finally organizational charts (Broning 2013). This study does not interview or refer to a single party member outside of the leadership, nor does it discuss what type of practices party members engage in. Palestinian political factions appear to exist independently from their members, which allows them to continue to exist even if they have no members. Indeed they become "empty buildings." Additionally, these buildings' defining characteristic is seen to be ideology. Scholars point out that Fatah is secular-nationalist, the Popular Front for the Liberation of Palestine (PFLP) and Democratic Front for the Liberation of Palestine (DFLP) are Marxist, while Hamas and Islamic Jihad are Islamic. In turn, the difference between the PFLP and the DFLP and between Hamas and Islamic Jihad is also explained as emanating from ideological differences, most notably from a different approach to militarism (Broning 2013; Hasso 2005) and *jihad* (Gupta and Mundra 2005; Milton-Edwards 1992; Abu-Amr 1994). This work questions this dominant understanding of Palestinian political factions. It asks, what is the ontological nature of factions?

In what sense can we say that factions are "entities" with lives of their own that are defined by ideology? And if indeed factions are not "actors" or "structures," then what are they? And why and how do they appear to be so if that is not their nature?

While the first set of questions—how unpopular and discredited political factions are reproduced in everyday life—was the initial drive behind this book, the second set of questions—how factions, which are clearly made of people, come to take on the appearance of a bounded structure defined by ideology that exists separately from the people it seeks to encompass—quickly came to the fore as I delved into my fieldwork. With time it became clear that the answers to these two sets of questions are closely intertwined. Through an examination of factions at the micro-level—the daily, mundane practices of Palestinian refugees in Nahr el-Bared camp—this book traces how factions are formed through local interpersonal relations imbued with high levels of trust, and how they take on the appearance of impersonal structures that exist separately and independently from those personal relations that form their very basis. In other words, this book explores how people coming together to form a political faction end up creating the appearance of a structure that can then be referred to in the singular as "Fatah did this" or "Hamas declared that," then studied by scholars as bodies through an examination of their ideologies, regional and international alliances, and sources of funding without examining the daily practices of the people involved in factional work. In contrast, this book, by focusing on everyday practices, argues that factions have a double nature: they are loose networks of people bound together by different degrees of trust and cohesion, yet they also appear as bounded structures defined by their stated ideologies. This book posits that it is precisely this double nature that allows unpopular and even despised factions to remain the center of political life.

A LATERAL APPROACH: EXAMINING FACTIONS THROUGH EVERYDAY LIFE

This study adopts an unconventional theoretical and methodological framework in the study of factions, what I refer to as a "lateral approach."[1] The book does not study factions based on their stated ideologies, publications or interviews with the leadership (the "top") (cf. Broning 2013; Cobban 1984; Cubert 1997; Gunning 2008; Hroub 2006), nor is it an ethnography based on what appears to be the "inside" of factions, such as factional offices, youth clubs, or associations (the "bottom") (cf. Hoigilt 2016; Jensen 2009; Roy 2011). Rather it explores how factions appear in the daily life of Palestinians, how refugees encounter them on a day-to-day basis. In other words, this study examines factions *laterally*, from what appears to be the "outside" of factions, from daily home life. By positioning myself on what appears to be "outside" of factions, I was able to look at how that very distinction comes into being, how factions appear as bounded structures, and how that line drawn between the "inside" and the "outside" produces power and allows discredited political factions to remain the center of political life in the face of widespread condemnation.

The "lateral approach" adopted by this study is largely inspired by the study of another "political structure" of great interest to both political scientists and anthropologists: the state. In doing so, I am not arguing that factions are like states, state-like, or quasi-states, nor am I ignoring the role the Lebanese state plays in the lives of Palestinian refugees. What I am arguing is that state literature helps me develop a novel analytical and methodological approach which provides me with fresh insights and allows me to denaturalize the nature of factions by investigating it through an exploration of everyday life.

The state has often been understood by international relations theorists to be an "actor," a "player," an "organ," or a "political structure" that exists "above" society and acts upon it. For example Asad (2004, 281) explains, "according to the modern concept, the state is an entity with a life of its own, distinct from both governors and governed." In other words the state is perceived to be an "entity" that exists separately and independently from those inside it (government employees) as well as those outside it (society at large), similarly to how Palestinian political factions are represented in academic scholarship and everyday speech. However, research on the state has gone a long way to question these assumptions and will help us develop an analytical and methodological way forward.[2]

Of particular relevance here is the argument that Timothy Mitchell (1988; 1990; 1991; 2002) has put forward regarding the "appearance of structure" of the state. Mitchell argues that the state *appears* to be a structure separate from society, due to the modern microphysical methods of order that Foucault (1977) calls discipline. Discipline refers to the meticulous organization of space, movement, position, and time sequences and the systematic methods of surveillance and inspection that were developed around the eighteenth and nineteenth centuries in factories, schools, prisons, hospitals, and government offices. Mitchell argues that modern disciplinary practices created a peculiar metaphysics, reordering the world into what appears to be two distinct entities: people and practices on one end and immaterial structures on the other.[3]

Mitchell illustrates his argument through the example of the army. The order, precision, and repetition of the disciplinary practices of the army, including the specific division of space, the regular timing, and the coordination of movements, all work to create "the effect of an apparatus apart from the men themselves, whose structure orders, contains, and controls them" (1991, 94). The army now appears as an "artificial machine" (92) that stands apart from the men and the practices that constitute it. This artificial machine is non-material, it cannot be touched, it is only represented through its soldiers, officers, emblems. . . . Mitchell contends that a similar two-dimensional effect is at work in other institutions of the state (such as the bureaucracy, organized schooling, and urban planning). This contributes "to constructing a world that appears to consist not of a *complex of social practices* but of a binary order: on the one hand individuals and their activities, on the other an inert structure that somehow stands apart from individuals, precedes them, and contains and gives a framework to their lives" (94, my emphasis). Reality seems to have a "two-dimensional form of individuals versus apparatus, practice versus institution, social life and its structure or society versus state."

The appearance of the state as an immaterial structure existing separately from society is therefore an effect of modern disciplinary practices. The state should not be studied as an actual structure but as "the powerful, metaphysical effect of practices that make such structures appear to exist" (Mitchell 1991, 94). By approaching the state as an effect Mitchell both acknowledges that the state *appears as a structure* and at the same time *accounts for its elusive nature*. Moreover, Mitchell insists that the appearance of separation of the state from society helps maintain a certain configuration of power. He argues that "the boundary of the state (or political system) *never marks a real exterior*. The line between state and society is not the perimeter of an intrinsic entity, which can be thought of as a free-standing object or actor. It is a line drawn internally, *within* the network of institutional mechanisms through which a certain social and political order is maintained" (90, emphasis original).

Building upon these insights I now turn to the ethnographers of the state, who similarly stress the importance of examining practices in order to understand the nature of the state. However, they focus on everyday practices and examine how individuals experience the state, and how the state appears in their daily lives. As such, they provide us with a method to trace empirically the creation of the "appearance of structure" identified by Mitchell. Ethnographers of the state refuse to look at the state as a coherent set of institutions working for public interest, instead arguing that one should seek to study the state by investigating the everyday practices through which people experience and therefore perceive the state (Das 2004; Das and Poole 2004; A. Gupta 2001, 2005; Ismail 2006; Wedeen 1999, 2010). The basic premise that underlies this work is that the mundane practices that bind the people with the state, such as applying for a passport, receiving unemployment benefits, watching a military parade, using an official letterhead, denouncing the corruption of the state, and so on, cause a certain popular and even scholarly imagination of the state (Sharma and Gupta 2006). One of the main contributions of this alternative approach of relevance is the way it examines how certain practices create a particular imagination of a structure that is separate and above society, while other practices break down this very idea (Asad 2004; Fuller and Harris 2001, 14–15; Hansen and Stepputat 2001, 5; Ismail 2006, xxxi–xxxiii). I will be focusing on this double movement of *building and breaking the appearance of structure*, as those are precisely the types of practices that I explore in this book.

Upon examining the practices that the ethnographers put forward as drawing the state as a bounded entity autonomous from society, we find that they relate to the imagination of the state as a protector of public good and justice.

Conversely, the practices that break down this image are practices of corruption and injustice. For example, Hansen's (2001, 33) study of the Indian state's response to the Mumbai riots in 1992–93 shows that the "'myth of the state,' the imagination of the state as a distant but persistent guarantor of a certain social order and a measure of justice and protection from violence" was shattered as the anti-Muslim bias of the Mumbai police became blatantly apparent during the riots. Interestingly, he shows how the myth was shattered differently for different communities (Muslims, middle-class Hindus, right-wing Hindus, and the high court judge), as they all had different imaginations of the state based on their different experiences with it. Nevertheless, even when the "myth of the state" was shattered, they all still remained dependent on the idea of the state, even if contesting it (63). More importantly, he argues that the state established a commission of inquiry and a special court to regain its appearance of autonomy from society, as it needed to re-establish itself as a provider of universal and impartial justice. Whether this move was successful is left open.

The lack of corruption and the presence of justice are not the only ways through which the state obtains its appearance of separation from society. Ferguson and Gupta (2002) examine how certain Indian governmental practices of supervision, registration, and mobility produce the spatial imagination of a high above and all-encompassing state in both popular and academic discourses. In this situation it is practices that create the imagination of the state as a "thing" that stands high above and all around society, as opposed to breaking down this imagination, as was the case with the practices of corruption. Ferguson and Gupta argue that surprise visits of inspectors, the mobility of the higher levels of the bureaucracy over the Indian territory and the amount of information that needs to be logged in by locals, verified by inspectors, and reported in official reports all serve to create rituals of surveillance. "What such rituals of surveillance actually accomplished was to *represent* and to *embody* state hierarchy and encompassment" (985, emphasis original). They argue that the mobility over the Indian territory of the higher levels of the bureaucracy is precisely what allows them to disavow the particular knowledge of the local NGO workers and "to claim to represent the 'greater' good for the 'larger' dominion of the nation and the world" (988).

These studies demonstrate how the examination of daily practices (such as corruption, criticism, and methods of surveillance) elucidates how the state can appear to be an entity in its own right as well as break down this idea—in other words how the line between the state and society is drawn as well as erased. This book follows this tradition by ethnographically examining the everyday practices of Palestinian refugees to trace how factions are produced through everyday life. It posits that daily life provides a crucial window through which to understand the forms of political organization that Palestinians adopt. The everyday practices of Palestinian refugees are the crucial ways through which the abstract notion of factions take concrete shape and form. Factions would simply not exist outside of those social relations, and their exploration is therefore essential. Using Mitchell's insights in dialogue with the work of the ethnographers of the state proves extremely helpful in studying the nature of Palestinian political factions. As we saw, Mitchell resolved the conundrum of how the state appeared to be separate from society while this was not the case. Additionally, he directed our attention to the importance of modern disciplinary practices. The ethnographic study of the state follows smoothly from Mitchell's argument, as it also focuses on practices. However, it emphasizes the everyday practices, and as such allows us to take people's experiences with and perception of the factions seriously.

By combining both approaches I advance a novel approach to the study of Palestinian political factions. Through an ethnographic study my work aims at highlighting *both* how factions are not bounded entities defined by their stated party ideology, and yet how they appear to be. To do so this book explores two sets of practices. Following a chapter on the ethnographic setting, it first looks at how Palestinians join factions (chapter 3) and how their relationship evolves over time (chapter 4). Exploring these practices and the personal narratives of Palestinian refugees reveals that Palestinians approached factions based on interpersonal relations imbued with high levels of trust: family, friendship, and neighborhood ties were the main vehicle behind factional affiliation. Palestinians seldom spoke of party ideology as an initial driver behind factional contact. Rather contact occurred depending on where people had friends or family, and sometimes depending on which faction had the closest youth center to their home. In fact, it is those personal relationships, including those developed with other faction members, that keep Palestinians affiliated to factions in spite of widespread criticism and disapproval. Factions appear as a loose group of people whose unity changes with time and context. This is their first nature.

Secondly, this book explores another set of practices: those of aid distribution (chapter 5), physical representation, and factionalism (chapter 6). This examination, in turn, exposes how factions gain a life of their own, how they metamorphose from loose networks based on interpersonal relations into impersonal structures defined by party ideology. This is their second nature. I show how these practices create the effect of structure, similarly to Mitchell's argument. These practices cause factions to take on the appearance of impersonal containers that exist separately from what they contain (their members). They also conjure up a line that seems to separate those on the "inside" (faction members) from those on the "outside" (independents). They create a new position from which an individual appears to be able to observe, grasp, critic, and study factions from the "outside" while being "inside" all along. Finally, they effect the appearance that factions are immaterial structures that exist independently from the very practices that bring them into being. Factions can never be touched; they are only represented in their emblems, stamps, flags, sports clubs, and so on. Additionally, this exploration brings to light the mechanism through which structures built on relations infused with high levels of trust end up inducing distrust in the community and controlling people's lives.

Finally, the book concludes (chapter 7) by showing, through two empirical examples—the 2012 protest movement that led to the annulment of the military permit system in Nahr el-Bared camp and the 2005 election of a "people's committee" in Shatila camp—how the double nature of factions allows them to remain in control of political representation despite their extensive unpopularity. It will elucidate how their first nature, as loose networks of people, allows them to "blend" into the masses at times of protest or dissent while their second nature, as structures, allows them to suddenly "appear" as actors in their own right when certain practices are needed, such as negotiating with official bodies like the Lebanese government or army. Like chameleons, Palestinian political factions have the ability to "appear" and "disappear" depending on the circumstances. This chapter will show how this chameleon nature, this "appearing" and "disappearing" act, allows unpopular political factions to continue to assert their relevance in the face of widespread dissent.

What is at stake in this re-conceptualization of Palestinian political factions is not just the definition of their nature; rather it is also the factions' source of power. By focusing on everyday life, this book shows that particular practices allow factions to metamorphose into structures while hiding the social relations that form their very core. The factions' chameleon nature is not out of some intrinsic aspect of their being, but simply due to practices. By providing a detailed account of these practices, by showing how intimate, interpersonal and kin-based relations are transformed into political networks and how these political networks are in turn metamorphosed into structures, this book exposes the process through which discredited factions remain in charge, helping us better understand the political impasse that Palestinians find themselves in with unpopular organizations representing them politically.

While this study was conducted within the specific context of the Palestinian refugee camp of Nahr el-Bared in 2011, its findings on the double nature of factions and the analytical and methodological "lateral" approach it suggests are not confined to those experiences. Finalizing this manuscript while living in Lebanon and experiencing first-hand the Oct 17, 2019 Lebanese uprising only reminds me that Palestinians are not unique in the situation of having unpopular political parties dominate their political landscape. Practices certainly change from one setting to another—for example, the practices that bind Lebanese citizens to their political parties are different from those examined in this study, and are certainly different from the practices that bind Palestinians in the West Bank and Gaza to political factions. However, the reality that political parties or factions are made of people, people who enter into different types of relationships with each other, still holds true regardless of the particular setting. In that sense the double nature of factions is not something peculiar neither to Nahr el-Bared camp nor to the Palestinian case. While more studies are needed to see how it is enacted and experienced in different settings, I see this study as a point of departure for our understanding of the double nature of political structures and not as a moment of arrival. What I hope to do in this study is to suggest a new way to study any "entity" that we commonly refer to as a "structure," or "agent," or "body," such as the state, political factions or parties, NGOs, or UN agencies, through an examination of the daily practices that constitute them and to question our taken for granted assumptions about the nature of those "structures."

Returning to my particular Palestinian case of Nahr el-Bared in 2011, it is important to note how my choice of place and time affected my findings. I conducted my research four years after the camp's destruction in 2007. This meant that the Palestinian political factions no longer carried arms within the camp, a situation which stands in sharp contrast to other places, whether within Lebanon, such as Ein el-Helwe camp,[4] or outside Lebanon such as in the West Bank or Gaza. I therefore could not directly experience the everyday occurrence of this practice and its ramifications on the factions' relationship with camp residents. This could be seen as a disadvantage as it meant that the context I was working in was vastly different from other contexts. However, I believe that this was an advantage, as I had to answer the more difficult question of how discredited factions are able to maintain monopoly over political representation in the absence of coercive measures. This made the question of their continued relevance even more puzzling and allowed the other roles factions played in everyday life to be highlighted, away from their more visible, abundantly photographed, and highly publicized armed component.

In this book I aim to describe in minute detail the texture of daily life and social relations that bind Palestinian refugees to factions. I strongly believe in the importance of giving an exposition of everyday life in the camp, an exposition that speaks for itself without it being overwhelmed by my own analysis. In that spirit I devote an entire chapter (chapter 2) to provide the ethnographic setting of this study, introducing the reader to the home and family that welcomed me, to their everyday struggles as well as to their endurance and ingenuity in building their lives. My rendering of everyday life is not confined to one chapter, however. Rather, throughout this book I employ a narrative format, quoting conversations verbatim to provide in-depth portraits of individuals and their highly political lives. In other words, I strive for a writing strategy "molded largely by the requirements of narrative rather than analysis" (Pachirat 2011, 18). I let the complexities and ambiguities of the stories take precedence over neatly packaged analysis to challenge the reader to think through what it means to be a Palestinian refugee in Lebanon today and navigate through the web of social and political relations in the context of chronic war, repeated displacement and longstanding legal discrimination.

The Palestinian National Movement in Lebanon:
"Some Built Castles and Some Built Graves!"

Palestinian refugees in Lebanon live on the margins of Lebanese society. Since the Nakba of 1948, the mass expulsion and de-Arabisation of Palestine at the hands of Zionist militias (Masalha 2012; Pappe 2006; W. Khalidi 1992; R. Khalidi 2007), their experience has been defined by war, displacement and discrimination. In the early years of exile, and especially after the Lebanese turmoil of 1958, Palestinians were severely restricted in all aspects of life. They needed permits to visit other camps, meetings of a non-domestic nature were not allowed, listening to the radio or reading the newspaper was forbidden, and building or repairing homes required an unobtainable permit. There were no private bathrooms or drainage systems and everyone, whether young or old, male or female, had to walk, night and day, to reach public latrines. Added to these practices were the daily harassments, humiliations, extortions, arrests and sometimes torture at the hands of the Army's Intelligence Bureau, also known as the Deuxième Bureau, who controlled the camps starting from 1958 (R. Sayigh 1994, 68–71; 2007, 139–47, 56–58).

During that period organized political mobilisation was clandestine, and first took the form of Nasserist pan-Arabism with the founding of the Arab Nationalists Movement (ANM) in the early 50s in Beirut (Y. Sayigh 1997, 71–75). It emerged around a group of predominantly middle- or upper-middle-class students from across the Arab world at the American University of Beirut. Its membership, though, encompassed all classes with a base in the refugee camps of Lebanon and Jordan, recruiting principally students and teachers in United Nations Relief and Work Agency for Palestine Refugees in the Near East (UNRWA) schools. It espoused a secular socialist pan-Arab ideology, believing that to liberate Palestine Arab unity had to be first achieved and that Gamal Abdel Nasser was the Arab leader able to achieve said unity (Baumgarten 2005, 27–31).

The defeat of the Arab armies (and Abdel Nasser) in the June 1967 war dealt a deadly blow to pan-Arabism and led to the gradual transformation of the ANM into the Popular Front for the Liberation of Palestine (PFLP) and the Democratic Front for the liberation of Palestine (DFLP). In parallel another group was beginning to form among Palestinian refugees from Gaza who had studied in Cairo or Beirut and later moved to the Persian Gulf States. Fatah, as that group came to be called, was a broad-based organization that adopted a Palestinian—as opposed to pan-Arab—liberationist nationalism. Founded in the late 1950s, it came to prominence after the 1967 war when Palestinian armed struggle appeared as the only alternative to the defeated conventional Arab armies (Y. Sayigh 1997, 80–87; Baumgarten 2005, 31–36).

Starting from the mid-1960s these organizations started to publish magazines, pamphlets and newspapers targeting the refugee camps (Khalili 2007, 47). They benefited from the increase in education levels, due to UNRWA's services, that created a generation of teachers and young professionals who would become the leaders of these organizations. In 1969, in an unplanned revolt, camp residents across Lebanon chased out the much-hated Deuxième Bureau (Kanj 2010, 64–70; R. Sayigh 2007, 169–70). The liberation of the camps ushered the era of the *thawra* in Lebanon, when Palestinians felt they had regained their self-respect, pride and dignity. They felt back in control of their destiny and struggling as part of a mass movement to return home. Um Nasser explained to me:

> The revolution was a sacred thing at the time; no one could even criticize it. We didn't see anything negative in it or rather we didn't want to see anything negative in the revolution. Due to the oppression we were facing, we were waiting for anything to save us from the situation we were in. And indeed after it people started to build. . . . People could enlarge their homes; there were no more restrictions. The people of the camp became responsible for the camp![5]

This mass uprising led to the signing of the Cairo Accords in 1969 between Yasir Arafat, who was soon to chair the Palestine Liberation Organization (PLO), and the Lebanese army commander.[6] The accord granted Palestinians the right to manage their own camps and to engage in armed struggle in coordination with the Lebanese Army (Cobban 1984, 47; Khalili 2007, 47; Peteet 2005, 7). Palestinian camps were thereafter administered by the combination of a popular committee, which acted like a municipality dealing with services such as electricity, water, and garbage collection, and the armed struggle command, which acted like a local police force (Peteet 1987, 32–33). Appointed by the Palestinian factions, rather than elected from the camp's residents, they were a welcome change to the rule of the Deuxième Bureau (R. Sayigh 2007, 179). Aided by the local population they quickly started to engage in infrastructural improvements and established health, economic, social and cultural institutions in the camps in addition to their recruiting programs and military training (Khalili 2007, 48; Peteet 1987, 33; R. Sayigh 1994, 95–96; 2007, 182–87).

Funding and resources started to flow to the PLO and the Palestinian political factions, especially from Arab oil-producing states, which allowed to them to expand the services and jobs they offered to Palestinian refugees. They soon grew dramatically in size and came to be known as the "Palestinian sector," absorbing about 65 percent of the Palestinian workforce (R. Sayigh 1994, 109). As the Palestinian resistance movement developed into a major force in Lebanon it increased its military operations against Israel, which augmented its air, naval and ground attacks, leading to heavy Lebanese and Palestinian civilian deaths with often minimal losses to PLO combatants, the presumptive target of any attack (R. Khalidi 1986, 20–21). This Israeli tactic was designed to alienate the Lebanese masses from the PLO and increase Palestinian-Lebanese tensions. Additionally, Palestinians became the target of right-wing Christian militias and continued to be attacked by the Lebanese army regardless of the Cairo accords (R. Sayigh 1994,

97). Allying themselves with the Lebanese National Movement, Palestinians were drawn into the Lebanese civil war.[7] With the breakdown of the Lebanese state the PLO continued to grow in influence until 1982, when Israel invaded Lebanon and expelled PLO forces.[8] The departure of the PLO and *fedayeen* forces from Lebanon was a critical turning point for the Palestinians in Lebanon, who lost an important source of employment and protection. The period that followed was marred with massacres and sieges and much of the PLO infrastructure was destroyed (Brynen 1990b, 180–81).

Meanwhile in the Occupied Palestinian Territories (OPT) of the West Bank and Gaza a popular uprising (*intifada*) erupted in 1987 and impacted the Palestinian community in Lebanon. First, Hamas, a new Palestinian political movement, emerged, growing out of the Muslim Brotherhood Gaza branch. Similarly to how Fatah presented itself as an alternative to pan-Arabism, Hamas presented itself as an alternative to secular nationalism by advocating "Islam as the solution and the alternative" (Baumgarten 2005, 37). Secondly, the attention of the PLO leadership shifted from Lebanon to the OPT, leaving the Palestinian refugees in Lebanon feeling abandoned (Khalili 2007, 54). This abandonment was concretised in 1993 with the signing of the Oslo Accords between the PLO and Israel. The Palestinian National Authority (PNA) was created as an authority over the West Bank and Gaza with no official ties to the refugees outside of Palestine (Hilal 1995). Starting from that date funding to the PLO was severely cut, with both the Palestinian leadership and the international community shifting focus from the PLO to the PNA (Frisch 2009; Hilal 2010, 27–30). Palestinian refugees, formerly the core of the *thawra*, felt a deep sense of betrayal and exclusion after years of struggle and sacrifice, which has led them to be called not only refugees of the *Nakba*, but also "refugees of the revolution (*thawra*)" (Allan 2014). This led the vast majority of the people to believe that the factions were not sincere in their initial calls for the liberation of Palestine. Abu Ali explains:

> This is what they make us feel, that [the stated goal of liberating Palestine] was a lie; that they were not honest. Those who accept Oslo and 27 percent of the West Bank can't be the same person that is holding the slogan 'Armed struggle until victory' and protecting it. It was a lie, unfortunately. We spend our life in the *thawra*. Some built castles and some built graves!

In the aftermath of the Oslo Accords, Palestinian political factions were split among supporters and detractors and thereafter the camps were internally governed by a web of complex power structures composed of the PLO popular committee, committees formed by dissident political parties, notables, factions, Islamist non-Palestinian groups, imams, PLO popular organizations, and UNRWA directors (Suleiman 1999). The post-civil war era brought an even sharper increase in the insecurity and marginalization of Palestinian refugees (Abbas 1997; Haddad 2003). While they were already excluded from key aspects of social, political and economic life in the country—for example, they were prohibited from practicing many professions—in 2001 they were also barred from owning property (Al-Natour 1997; Saghieh and Saghieh 2008; Suleiman 2006). Restricted to working in menial jobs, and unable to achieve a minimum of stability in the form of homeownership, Palestinians have been pushed to emigrate (Al-Husseini and Bocco 2011, 133–34; R. Sayigh 2001, 100). Those unable to escape from Lebanon's suffocating laws lived in physical misery and with the constant fear that even the precarious lives that they had painfully built for themselves could be taken away at a moment's notice, and with impunity, as the 2007 Nahr el-Bared conflict taught them.

NAHR EL-BARED CAMP AND THE 2007 CONFLICT

Sadness is our fate
Trouble is our fate
Our dreams cannot be measured
And by God no one cares
I swear I miss our neighborhood
I swear I miss our home
I miss the shouting of our neighbor
I wish I stayed in Nahr el-Bared

—10-year-old Palestinian girl displaced from Nahr el-Bared camp, singing and drumming in the courtyard of the UNRWA school in Beddawi camp where she was sheltering with her family, June 2007

FIGURE 2. Hanging laundry. Photograph: Ali Alloush.

Nahr el-Bared was the second-largest Palestinian refugee camp in Lebanon, housing in 2007 about 33,000 refugees (Sheikh Hassan and Hanafi 2010, 31). It was situated on the Mediterranean shoreline, on a main road connecting the northern Lebanese city of Tripoli to Syria. After the end of the Lebanese civil war in the 1990s residents used the camp's strategic location to turn it into an important commercial hub. It was a trading center for goods smuggled in from Syria, for agricultural products going from the countryside into Tripoli, and for cheap manufacturing goods moving from Tripoli to the villages (Sheikh Hassan and Hanafi 2010, 31; Quilty 2007b). This commercial activity meant that Nahr el-Bared had strong economic and social ties with the adjacent area, which translated into many mixed marriages between Lebanese and Palestinian refugees.

However, things changed dramatically and fast at the end of 2006 and early 2007 with the arrival of Islamic militants, who later called themselves Fatah al-Islam. The story of Fatah al-Islam is difficult to piece together, as many of its alleged members are either dead or in prison. However, its composition of mostly

FIGURE 3. A commercial street in Nahr el-Bared before its destruction. Source: Wikimedia.

non-Palestinians is not in dispute, as even the Lebanese Judiciary Council confirmed it (Haddad 2010, 559). Its origins, by contrast, are debated. The Lebanese government of the time, led by Prime Minister Saad Hariri, saw Fatah al-Islam as a Syrian implant in Lebanon with ties to al-Qaeda, while the opposition, led by Hezbollah, saw Fatah al-Islam as the creation of the Future Movement, accusing it of wanting to create its own militia. Ultimately, what became apparent was that all parties, including the Lebanese government and its armed forces, were well aware of the movement and settlement of these militants in the Palestinian camps in the north of Lebanon (International Crisis Group 2009, 26; Khalidi and Riskedahl 2007, 28–29).The newcomers were not welcomed by the camp population (*The Daily Star* 2006). Instead, many residents staged protests demanding that Fatah al-Islam leave the camp (Bathist 2007a; Ramadan 2009, 155; Taarnby and Hallundbaek 2008, 5–6). Two separate armed incidents ensued in which one member of Fatah al-Islam was stabbed to death (*The Daily Star* 2007); a month later a member of Fatah was shot dead (Bathist 2007b).

On May 19, 2007, members of Fatah al-Islam robbed a bank in Amyun, a small town south of Tripoli. Subsequently, the Lebanese Internal Security Forces (ISF) raided their apartments in Tripoli and a firefight ensued (Sheikh Hassan and Hanafi 2010, 34). In response, Fatah al-Islam launched a brutal night attack against the Lebanese army barracks outside Nahr el-Bared camp. Twenty-seven Lebanese soldiers died, some of whom were killed in their sleep (Human Rights Watch 2007c; Khalidi and Riskedahl 2007, 28–29).[9] The army responded by carrying out heavy and indiscriminate shelling of the camp. The battle turned into a hundred-day conflict and was framed by the Lebanese government in terms of the global "war on terror," with Fatah al-Islam labeled an international terrorist organization linked to al-Qaeda.[10]

At the time, there was no public criticism against the army's actions in Nahr el-Bared (Sheikh Hassan and Hanafi 2010, 34; Quilty 2007b). Instead, strong support was shown across the entire Lebanese political spectrum.[11] While it was the Hariri government that led the offensive on the camp, Nasrallah, the Secretary General of Hezbollah, labeled both the attacking of the camp and the army as red lines. However, no action was taken as the army systematically demolished the camp. While all parties claimed that the battle was against Fatah al-Islam rather than Palestinians, the newly displaced refugees were routinely detained and abused by the Lebanese military as they were fleeing the camp and at different checkpoints around Lebanon. Harassment included being stripped, forced to lie on the ground, being kicked, beaten, insulted and humiliated (Amnesty International 2008; Human Rights Watch 2007b).

Initially the attack continued for three consecutive days, causing the death of twenty-seven Palestinian civilians, before a cease-fire was declared which allowed the first wave of refugees to flee (Human Rights Watch 2007c). Most of the displaced went to Beddawi camp to stay with relatives and friends or to shelter in offices, garages, storerooms, and schools (FAFO 2007, 3). The refugees initially thought that their displacement from their camp was temporary; however as days turned into weeks they soon feared that there would not be a return to Nahr el-Bared camp. Young children and adults alike began to voice their fears, despair, and most importantly their longing for their homes and neighborhoods, regardless of all their drawbacks, as expressed in the song quoted at the beginning of this section.

The position of the Palestinian leadership was deeply unpopular during the conflict. On the fourth day of fighting and as civilians were being killed indiscriminately, the PLO representative to Lebanon, Abbas Zaki, declared to the media that the PLO had no objections to the Lebanese military sending troops to Nahr el-Bared, that "this is a Lebanese decision" (quoted in Qawas and Zaatari 2007). Many also pointed out that if the Palestinians had a united and effective leadership, then the conflict and the camp's destruction might have been averted as the armed factions themselves could have acted against Fatah al-Islam (Sheikh Hassan and Hanafi 2010, 33; Ramadan 2009, 161). Abu Ali, a resident of Nahr el-Bared in his fifties, expressed this commonly held-view:

> The crisis of Nahr el-Bared was the biggest indicator of the weakness of the factions and our leaders. Look at where we are today! They took the decision to displace 30,000 refugees! For what? Because they were not able to take a decision to fight a gang?[12]

The battle continued until September 2, 2007, when the Lebanese army declared its first victory over global terrorism. Chawki Masri, the army chief of staff during the conflict, later declared:

> The LAF's [Lebanese Armed Forces] morale was very high after the conflict and we were proud that all the Lebanese, and the US, UK, Spain and other friendly countries, were astonished by how we were able to throw a 4,000-pound bomb. They came here and asked how we did all this with such limited capabilities, and they told us they were very proud. It was a very good sign for us that not only the Lebanese but also the great armies from around the world said they were proud of what we did in Nahr el-Bared (International Crisis Group 2012, 3).

The army had effectively won a battle fought against a group of militants whose numbers, even by the account of the Lebanese government, did not exceed 450.[13] In the process, the conflict led to the death of 42 civilians, 168 Lebanese soldiers and 220 militants, as well as the displacement of over 30,000 refugees (Amnesty International 2008). All 1700 buildings in the old camp were reduced to rubble (Sheikh Hassan and Hanafi 2010, 34), and about 65 percent of the new camp buildings needed repair (IRIN 2007), including 100 totally demolished buildings (Sheikh Hassan and Hanafi 2010, 34).[14]

Once the battle ended residents were denied access to the ruins of their own homes. While the army had declared that the camp was disarmed and free from Fatah al-Islam, they still did not allow Palestinians to return. Instead, they surrounded the new and old camps with two sets of barbed wire and concrete blocks. Checkpoints, manned by the Lebanese army, now controlled the entrance of people and goods. The old camp was completely off-limits to its previous residents.

This was the continuation of a long series of humiliating experiences for the residents of Nahr el-Bared, who now needed a military permit to access rubble. Even more upsetting was that once they got access to their homes and businesses in the camp they found them vandalized, looted, and burned. Racist graffiti had been written on the walls insulting Palestinians (Amnesty International 2008; Ramadan 2009, 2010). Upon visiting a burned-out and looted dental clinic in Nahr el-Bared camp in October 2007 I saw "Fuck you Palestine! With regards from the 5th Brigade" spray painted on the walls. While it is hard to believe that the destruction of the entire camp was a military necessity in a fight against a group of 450 militants, the accompanying looting, burning, vandalism, racism, and the subsequent militarization of the disarmed camp made it clear that Palestinian refugees were being treated as a guilty party. Although Lebanese officials repeatedly declared that Fatah al-Islam was not a Palestinian entity, they nonetheless seemed to blame the Palestinian community for their emergence (International Crisis Group 2009, 12). Residents felt used as scapegoats yet again, as they knew full well that the Lebanese government and its security apparatuses were all well aware of the presence of the militants who formed Fatah al-Islam, and had allowed them to move around and operate openly. Furthermore, Palestinians felt that by leaving the camp they had in effect sided with the army. They saw their departure from the camp as supporting the military campaign, as the army could lead a more aggressive assault on the camp without the fear of civilian casualties. Their subsequent treatment by the army as a suspect community only aggravated their feelings of betrayal and distrust.

Finally, in May 2008 the army commander during the conflict, General Michel Suleiman, became the consensus presidential candidate for the two main rival political coalitions who had been deadlocked for months (Quilty 2008). To mark the occasion, Lebanese newspaper *The Daily Star* published a biography of the general entitled "Nahr al-Bared victory launched Suleiman to Baabda" (Elghossain 2008). Simply put, the destruction of the second largest Palestinian camp in Lebanon became a source of unity for Lebanese politicians.

PRODUCTION NOTES

Like any researcher, I started my fieldwork with my own set of ideas and goals (Abu-Lughod 1991; Fontana and Frey 2005; Shehata 2006). I am a Palestinian refugee, but one who was born with Lebanese citizenship and who has studied and lived in the West for many years. My first visit to a Palestinian refugee camp was in 2005 when I volunteered to teach English in Shatila camp in Beirut. However, my formative experience came at the end of 2006, when I began working with

FIGURE 4. Marching cows. Photograph: Perla Issa.

Palestinian refugees from Iraq. They were being kidnapped, tortured, killed, expelled from their homes, and their neighborhoods were being shelled. Neighboring countries closed their borders to them and four different camps were erected on the borders between Jordan, Syria and Iraq. This experience opened my eyes to the inadequacy of the current Palestinian political leadership, as neither the Palestinian Authority (PA) nor the PLO were willing to act.

As an outcome of this experience, colleagues and I decided to make a six-part documentary series exploring the experiences and opinions of Palestinian refugees around the world.[15] Through the making of the series and its screening I came to be exposed even more to Palestinians' dissatisfaction with their leadership. Out of the three hundred interviewees only one person responded positively to the question: "Does anyone represent you politically today?" The remaining interviewees responded negatively. The uniformity of the "No" answer across geography, age, and socio-economic status was striking.

At around the same time I began to visit Nahr el-Bared and Beddawi camps in the north of Lebanon. I became involved in local initiatives trying to rebuild the camp and to break the military siege that was imposed on the camp after the end of the battle. Throughout these times the inadequacy and impotence of the Palestinian factions and leadership was painfully visible and a constant source of discussion among local activists. These experiences made me begin my research project, at the onset of which I believed that there was no greater, or more important, step for Palestinian activists to work on than on finding a way to change our current political representation. I wanted to know how discredited factions remain the center of political life in spite of widespread condemnation.

I decided to carry out my research in Nahr el-Bared camp, as I had developed sustained relationships with many of its residents over the three years of my involvement. However, this prior engagement with my eventual "field site" did not shield me from experiencing ethical dilemmas, which can be conveyed through one simple incident. About a month into my fieldwork, I was introduced to a group of young kindergarten teachers. The head of the NGO explained that I was a PhD student doing research in the camp. She then left the room to attend to other business. The young women all looked at me, waiting for my questions. When I did not come forward with any, one of them asked me, "What do you want? You want to solve our problems?" The sarcasm in her voice could not be mistaken.

This incident brought to the fore all the dilemmas I experienced conducting research in an over-researched and under-privileged community (Sukarieh and Tannock 2013). Switching from being an "activist" to a "researcher" in Nahr el-Bared, I found it difficult to accept my new position. It seemed so passive. In the past I always felt, rightly or wrongly, that I was part of some immediate action. I believed that I was active, debating particular strategies as well as suggesting and working towards certain courses of action. In contrast, as a researcher, I was trying to go along the normal course of the day and was more interested in listening than talking. This was, after all, the reason why I had chosen to do a PhD. In my prior work I felt I was in too much of a hurry, always visiting the camp with a certain objective and never stopping to just hang out with people. I now wanted to take my time, to observe and listen. This yearning to take it slow continuously clashed with my desire to be—or maybe it is just to feel—more useful. While I told myself that I was doing this research with the hopes of bettering our understanding of the dynamics of the community, I could never ignore the fact that it was I who would ultimately benefit from this research, as I would gain a PhD while the circumstances of the community would remain the same. This point was certainly not lost on the young women meeting me in the NGO that day. They were highlighting the role often taken by researchers, who would express sympathy and exhibit a desire to form friendships only to disappear after their fieldwork was done (Sukarieh and Tannock 2013, 504–5). Respondents in the field continuously expressed their fear that I would soon forget about them. It was in great part for this reason that I chose to conduct research with individuals and families I had known for several years prior to my research. These refugees already had longstanding relations with me. I hoped that their fears would therefore be minimized.

There was an additional reason for wanting to work with past acquaintances. In short, they already knew me. They were familiar with my background, my past experiences and stances on political issues. This created a sense of openness and honesty conductive to building trust (Hammersley and Atkinson 1983, 77–88; Kanaaneh 1997). In order to study the everyday interactions of Palestinian refugees with political factions I needed my respondents to understand my opinions and thoughts as much as I needed to understand theirs. I wanted to know how and why people joined factions, how they obtained aid, how and why they did or did not participate in factional events, how their relationships evolved over time, what their fears, doubts, and regrets were over the years. Those were private and sensitive issues that I could only explore through knowing people intimately and over time (Schatz 2009). Therefore, I considered mutual trust to be the most important factor in determining my choice of camp, host family, and interviewees. While I certainly did not shy away from meeting new people, I only performed in-depth conversations with people that I felt trusted me and understood my research and my motivation.

In my research I did not prioritize or focus on a given faction; again, my criteria in selecting my interviewees was mutual trust. In an effort to obtain more honest and sincere answers I believed that it was important that I only interview people whom I felt understood why I was asking the questions I was. These people, as it happened, were affiliated with different factions. This was an advantage, as I was able to look at political membership across factions. However, my choice of Nahr el-Bared camp implied that a good majority of my respondents would be linked to the PFLP and DFLP, as those two factions had the largest presence in the camp in the form of well-funded and large NGOs. Nevertheless my interlocutors did encompass a number of other factions, including the Islamic Jihad, the PFLP-GC, Fatah, Fatah al-Intifada, and Hamas.

I lived in Nahr el-Bared camp, in the north of Lebanon, for seven months with the Talal family, whom I had known for over three years prior to my research. The family was very generous to allow me to stay with them as long as I needed, even though their financial situation was very difficult. I accepted the family's offer to host me for two reasons. First, I was acquainted with their extended family. In particular, I was close to Um Muhammad's, the mother's, family. I knew her brother and his family very well, as well as her own mother. Those relationships made my presence in the Talal family's home less peculiar. Second, I was encouraged by the fact that in the previous three years they had never treated me like a special guest that needed to be pampered. They always made me feel welcomed without ever making me feel like I was burdening them with, for example, the cooking of special meals. While I never really lost the status of guest, I nevertheless felt like I was part of the household. Family fights would happen in front of me and people would often ask me for my opinion on personal matters. The Talal family's household became my home in the camp, where I was able to rest, read, write notes, or just relax. I usually spent my mornings and evenings with the family, and in the afternoon I visited other acquaintances. I was free to come and go as I wished, as the family provided me with a key to their home, although I took care never to be out past 9:00 p.m. They were always very considerate of my "work," although it was sometimes obvious that they did not understand why I was troubling myself so much with Palestinian politics and not just getting married and having children.

In addition to participant-observation, my research was also based on open-ended Arabic-language interviews (Bevir 2006; Maynard-Moody and Musheno 2006; Maynes 2008). In total, I conducted seventy-three in-depth interviews: fifty-one with people I had known for at least two years prior to my research and twenty-two with those I met during my fieldwork. For the remainder of the book I will refer to those two categories as "close" and as "newly-met" Palestinians. In my interviews I included both women (thirty-one) and men (forty-two), as well as thirty Palestinians of the *thawra* generation—the generation that lived through the Palestinian *thawra* and the Lebanese civil war, born before 1975—as well as forty-three members of what I refer to as the "young generation," born after 1975. As mentioned earlier, in selecting the interviewees I took extra care to approach people whom I felt knew me and understood my research. In this sense my discussions with the refugees resembled more a mutual exchange of experiences than interviews (Kanaaneh 1997, 5; Soss 2006, 135; Worth 2006) and I was able to tape-record forty-three interviews without feeling like the technology was intruding on our conversation. All names have been altered to preserve the anonymity of my interviewees.

ACCESSING NAHR EL-BARED CAMP

In December 2010, when I began making arrangements to move to Nahr el-Bared, I needed a permit from the military to access the camp. I began by asking fellow Palestinian and Lebanese activists for advice. Everyone's answer was less than encouraging—that is, until I met the wife of a prominent businessman who offered to help. Her staff submitted an application for my permit and I received a call on the following day from the army asking me to meet with the head of the Lebanese Military Intelligence (LMI) in the North. I went to the appointment with a heavy heart; it is never an enjoyable experience to meet with military intelligence in any country. The head of the LMI in the North asked me about my research and for whom I was doing it. Once he realized that I was a PhD student and not an NGO worker he called the army's Chief of Staff on the phone in my presence. They discussed my situation and the Chief of Staff asked to see me in person. My heart sank even further; I now needed to go to the Ministry of Defense and meet with the Lebanese army's second-in-command to be able to conduct research in a Palestinian refugee camp, which was already under heavy military surveillance.

FIGURE 5. Barbed wire fence around Nahr el-Bared camp. Photograph: Perla Issa.

I went to the appointment but was thankfully accompanied by an aide of the businessman, and surprisingly—or maybe I should not have been surprised—the meeting went very smoothly. I was not even asked about the topic of my research as the conversation revolved around the weather and the political situation in Lebanon. I was then taken to a different room with a couple of officers and I wrote down a brief description of my research. The officers proceeded to tell me about the "liberation of Nahr el-Bared" while showing me pictures of the different types of bombs and ammunition that were used in the war that obliterated the camp. At the end of the encounter I was told that my permit was approved for a full year but there was still a simple bureaucratic procedure they needed to perform and that they would call me once it was ready. I was ecstatic and a bit in shock about how unreal the meeting was.

About two weeks later I received a phone call from an army officer informing me that the permit had been granted. I was delighted and I asked him where I should go to obtain it. He replied that he did not know, that his job was simply to inform me of my permit's approval. The very next day I received another call from yet another army officer who explained that he had been informed that I obtained a permit to conduct research in Nahr el-Bared but that he regretted to inform me that "Nahr el-Bared was empty." I did not understand and asked him to elaborate. He explained that the residents of Nahr el-Bared had not returned to the camp yet; that no one was there. I responded that I was aware that the refugees had not returned to the original camp, but that my permit was for the adjacent area where Palestinians currently lived. The fact that I had applied to the adjacent area of Nahr el-Bared was actually written on the permit and the officer should have known this. He excused himself and hung up.

A few days later I received a call from the businessman's aide, telling me to go meet again with the head of the LMI in the north, this time to get my permit. I went back to Qobeh on my own, and I was told that I had obtained the "approval" for my one-year permit from the Chief of Staff's office but that they—the northern LMI office—were the ones who issued the permit and had the last word. I was again asked about my research topic, which I again explained. I was then issued a two-month permit and was told that I needed to visit them every two months to renew my permit and to provide them with a copy of "what I write." I explained that I would not be writing anything immediately and that I would be happy to provide them with a copy of what I would publish. They responded that, no, they wanted a copy of my field notes. I objected and explained that it was against my ethical standards and against university rules. They said I had no choice. I left the office very angry, with a two-month permit in my hands.

For the next two months I lived in Nahr el-Bared camp. Once my permit expired I went back to the head of the LMI in the north; he was not present and I went to see his lieutenant. Sitting in his office and facing a series of framed joint Lebanese and American training certificates in "interviewing" and "counter-terrorism," I explained that I could not hand in my field notes and that I could provide them with my work once it was published. I added that it would be unfair to hold me accountable for what I wrote in the field, that my ideas were not fully developed yet, and that I should be held accountable for my ideas once I deemed them ready to be published. I was told bluntly, "we are not interested in your ideas but in *information*!" I pointed out that the Lebanese army was in the camp, so they did not need me to gather information for them. The lieutenant's only answer was that "Nahr el-Bared is special." I was given another permit for ten days and told that by then I needed to give them my notes. I took the permit and decided to leave the camp within ten days. I spent those remaining days in the camp inform-ing my friends of the situation and explaining why I had to leave. Then I went to Beirut and did not attempt to renew my permit any longer.

Later during the month of July, my friends in Nahr el-Bared called to inform me that the army had announced that women no longer needed a permit to enter the camp. I decided to give it a try and went to one of its checkpoints, which consisted of two military posts, the first manned by the LMI and the other by the army. At that point in time women no longer needed to stop at the LMI post but could proceed directly to the army's post. I just walked past the LMI officers and went straight to the army's post. A soldier took my ID, wrote down my information on a notebook, and told me I could go in. He did not call headquarters. This was how I entered the camp for the remainder of the year.

This story shows how arbitrary rules regulating Palestinian life in Lebanon can be. A permit system was enacted and then revoked without explanation and without any change in the camp's situation. An officer of the LMI was unable to explain to me why he needed me to be an informant, his only answer was that "Nahr el-Bared was special."

. . .

Living in Nahr el-Bared camp was a deeply humbling experience. Not only was I constantly made aware of my privileges as a Palestinian with Lebanese citizenship, but more importantly, I was repeatedly faced with the inadequacies of my own explanations and understandings of Palestinian politics and of life in the camps in Lebanon (Pader 2006). My interlocutors in the field often asked me what I had learned from my research, what I had "uncovered." Nothing was more humbling than relating to them what had taken me several months to understand only to be met with a "that's obvious" stare. Refugees saw little value in my attempts to grasp their understanding of their world. What was the point of me learning what was so obvious to them? Wasn't my time better spent exposing the complex and multilayered system of domination that Palestinian refugees were subjected to? While the latter project is certainly crucial, I contend that understanding the internal dynamics of an oppressed community is just as vital (Ortner 1995). Exploring the quotidian interactions and encounters between Palestinian refugees and factions brings us valuable insights into the nature of factions, how we should study them, or work with—or against—them as activists interested in bettering Palestinian political representation. Indeed the very questions I ask about our conventional understanding of factions as building-like structures were directly precipitated by the alternative methodological approach I adopted.

FIGURE 6. Women carrying eggs in Nahr el-Bared camp. Photograph: Ali Alloush.

"The Nest of the Crazy"

The Ethnographic Setting

Prior to starting my research, I visited Nahr el-Bared camp numerous times. The experience was always the same. Upon approaching the Lebanese army's checkpoint, my stomach would tie itself in knots as I found myself entering a different world; a world of military control and surveillance, destruction, destitution, and injustice. The proximity of this world to the world I was coming from always overwhelmed me. I have to confess, even if I run the risk of sounding weak and self-centered, that as I made plans to live in Nahr el-Bared I worried about how it would affect me. Would I become depressed? Would I be able to handle it?

Amazingly, what I found was that the overt signs of poverty, misery, and hardship, so visible to me on my visits, actually disappeared. I no longer noticed the holes in buildings, the dark alleys, the corrugated iron roofs, the piles of rubble, the bullet- and shell-holes. It is not that they went away, but they just melted into the background; what became visible in their place was misery in its detail and daily occurrence. No longer in the forms of buildings or roads, this misery was instead to be found in mundane things, such as the choice of room to sit in, of fruit to buy and of hot drinks to consume, as well as in life-changing decisions about pursuing an education or searching for employment. Everything that a person did or did not do was determined by material necessity. However, what this misery in its detail revealed in turn was the survival techniques, the ingenuity of the refugees in making their lives. To me, Nahr el-Bared was no longer just a place of destitution, but also, and more importantly, a place of collective survival and great inspiration.

THE SETTING

When I first moved in with the Talal family, they lived in a rented apartment in a partially destroyed building situated on the main road of the new camp. The owner

FIGURE 7. Snow-capped mountains surrounding Nahr el-Bared camp. Photograph: Perla Issa.

had repaired part of the floors while others still bore the signs of war with large shell holes visible.[1] The outside of the building was not completed, with cinder blocks and concrete pillars remaining exposed. A series of shops lined the ground floor. There was a computer and internet store, a vegetable seller, a grocery store, and a calling center. The building stood next to an open field of gravel, which extended to its left and behind it. The winter rains had created large puddles of water in which wild vegetation was growing. The field was used as a storage place for cinderblocks for sale, as a parking lot for cars, and as a playground for children.

The building's entrance, situated at the back, was reached through a slightly elevated path that circled around the structure. A few steps led up to the building's concrete hallway, where electric cables dangled out of countless circuit breakers and the occasional electricity meter. On the left, next to an apartment door, stood a concrete stairwell leading to the upper floors. The rough and uneven finishing of the concrete made cleaning the stairwell and the hallway very difficult. Despite the frequent attempts of residents to sweep them or hose them down with water, they would remain dirty and dusty.

The Talal family lived on the third floor in an apartment that faced the main street. The apartment consisted of three bedrooms, a salon, a short but wide hallway that had been turned into a living room, a kitchen, a bathroom, and two balconies on the eastern and southern sides of the building. A rarity in the camp, their home had a lot of natural light, a nice breeze when doors and windows were opened, and a great view of the snow-capped mountains of Akkar in the distance. When the family first moved back to Nahr el-Bared camp after the war, they had lived in a two-room apartment, where Um and Abu Muhammad shared a room while their children slept in the other. On my earlier visits to Nahr el-Bared I often visited them in that home and would even take the opportunity to nap to beat the afternoon heat. However, once Muhammad got married and was working on a project with a local NGO, they moved into the present apartment. Here Muhammad and his wife occupied one room, Um and Abu Muhammad took another, and Mahmud, Ahmad, and Nadia shared the third. The rent was partially covered by Muhammad and by a rent subsidy that UNRWA provided for displaced Nahr el-Bared families whose homes had been demolished. However, after a few months the project on which Muhammad was working ended. Despite assurances from the NGO that they would keep him on staff after the end of the project, they did not do so and he lost his job. Looking for new employment, Muhammad found a position in another NGO in the south of Lebanon, where he relocated. At that point the family began to look for a smaller home to rent, as Muhammad was still helping them and they wanted to eliminate that expense for him. Homes were difficult to find in Nahr el-Bared as few of them were left standing after the war and there was a large number of families who, like the Talal family, had been made homeless by the war and were searching for housing. Throughout my stay with them, the family was not able to find a cheaper apartment to rent.

At the time of my arrival, Nadia had moved into the room that Muhammad and his wife used to occupy, and it was this room that I shared with her. The house was scarcely furnished, mostly with foam mattresses that doubled as beds at night and as sitting areas in the day. There were two different kinds: a thicker and harder mattress that was in the salon, handed out by Hamas after the war, and a thinner and softer type that was used in the sitting area and the children's bedrooms, distributed by UNRWA. The rest of the furniture consisted of one bed that Um and Abu Muhammad used, two old wardrobes, and a plastic kitchen table with four chairs. In the winter, the tile floors of the living room and salon were covered with plastic rugs, handed out by UNRWA, in an attempt to insulate feet from the cold. The walls were bare. The kitchen had second-hand appliances with a gas stove, a washing machine, and a fridge notorious for its breakdowns. There was an electric heater with "donated by ECHO" (for the European Community Humanitarian Office) printed in large letters on it in the hallway. Finally, their son Mahmud had bought a used computer and he obtained a wired Internet connection from the ground floor shop.

Most of the time at home was spent in the hallway that had been turned into a sitting area. Connecting the bedrooms at one end of the apartment to the kitchen and salon at the other, three of its walls were lined with mattresses; a television set was against the fourth. It was a windowless room with little natural light. I always wondered why the family picked this room to spend so much of their time in, when the rest of the rooms were well-lit, with either windows or balconies that had such nice views of the mountains. At first I wondered if the Nahr el-Bared conflict had had a lasting impact on the family, who now always worried about sudden and indiscriminate bombings. Hallways were always deemed the safest in times of war as they increased the number of walls between the person and incoming missiles; maybe the family was continuously worried about its physical safety. However, I soon realized that that my preference for a well-lit room with a mountain view reflected my privilege. I was thinking of looking at nice scenery, while they were worried about saving money. Being the smallest room in the house, the hallway was the easiest and therefore the cheapest room to heat during the winter. Often, just the heat of our bodies under a pile of shared blankets would be enough to warm it up; if not, then a small electric heater would suffice. In the summer, with the lack of electric fans, let alone air-conditioning, it was important to look for the coolest room in the house. The lack of direct sunlight turned into a blessing, which kept the hallway cooler than other rooms; a breeze still crossed it when windows and doors were opened.

Evening family gatherings soon became one of my favorite times in the camp. Ahmad would often be on the computer browsing the Internet for news about the Arab Spring, Mahmud would try to distract him by making jokes, while Abu Muhammad would purposely tease his sons by commenting that the only "real *thawra*" was the one of his generation. This would have the intended effect of pro-voking Ahmad, who would get angry and tell his father not to talk to him of a *thawra* that ended up in the Chadian desert of Aouzou, referring to his father's six-month involvement in the 1987 Libyan-Chad war. In the meantime, Um Muhammad would tap her husband on his shoulder, telling him not to instigate trouble, while Nadia would laugh and tell me "see, this is why I don't like politics." It is those evenings that made Um Muhammad call her family "the nest of the crazy" (*'ish al-majānīn*) and it is those evenings that warmed my heart and made me look forward to visiting Nahr el-Bared. Abu and Um Muhammad's life course and past political engagement were often the topic of conversation in these nightly gatherings and these helped me better understand the challenges facing the family and the strategies it adopted to overcome them.

Abu Muhammad

Abu Muhammad, a humorous man, often told me that if I wanted to under-stand Palestinian politics all I had to do was listen to his personal experience. In many ways he was right. His story featured many of the defining experiences of the *thawra*: the initial enthusiasm, the suspension of education in favor of join-ing the struggle, the witnessing of corruption, the subsequent disillusionment, the betrayal and abandonment by the leadership, the retreat from politics and finally the attempt to make a living, and raise a family, as an unskilled laborer. However, what was even more telling about Abu Muhammad's experience was his lack of desire to talk about it. Indeed, despite his insistence that his life story alone would be enough for me to "complete my research," he did not like to elaborate on it. Later, Um Muhammad explained that he did not want to talk about his experience in too much detail in front of his children, afraid that his stories would inspire them to partake in political work that could jeopardize their lives or their futures. This did not mean that he was not proud of his past actions, but the lesson he wanted his children and me to learn was: don't get involved with the factions, don't waste your time with Palestinian politics, it is all "nonsense" (*ḥakī fāḍī*), it is better to build a future and raise a family.

Abu Muhammad was born in the Zarqa Palestinian refugee camp in Jordan in the mid-1950s. At the age of fifteen he became a *shibil* in Fatah, following in the foot-steps of an older cousin who was a *fidā'ī*.[2] This was in 1969, two years after the Arab defeat of 1967, and as Fatah increased its military operations against Israel. During Black September in 1970 he was imprisoned for several months by the Jordanian authorities at the age of sixteen.[3] When I asked him if he was beaten, he laughed and told me that I better not ask and then recounted how his older cousin, who had initially inspired him to join the struggle, had been shot dead outside his family's home by the Jordanian authorities. After his release from prison in Jordan, Abu Muhammad still feared for his life and hid for a year in the hills, until his parents used their connections to fly him out to Kuwait to join his brothers. There, he worked as an electrical technician. He remained active in Fatah and in 1976 went to Lebanon to help in the defence of Tal al-Za'tar camp.[4] The camp fell three months later and Abu Muhammad went back to Kuwait for another three years. In 1979, he left Kuwait permanently to join Fatah's Force 17 in Lebanon.[5]

Abu Muhammad did not like to talk of his experiences in Tal al-Za'tar or as part of Force 17. He was more interested in discussing the dual effect of petrodollars. He would highlight how the money pouring from oil-rich countries made many Palestinian fighters prefer to be in office jobs in Beirut rather than on the frontline in the south, and how the influx of money gave foreign countries influence over Palestinian decision-making. However, when I asked him how he lost his passport and became a non-ID,[6] I learned that during the 1982 Israeli invasion of Lebanon Abu Muhammad had taken part in famous battles at Khalda and the Beirut airport.[7] To my great disappointment he did not provide me details of these battles, which I had only read about in books and which I had been longing to hear about from people who had fought in them. Instead, Abu Muhammad just recounted how, during the airport battle, they were able to repel the Israelis on two occasions, but on the third attack Israeli tanks managed to reach the runway. Abu Muhammad explained that as the tanks were driving down the runway, he and fellow fighters asked the leadership to bomb the tanks, which they refused to do. He then added that he witnessed the looting and burning of the airport by fellow Palestinians. When he attempted to call the firefighters, he was told by a commanding officer that "there is no need for that." This, he said, was the beginning of his troubles with part of the Fatah leadership.

Following the fall of the airport Abu Muhammad went back to the offices of Force 17 in Beirut, where he had left some of his clothes and passport; however, he found his bag open, his clothes spread everywhere, and his passport gone. He assumed that it had been burned. The loss of his passport was a major problem, as the Jordanian Embassy refused to issue him a new passport, and thereafter he became a "non-ID." In September 1982 Abu Muhammad left Beirut with the departing PLO forces for Tunisia. He had little to say about his stay in Tunis other than the fact that it basically consisted of "eating, drinking, sleeping, and sitting." But crucially, it was in Tunis that he learned that his passport had not been burned, but had been stolen by a Fatah official in Beirut. Abu Muhammad was keen on naming the given official, whom I will call Official X. He mentioned that, in the post-Oslo years, he often saw Official X standing behind Yasir Arafat on television.

Upon confronting Official X, Abu Muhammad was accused of being a Jordanian spy and imprisoned in the hotel nightclub in Tunis. Abu Muhammad laughed, saying that they had turned the nightclub into a prison just for him. However, security was lax and Abu Muhammad was able to escape within a few days and then hid in Tunis for the next seven months. He later made contact with a friend, who informed him that both Fatah and the Tunisian police were looking for him and advised him to leave the country. Abu Muhammad thought of his aunt, who lived in neighbouring Algeria, and decided to attempt to cross the border on foot. He took a train to the last town before the Tunisian-Algerian border and started walking along the train tracks. Soon his shoes fell apart and he continued barefoot until he reached a small village. Tired and hungry, his only option was to knock on someone's door and hope that they would help him. He heard the voice of an elderly woman coming from one house and decided that this was probably the safest place. He knocked on the door but, to Abu Muhammad's surprise, the door was opened by a young man, not an old woman. Once the young man realized that Abu Muhammad was Palestinian, he invited him inside, served him food and tea, and gave him a pair of boots. Abu Muhammad learned that he was still in Tunisia and the young man directed him on how to walk the rest of the way to Algeria.

He walked all night until he reached a river and found a fisherman. Again, once the fisherman realized that Abu Muhammad was Palestinian, he offered him food and a place to sleep and informed him that he had now crossed over the border. The next morning Abu Muhammad took the train to his relative's village, where he spent a week until he heard that there would be a meeting of the Palestinian National Council (PNC) in Algiers.[8] He decided to go to try to speak with the head of the Palestinian Liberation Army (PLA) and seek his help.[9] Upon meeting him, the head of the PLA, to Abu Muhammad's distress, called Official X, who was also at the PNC meeting. After a heated argument they agreed to give Abu Muhammad a six-month Tunisian travel document, a one-way ticket to Cyprus, from where he could take a boat to reach Tripoli in Lebanon, and a small amount of pocket money. He arrived in Lebanon just as the Fatah mutiny was taking place.[10] The mutineers called themselves Fatah al-Intifada and were engaged in armed combat against Fatah. Upon reporting to his assigned commanding officer, Abu Muhammad was put in charge of a hill facing Fatah al-Intifada and asked to lead an attack that evening, even though he was unfamiliar with the terrain and didn't know any of the men he was supposed to lead. In fact, it was his first time in the north of Lebanon. Abu Muhammad felt that he could not obey his orders; he had lost trust in the leadership of Fatah and was even afraid that they might want him dead. He thought that maybe they wanted him to lead an attack either to get killed by Fatah al-Intifada or to get killed from behind. He decided to disobey his orders and fled to Tripoli, where he hid in a school that was sheltering newly displaced Palestinians from the fighting. He spent three days thinking about his options. Without a valid passport he could not leave Lebanon, and certainly could not return to Jordan. He could not stay in Tripoli, for Fatah would soon find him and he feared what would happen to him if they did. He thought that his only option was to defect to Fatah al-Intifada.

He knew that Fatah al-Intifada now controlled Nahr el-Bared camp. However, two Fatah checkpoints separated him from it. He carefully selected a shared taxi with two women as passengers, thinking that it would not be stopped at the checkpoints. Indeed he was right. He reached Nahr el-Bared safely and defected to Fatah al-Intifada, with one condition. He argued that, since he refused to lead an attack against Fatah al-Intifada, similarly he would not fight Fatah. They agreed that he would go to Syria until the end of the battles. Two weeks later, as Fatah forces withdrew from Tripoli, Abu Muhammad returned to Nahr el-Bared and became a guard at one of the camp's checkpoints. This was how he met Nasser, Um Muhammad's brother-in-law, who introduced them to one other. They were engaged a few months later and married in the summer of 1984. The following year their first son, Muhammad, was born.

Over the next two years Abu Muhammad continued to work as a guard for Fatah al-Intifada, until Qaddafi went to war with Chad over control of the Aouzou strip in 1987. Fatah al-Intifada, which had close ties to the Qaddafi regime, gave its fighters the option of going to fight in Aouzou, northern Chad, offering double pay if they did so. One salary would be paid immediately to the fighter's wife in Nahr el-Bared, while the second installment would be paid to the fighter upon his return from Aouzou. However, Abu Muhammad explained that it was not money that made him go, but a friend who had signed him up without his knowledge. He smiled as he told me that he would have been deemed a coward if he had removed his name. He therefore went to Aouzou while Um Muhammad was pregnant with Ahmad. He stressed the fact that in Aouzou there was in fact no fighting and that they basically just sat around in their barracks in the desert.

Upon returning from Aouzou Abu Muhammad was asked to fight in Shatila. The War of the Camps was over, but a battle between Fatah and Fatah al-Intifada erupted when the splinter group wanted to expel the remaining Fatah loyalists from Shatila and began bringing in fighters from other camps.[11] Abu Muhammad refused to join the fight. He remembered how he told his leadership that "my fingers don't know how to shoot" (*aṣābi'ī mā bya'irfū yṭukhkhū*). He explained that he stayed home, at which point they refused to pay him the remaining six months of pay they owed him from his trip to Aouzou.

I realized that there were several reasons why his children often mentioned this trip to Aouzou. It not only reflected how the *thawra* went astray by fighting other people's wars, but also referred to what Abu Muhammad had to leave behind when he refused to fight in Shatila. The renunciation of six months of pay was not a small sacrifice. I learned from Um Muhammad that at the time she had just given birth to Ahmad; they were still living in a rented apartment and were desperate for money so they could settle down. Abu Muhammad's dissociation from Fatah al-Intifada also meant that he now had to fend for himself. His children had not missed this important point. One night, Mahmud pointed out to his father that former Fatah fighters now received a pension from Fatah, and suggested he could try asking for it. Um Muhammad laughed, telling Mahmud that his father gave up six months of salary not to fight in Shatila—did her son now want him to beg Fatah for a pension? Abu Muhammad added that Fatah never forgave the Intifada people and he would not go to them.

Abu Muhammad finished his story by saying "My dear, I became a porter at the port from that day until now, twenty-two years" (*yā sittī 'attāl 'ala bawwābat al-mīnā min waqtha lal-yawm, 22 sana*). Abu Muhammad's past involvement in the *thawra* meant that he had no particular skill or trade, let alone education, in order to find a stable job. His only choice was to find work as a day laborer, which he did as a porter at the Tripoli port. Abu Muhammad was a hard-working man, waking up everyday at 6:00 a.m. except on Sundays. I never saw him tired, nor did he ever complain of any ailment, although he was approaching his sixties and was performing physically taxing labor everyday. His life experiences taught him to be wary of grand political claims, stating that "all look for their interests and if someone comes and talks to me about freeing Palestine from the water to the water I will bring out my shoe and hit him in the head."[12] He often said that the best thing he did in life was to start a family with Um Muhammad.

Um Muhammad

Um Muhammad was the family's center of gravity and kept everyone on their feet and well-balanced. She was the one who knew where everyone was, what they were doing, when they would come home, what they needed, whether they had problems, and what to do about it. At the time of my research, Abu Muhammad's role was to make money, while Um Muhammad's was to find ways for the family to survive using that money. Faced with this daunting task, she never complained.

Um Muhammad was born in Nahr el-Bared camp in the early 1960s and lost her father in her teens. Her oldest brother, Muhammad, who resided in the United States at the time of my research, soon dropped out of school and began to work in different electrical jobs in the camp. Um Muhammad, the second-oldest daughter, decided to also help the family. While she worked during the summer picking and sorting tobacco, she felt it was not enough, and participated in a sewing workshop offered by the General Union of Palestinian Women in Nahr el-Bared camp. She explained that this was how she began her involvement with Fatah. Um Muhammad often used Fatah and the Women's Union interchangeably while she spoke. While she was certainly aware that the Women's Union was supposed to be an umbrella organization for all Palestinian political factions, she also knew that it was controlled and funded by Fatah, so for her there was little difference. She explained that once she became involved in the workshop, she started participating in different political events, marches, and conferences. At that time, Israeli raids and incursions into the camp were frequent and she often helped deliver food to the fighters and provided first aid to the injured. Her family's home was itself destroyed at least three times by Israeli bombardments and she helped rebuild it, both by partaking in the physical labor of rebuilding the house and by funding the purchase of required materials through her earned income.

In addition to her sewing activities, Um Muhammad started working in Fatah's radio communication department and later worked in "the cooperative" (*taʿāwuniyya*) operated by Fatah, where the popular committee was located along with several shops selling household items from furniture to cleaning products, all at a lower price than in the market. Um Muhammad ran a small cassette shop. She explained that after the 1983 Fatah mutiny she left her job and went home (*rawwaḥit ʿal-bayt*). She did not work after that, and although Fatah told her that they would keep on paying her even if she remained at home, she told them to stop as she worried that the Syrian authorities would know of her involvement with them.

This was also when she met Abu Muhammad. She explained that the first time she met him and learned that he was with Fatah al-Intifada, she argued with him. She told him that she disliked them and accused them of destroying the camp. He apparently smiled and told her that she was right and that all Palestinian factions were bad. After that they got along, she explained. Although Um Muhammad did not seek formal employment after her marriage, this did not mean that she was not working: it was rather that the nature of her work changed. She was now responsible for raising a family and making ends meet with the income that Abu Muhammad brought home. Daily survival soon filled her days.

DAILY SURVIVAL

Abu Muhammad went every day to the port of Tripoli to look for trucks to load or unload for a wage. Occasionally he would be hired for petty jobs such as taking furniture apart and helping in a move. Throughout my stay with the family they never discussed in front of me whether Abu Muhammad was successful at finding work on a given day or not, and I never asked. They seldom spoke to me directly of their financial difficulties, but these were visible in every detail of their lives.

A Day

A typical day for Um Muhammad started at 6:00 a.m. when her husband rose. While he would always tell her not to get up, as he liked to prepare his own breakfast, she argued that she didn't like the mess he usually left behind. Nadia would soon wake up too and begin her studies for the baccalaureate exam. Having failed the matriculation exam the year before, she wanted to retake it, but decided not to go back to school and to prepare for it on her own. Mahmud, who was working as a day laborer in the old camp, would be next to wake up. After a quick breakfast he got ready to leave and soon a discussion with his mother began about which clothes he could wear for work and which boots he could use. The debate about clothing and footwear was fuelled by necessity. The Talal family had some old clothes that Mahmud could use for work and they did not want to damage good clothing during construction work. This meant that Um Muhammad had to wash Mahmud's work clothes almost daily in order to make sure that he had clean clothing to wear the next day. However, shoes were the real cause of concern. At the construction site where Mahmud worked there was a large number of nails on the ground, which frequently pierced his flimsy shoes and caused injury. His mother feared that he would contract tetanus. Mahmud had already used—and pierced—most of his old shoes, and discussions would revolve around the possibility of getting new, tougher shoes, or which old shoe would withstand the day better.

Soon after Mahmud's departure, Ahmad would wake up and have his breakfast. By that time, Um Muhammad would have decided what the daily meal would be and would send Ahmad on errands to obtain the required ingredients. After this errand Ahmad would go to college and it was at that point that Um Muhammad, Nadia, and I would have our breakfast, before starting our cleaning chores. Um Muhammad always insisted that Nadia should concentrate on her studies and not partake in them, but Nadia continuously refused. However, they would both agree that my cleaning skills were even worse than mediocre. They would therefore assign me easy tasks such as doing the dishes, cleaning the stove, and putting the bedding away. They also both agreed that my sweeping skills, with or without water, were not good enough and far too slow. While I was always impressed by the speed and effectiveness of their work, I suspected that the real reason behind their insistence on doing most of the cleaning was simply kindness.

After the cleaning chores were done, the cooking started. This, along with the evening gatherings, was my favorite moment of the day. In addition to my learning how to cook many Palestinian and Arabic dishes, it was also the only time that Um Muhammad and I had on our own to talk. I would often tell her about the people I would be visiting that day, or the stories I had heard the day before. To my continual amazement, she seemed to know everyone in the camp, often correcting certain information I had misunderstood, or giving me more background information about the family history of a certain person I would meet. Time always flew by before we could finish our conversation, as Mahmud would be back for his lunch break and food needed to be ready so he had time to eat before going back to work. Then the conversation would invariably turn again to the shoe situation. After Mahmud's departure, Um Muhammad had a few hours where she would leave the house. She usually went to different NGOs if paperwork needed to be handed in, visited her sisters in the camp, or else stayed home to relax—or, more often, to wash laundry.

Um Muhammad's extended family was an essential component of the family's daily life. She had two sisters, Mariam and Fatima, who returned to Nahr el-Bared after the war, and another sister, Najah, and a brother, Sami, who preferred to remain in Beddawi camp. Mariam was not married and Nadia often slept over at her house with her other female cousins. In actuality, Mariam never slept alone as far as I could tell: every day a different cousin would stay over with her. Um Muhammad, Mariam, and Fatima visited each other almost daily. Their children's work, education, and study efforts would be discussed as well as everyone's health. News of new NGO or UNRWA programs would be spread and advice would be sought if needed.

In the early evening Um Muhammad would go back home. She liked to be home whenever her husband or children came back. In addition to making sure that they were eating well, by reheating the meal she cooked earlier in the day and making sure that it was enough for everyone, she also had the opportunity to hear about their day and get the latest news of what was going on. I suspect she also wanted to make sure that they were not facing any problems. I soon realized that she was the confidante of her children, who always came to her with their worries and not to their father. Mahmud's schedule was the most erratic as he worked several jobs, but Um Muhammad always knew when he would be coming home and always made sure that he had food ready to eat whenever he did, even if it meant that she stayed up late. Food, I soon realized, was a major cause of concern for the family.

Food (In)Security

During one of my mornings cooking with Um Muhammad, I learned that UNRWA considered them a special hardship case. I was helping Um Muhammad make a dessert by mixing milk powder with water in a saucepan on the gas stove and Um Muhammad explained to me that it was milk from UNRWA. She showed me the grey milk bag, which had the French flag on its upper half. She explained that the milk was bad quality and did not dissolve easily, which was why the water needed to be heated. UNRWA special hardship cases were considered amongst the poorest in the camp and they received food aid. Um Muhammad explained that it was dispensed every three months and that each person was entitled to

2.5 kilos of rice (which Um Muhammad added was bad quality, as it required a lot of cooking time to become tender and it would then be sticky), 2.5 kilos of sugar, 3 liters of oil, 2 kilos of milk powder, 2.5 kilos of lentils, 2.5 kilos of beans (also bad quality, according to Um Muhammad, as again they required a lot of cooking time and would still remain hard to eat). She added that they used to receive chickpeas, which she appreciated, but that had stopped for a reason unknown to her. Um Muhammad did not like grains that took a lot time to cook, as that meant that they consumed a lot of cooking gas. Over the next few months I witnessed the family going to an UNRWA food distribution center to collect the aid in boxes with stickers of the European Union flag. Individual food bags inside also often exhibited the donor country's flag.

A family needed to qualify to receive the food aid. This was done by proving that the main breadwinner, in this case Abu Muhammad, was not earning enough to feed his family. In Um Muhammad's case, she also had to justify the fact that Mahmud was working, as that usually meant that the family would be "removed from the list," as Um Muhammad put it. However, in this case, Um Muhammad was able to convince the UNRWA social worker overseeing her case that Mahmud's income was essential to help pay for Ahmad's tuition. The social worker agreed but told her that as soon as Ahmad graduated they would be "removed from the list." In addition, the family was the target of annual surprise visits from that same social worker. Um Muhammad explained that she could run into her in the street and the social worker would still not tell her that she was coming over to visit. Soon I realized that they also received surprise visits from another UNRWA employee, from the rent subsidy department. This employee came every three months, also unannounced. However, Um Muhammad did not like this particular worker. When she visited, she would not take off her shoes. Camp roads and alleys were notorious for being dirty and muddy, so residents and visitors would always remove their shoes upon entering a home in order to keep them clean. This was why Um Muhammad and Nadia cleaned the floors every day in order to keep them spotless, as everyone walked barefoot. The UNRWA employee, who came from the camp, certainly knew this, but showed her superiority over the family by not abiding by the custom. Um Muhammad explained to me that not all UNRWA employees were like that, but that some enjoyed being part of UNRWA "to be able to control people" (*tayiṭhakkamū bilnās*). The stated purpose of the surprise visits was to verify the information given by the family, such as who was living in the house, the size of the home, and the type of furniture in the house, which might disclose that the family had an additional income.

However, the family's level of food insecurity was revealed to me when I attempted to buy supplies for the household. Living with them in their home, I was fully aware that I was an additional mouth to feed. I was concerned about the extra burden that I represented, especially since the family categorically refused any attempt on my part to help them financially. I therefore decided that I would just buy groceries for the house from time to time. I thought that I better pur-chase a few items at a time, hoping that they would go unnoticed. I started to be on the lookout for items that they might need and soon I noticed that they were running low on tea and oranges, which they had a big stock of when I first moved in. Therefore, on my next errand outside of the house I came back with a box of tea and some apples, thinking that maybe they would like some change from oranges. When I got home my actions were contested and I protested that I could not feel at home if I did not also contribute to the house. Um Muhammad looked unconvinced but she did not reprimand me for too long and I thought that I had done well. I did not want to offend the family by acting in a way that openly acknowledged the extent of their poverty, but at the same time I could not ignore the extra burden that I represented for them. I wanted to find a way to contribute without upsetting them, and I thought that I had found it. A couple days later, Um Muhammad asked me if I liked apples. Her question took me off guard. I didn't know what to say, I thought we had settled the matter, but I realized that there was something special about the fact that I got apples. I finally answered that I didn't like fruit in general. She nodded and changed the topic of conversation. On my next errand outside of the house I passed by a grocery store and noticed that apples were in fact more expensive than oranges. I realized that variety was a luxury that the family could not afford. I never got apples after that and I became especially cautious to not only look for what they needed but also to learn which brands they bought to get the exact same items. This incident revealed to me just how precarious their situation was.

However, the biggest difficulty that the family faced, beyond their low income, was its unpredictability. I didn't realize the full implications of that until a few months into my fieldwork. It came to my attention when I was talking with Um Muhammad and Nadia about their participation in *jam'iyyāt*, informal savings associations.[13] Nadia was telling me that she and two of her friends from school, as well as their mothers and sisters, made a *jam'iyah* where they would each contrib-ute 500 LBP a day, the equivalent of 0.33 USD, and that each in their turn would get 10,000 LBP, the equivalent of 6.67 USD.[14] Um Muhammad told me that she did not participate, as she was unsure she could afford to pay 500 LBP every day, since Abu Muhammad did not work every day and she might need the money to purchase food instead. I was taken aback that Um Muhammad could not commit to such a small sum. The implications of a daily wage were suddenly clear to me. Although the signs were all around me, I hadn't put it all together until Um Muhammad put it plainly enough for me to hear. I now understood what initially puzzled me about Um Muhammad's daily routine. As I explained earlier, every morning Um Muhammad decided what would be the meal of the day and she would send out Ahmad to buy the required ingredients. They always purchased food items in small quantities, just enough for one meal. That surprised me, since buying in small amounts meant that they would not take advantage of bulk prices and also that Ahmad had to go on errands every day. But now it made sense. Since income was unpredictable it meant that Um Muhammad could not commit a large sum to buy, for example, a large quantity of soap, since she could not be sure that there would be money made in the next days to cover, for example, the price of bread. Um Muhammad had to purchase items on almost a daily basis, adjusting her expenditures to the immediate financial situation.

I realized the difference between Um Muhammad and her brother, Sami, who worked as a driver for a Tripoli businessman. Sami had explained to me that although his wage was lower than the other Lebanese drivers working for the same businessman, and although he did not receive the school aid for his children that the other Lebanese drivers got, he was grateful that the job was at least stable. Sami's wife could therefore plan her monthly expenses. At the beginning of every month she would buy all non-perishable food items for the month, taking advantage of bulk prices; she highlighted that she even bought the meat once a month—a package of 2 kilos, that she divided into ten smaller packets of 200 grams and froze individually so that she could make ten different meat dishes a month. I could not help but remember how my mother taught me when I first went to university that whenever I cooked I should plan for 200 grams of meat per person per serving. Sami's wife would plan the same amount for a family of five. The difference astounded me.

Um Muhammad's occupation, round the clock, was to save money. No member of the family ate outside the home. The daily meal that Um Muhammad cooked would be both lunch and dinner. Breakfast usually consisted of tea accompanied by bread and *labna* (strained yogurt) or sometimes eggs. Sweets were never bought but were always made at home. Soon I realized that fruit in general, not just apples, was a luxury. The stack of oranges I saw initially was probably purchased in my honor, as I was just moving in. A one-cup bag of Nescafe, priced at 250 LBP, about 0.17 USD, was a special treat that Nadia saved for particular occasions, usually when her close friend visited her. The more usual hot drink was tea. One tea bag boiled with several cups of water for a few minutes could provide a hot drink for the whole family, so it was much cheaper. The usual Arabic coffee was also made daily, but the used ground coffee was kept, mixed with fresh ground coffee, and reused. The family never bought fresh milk, yogurt, *labna* or cheese. Rather Um Muhammad would make yogurt and *labna* from milk rations she got from UNRWA, which always ran out a month before the next scheduled food aid distribution. They reused water bottles, and when the plastic turned opaque from usage, Um Muhammad poured grains of salt in them with a little bit of water and shook them vigorously. This cleared the plastic bottles and they would be ready to be refilled again. Children's spending would be discussed and compared between family members. Stories told about anything and everything would be punctuated with details of the price of things. When Muhammad's first daughter was born, Um Muhammad visited him and wondered how he paid for the pistachio that he used to garnish the usual desert of *mughli* that was offered by new parents to their visitors.

The importance of shoes was made clear to me again and again. It was not just an issue for Mahmud, but for most people in the camp. In the winter months, rain was common, and with the lack of proper street drains, the camp alleys quickly accumulated water. In the absence of proper heating, wet feet would remain wet for the rest of the day, increasing the chances of illness among children and adults alike. This explained why many parents worried about the distance that their children needed to walk to reach school. I realized that my waterproof boots were a marker of wealth in the camp. When I would go out on rainy days, Um Muhammad and Nadia always protested that I should stay home because of the rain. I was surprised. Um Muhammad had lived through countless Israeli bombings and the destruction of her home, not to mention the latest Nahr el-Bared war, and she worried about the rain? However, as often happened during my stay in the camp, my lack of understanding, and often my hasty judgment, was a reflection of my privilege. Material necessity regulated every aspect of the family's existence: the structure of their daily life as well as the long-term options available to them.

STARTING A LIFE

Mahmud, the youngest son of the family, was a tall, skinny, and highly energetic young man. He was outspoken and outgoing, rarely home, but when he was, he usually created a festive mood, making his mother and sister laugh at his jokes. On paydays he would bring home a bottle of juice and some Nescafe "one-cup" bags for his sister. He was also the one who used to give her pocket money. In this section, I trace the life choices and opportunities available to Mahmud as an example of how young Palestinian males "make it."

During the Nahr el-Bared war of 2007 Mahmud was studying hospitality management at a technical college in Tripoli. When the war started and his family took refuge in Beddawi camp, Mahmud stopped studying for his upcoming exams and instead volunteered with an NGO in the camp. He helped in the distribution of aid, and was an entertainer for children, organizing activities in the UNRWA schools where fleeing refugees had found shelter. This was not Mahmud's first encounter with NGOs. As I mentioned earlier, Muhammad, Mahmud's older brother, had been working with different NGOs for several years. He had introduced his younger brother to this line of work and Mahmud had already volunteered for several NGOs prior to the war.

Typically NGO volunteers were paid a nominal sum on a month-to-month basis, varying from 100,000 LBP (about 67 USD) to 100 USD. Volunteering was often a time when young Palestinians, men or women, attempted to prove to the heads of NGOs that they might be capable of a paid position. They provided a lot of their time, and sometimes even put in a bit of their own money on things such as trans-

FIGURE 8. Playing football in Nahr el-Bared camp. Photograph: Perla Issa.

portation or phone calls in the hope that they would be made part of the NGO's permanent staff. Mahmud volunteered for a total of two years after the war and worked on several projects. However, the experience left him bitter. He explained to me that towards the end of his two years and as he began to work on a new project, his superior told him that he needed to prove himself before they would hire him. Mahmud in response worked for two months without pay, organizing activities for other youth in the camp and even buying juice boxes for the participants from his own money. Following these two months, his superior told him that they did not have the funds to continue the program. Mahmud felt betrayed and left them.

Mahmud's efforts to search for employment were not confined to NGO work alone; he was active in seeking any type of occupation. He worked in Tripoli as a painter for a contractor and was paid 10 USD a day. He worked in a restaurant located across from one of the main entrances of Beddawi camp where he made 40 USD a week working twelve hours a day from 2:00 p.m. to 2:00 a.m. He worked in a restaurant in Tyr, where his older brother lived, making 10 USD a day. At the time of my fieldwork he was working as a day laborer in the old camp, making 20 USD working from 7:00 a.m. to 4:00 p.m., with an extra 10 USD if he worked overtime from 4:00 p.m. to 7:00 p.m., which he usually did. This made a total of 30 USD for twelve hours of work and was certainly the best-paying job he had had up until then. Additionally, he worked on a part-time basis with a new NGO in the camp, entertaining children with clown activities and theater and helping in the distribution of aid when available. Finally, throughout his previous years of work, he had saved some money to be able to buy a set of speakers, a mixing console, two microphones, and a used laptop. This allowed him to begin operating his own DJ business and he performed at weddings, bachelor parties, engagement parties, as well as political protests and conferences. When I asked Mahmud what work he preferred, he explained that he most enjoyed being an actor and an entertainer for children but, at this point, the only thing he wished for was stable employment.

Um Muhammad disliked the fact that Mahmud was working. Although the family was in dire need of the additional income he earned, she wanted him to continue his studies. She believed that the war was to blame for his renunciation of an education, as well as for his recent habit of smoking *narghile*. However, she was happy that he was now toiling in the hard work of construction, hoping that this experience would teach him that it was better to obtain a degree than to labor for a daily wage. She had therefore stopped arguing with him, and was patiently waiting for him to reach his own conclusions in due time. At the beginning of the next school year, Um Muhammad was almost proven right as Mahmud went back to college to continue his degree in hospitality management.

However, a few months into the semester he quit again. His reasons for quitting were numerous. Firstly, he no longer believed that education would allow him to be more successful in life. While working on the construction of the old camp he met countless college graduates who, due to Lebanon's discriminatory laws, could not find proper employment and who, like him, had to work as day laborers in construction. Um Muhammad disliked this line of argument the most, as she felt it encouraged Nadia not to study hard to obtain her baccalaureate. Second was the ever-repressive issue of money. Mahmud was well aware that by going back to school, he stopped bringing an additional income into the household, and became a burden again on his parents, having them spend money on his expenses and tuition. Thirdly, the prospect of potential failure loomed. Failure in his exams would not only represent a personal disappointment but would also mean that the money spent on him would have been lost for nothing. That was a heavy burden for him to carry.

Finally, he saw what his older brother, Ahmad, had to go through to obtain enough aid to cover his tuition. As I will explain in chapter 5, Ahmad's tuition was paid from four different sources: a Palestinian political faction, the Palestinian embassy, an international NGO, and finally the family itself. His tuition cost 2 million LBP, the equivalent of 1,334 USD. However, at no point in time did the family know how much each party would be paying, so as to know how much would be left over for them to cover. Mahmud explained that he could not live with this type of uncertainty, preferring instead to live with the uncertainty of a daily wage. Uncertainty and precariousness were features of Palestinian life in Lebanon, and the daily struggle to make ends meet was often punctuated by conflicts which only furthered people's sense of insecurity and vulnerability, such was the case with the 2007 Nahr el-Bared conflict.

LIVING THE 2007 NAHR EL-BARED CONFLICT

In the early hours of May 20, 2007, the Talal family woke to the sound of bombs. Abu Muhammad got up and went up on the roof to see what was going on. Having been a fighter for eighteen years, Abu Muhammad had developed a sense of invulnerability to physical danger. He watched the bombs fall on the camp and called the rest of his family to come up and join him. He initially thought it was an Israeli attack on the camp, as those had been frequent in the 70s and the 80s. After all he had initially met Um Muhammad while she was carrying cement blocks to rebuild her parents' home after it was demolished by an Israeli attack. Over the years that home was to be bombed and destroyed by Israel and rebuilt by Um Muhammad's family three times. However on this occasion the shelling was from the Lebanese army stationed not far from Abu Muhammad.

Um Muhammad, less interested in the theatrics of war and more concerned with the practicalities of survival, took a shower right away. The electricity had been cut off and she thought that it would take at least a week for it to be repaired again. Without electricity there would be no hot water and more importantly, within a couple days, there would be no water at all, as the water pump would stop functioning. She told her husband that since he was enjoying himself on the roof he might as well bring down the laundry she had hung out to dry the night before, otherwise it would soon smell like gunpowder. She woke up her two sons Mahmud and Ahmad, asking them to shower too, but they refused to get out of bed. Their sister Nadia was sleeping at her grandparents' home in the old camp, and their eldest brother Muhammad was working with an NGO in the Buss camp in Sour. Everyone thought that the clashes would last a few hours, or maybe a few days, but that it would be over soon. No one thought that this would be the last time they would see their home, their neighborhood, and the entire camp. Abu Muhammad went out to get some food and heard from other people in the camp that it was a battle between the Lebanese Army and Fatah al-Islam.

Abu Muhammad was unhappy with the news. He had first heard of the newcomers to the camp at the end of the previous year. Rumours started circulating that Fatah al-Intifada was bringing in people into the camp, people who didn't even speak Arabic. Then at the end of November 2006, his son read to him the public statement distributed in the camp declaring the establishment of Fatah al-Islam and announcing its split from Fatah al-Intifada. Next, when members of Fatah al-Islam took over the main office of Fatah al-Intifada, which lay on a main crossing between the old and the new camp, Abu Muhammad stopped walking on the main road, not wanting to come face to face with them and have to salute people he distrusted. Um Muhammad would always tease him that he would take the long way home just to avoid them. In contrast, Um Muhammad and her daughter Nadia welcomed their presence at the main intersection, as they could now take that road to the market. When the office had been under the care of Fatah al-Intifada, their members had been notorious for sitting outside the office, occasionally harassing women passing by. But since Fatah al-Islam took over the space, no such incidents occurred; they were most often seen reading the Qur'an.

Several members of Fatah al-Islam rented apartments close to where the Talal family lived. On one occasion the wife of a member of Fatah al-Islam asked Um Muhammad for advice on where to seek medical help for her sick child. Abu Muhammad was unhappy about that; he didn't want any member of his family to have contact with Fatah al-Islam. He was suspicious of their presence and felt that trouble was about to befall them. He told Um Muhammad that he wanted to leave the camp but he did not want to sell his home to members of Fatah al-Islam, the only people buying apartments at that time. Um Muhammad, on the other hand, would argue that if these people were here to fight and cause trouble they would not have brought their families with them.

Regardless of their past positions towards the newcomers, both Um and Abu Muhammad were now in agreement that they had to leave their house immediately. They feared that their area, inhabited by several families of Fatah al-Islam, would be targeted by the Lebanese army. Um Muhammad called her sister Najah and learned that her extended family was congregating at Najah's house. Located in the middle of the old camp, it was deemed the safest as it was far from Fatah al-Islam and far from the edges of the camp that always bore the brunt of any attack. Um Muhammad put an 'abaya over her nightgown and took her most precious possession: a plastic bag full of documents. Abu Muhammad, and all of his children, were not legally recognized by the Lebanese government. As we saw, Abu Muhammad lost his Jordanian passport in 1982 during the Israeli occupation of Lebanon. Thereafter the Jordanian government refused to issue him a new passport. His four children, born in Lebanon, were not recognized by either the Jordanian or the Lebanese government. Legally, they did not exist. Their mother Um Muhammad, a holder of the blue identity card issued by the Lebanese government for Palestinian refugees, could not register her children under her name according to Lebanese law. During the 2006 war with Israel Um Muhammad had collected all papers into a plastic bag, with a sturdy handle, that was ready to be taken at a moment's notice. No paper, no matter how insignificant, was deemed unworthy of protection. Abu Muhammad laughed at her when he saw her taking the bag, but it was Um Muhammad who later laughed at him, pointing out her foresight. With the bag in hand, they waited for a lull in the bombings, but no such moment occurred, so they dashed through the alleys as quickly as they could and made it to Najah's house safely.

They found the three-floor house bursting with people. Um Muhammad's brother Sami was present with his wife and three children, her other sister Fatima was also there with her husband and four children, and her third sister Mariam and her mother also joined them with Um Muhammad's daughter Nadia. Finally, looking for safety in numbers, neighbors had also converged onto the house. Everyone discussed the latest political developments, as well as any updates as to which homes got hit, who got killed and who got injured. The third floor of the house was left empty as it was deemed to be too dangerous. At times of war the number of walls and roofs separating people from the outside world were counted as a form of protection against deadly flying missiles. Following that logic, the women settled into the bottom floor of the house, considered the safest, and the men on the second floor. The children could move from one floor to the other in an attempt to deal with their fears and the feelings of confinement caused by being indoors surrounded by so many people.

On the second day of bombing Abu Muhammad decided to go and check on his home. It had taken him and Um Muhammad twenty-two years to secure a small home which possessed two critical features: it was theirs and it had concrete walls and roofs. It initially took them fifteen years to be able to secure one room that was five by seven meters with a small kitchen and bathroom attached. That room was allocated to them by the popular committee of Nahr el-Bared in an area called *al-muhajjarīn*, which in Arabic means "the displaced." *Al-muhajjarīn* was initially built to accommodate the refugees who had been displaced by the Tal al-Zaʿatar massacre in 1976. The Talal family had only able to obtain that room once it was considered unfit for living and UNRWA, under an agreement with the PLO, built new housing units for those previously living there. As the previous residents of *al-muhajjarīn* moved into their new units, their old unlivable homes were given to people who were desperate for any place to call their own.

At first the family divided the space into a two-by-five-meter room where Um and Abu Muhammad slept while their children slept in a five-by-five-meter room that was turned into a sitting and study area during the day. The roof was made of overlapping zinc metal sheets. With the pouring of concrete roofs banned by the Lebanese authorities, they had to live under these flimsy metal sheets that were notorious for water leakage during the rainy and cold winter months, then transformed homes into ovens in the summer as the metal radiated the sun's heat into their small living space. It took three years and a Norwegian NGO to convince the Lebanese government to allow them to pour concrete roofs. Then it took two more years and the help of Um Muhammad's brothers to pour a second concrete roof, which gave the Talal family another floor. However, they had to wait yet another year in order to save enough money to be able to buy the concrete blocks to add walls to it. They first built one room, and then later added another. Finally, a few months before the war, they bought a new batch of cinderblocks, which now laid on the roof, as they were planning on adding a third floor to the house to make room for their eldest son Muhammad, who was starting to make marriage plans.

However, those plans and the house itself were now under threat. Abu Muhammad found that a missile had struck the outer wall of their neighbor's house but had not detonated. Members of Fatah al-Islam used that house. He went in to tell them that an unexploded missile lay outside their wall, but they did not speak any Arabic and seemed lost and confused. He gave up on trying to communicate with them and instead decided to remove the missile himself. From his past training he had learned that if a missile doesn't explode once its head explodes, which had happened when the missile struck the wall, then it was safe to manipulate it. He therefore carried it to Najah's house. When the women saw him approaching carrying a missile in his hands they started screaming at him. He tried to reassure them that it was not dangerous but they told him to get rid of it. The question for him was, where? He went to the office of the PFLP, who again screamed at him, and in the end he decided to throw it into the sea.

Um Muhammad, meanwhile, ventured out of the house occasionally with her sister Mariam. They would wait for the bombing to decrease and they would run through the alleys to go to their mother's house, which was the closest, in order to get additional food supplies. They didn't want to use up all of Najah's food reserves, believing that it was unfair for her to carry alone the financial burden of feeding five different families.

Finally, on Tuesday May 22, after three days of indiscriminate and continuous bombings, a cease-fire was declared. Rumours circulated that UNRWA had sent trucks full of bread into the camp. Abu Muhammad collected the UNRWA ID cards of all the different families present and was happy to go out and collect their rations. Mahmud, Um Muhammad's fifteen-year-old son wanted to go out with his cousins, Aboud and Ammar. Mahmud and Ammar in particular had a very special relationship; they both had cheerful dispositions and were always seen together laughing and joking. However, Um Muhammad did not let Mahmud go, telling him that she needed him with her. Ammar, who was studying in the UNRWA technical school in Sibline, had come home on Saturday for the weekend and bought a new outfit. Unable to leave again for his classes on Monday due to the bombings, he was eager to go to his home and change into his new clothes. His brother Aboud accompanied him and as they sat outside their home, Ammar in his new attire, they heard that the media was present with the UNRWA bread trucks. They decided to seek them out.

As they reached the bread truck, and as Abu Muhammad was walking away from it, loaves in hand, a missile struck the truck. Abu Muhammad felt the blow but was not injured; Aboud was thrown to the ground; and Ammar was killed. In the great commotion that ensued Aboud could not locate his brother and he simply thought that Ammar must have returned home on his own. He therefore got up and went home. In the meantime Jihad, the cousins' father, had heard the explosion and went out to look for them. He overheard people saying that "ibn Jihad" ("the son of Jihad") was killed. He asked them where the bodies had been taken without telling them that he was Jihad. There were, after all, many Jihads in the camp. He went to the clinic and to his great distress he found his son's body.

He pushed himself to go back home and tell his family. His wife was devastated. Everyone was screaming. Aboud could not believe it. "He was standing right next to me," he kept repeating. At that moment, Um Muhammad's oldest brother, also named Muhammad, called from the United States. While speaking to him Um Muhammad dropped the phone on the floor and all that could Muhammad hear on the telephone was screams; he thought that the house had just been hit and began to go crazy in distant Washington, DC. In a desperate attempt to keep some cool he called the one person he knew who was not in the house, the sister of the wife of his brother Sami. Fortunately, she answered the phone, and living nearby she went to check on them, learned the news, and reported back to Muhammad.

The shelling of the camp had now started again and Jihad urgently needed to go back to the clinic to bury his son. His two brothers-in-law, Abu Muhammad and Sami, decided to accompany him. Upon arriving they discovered that the staff of the clinic, due to the renewal of the bombing, had already buried Ammar in the mass grave they had dug for those who were killed in the previous three days. The mass grave was partitioned so that each person buried had a specific spot. However, when Jihad asked which spot was his son's two were indicated. To this day, when Fatima goes to pray for her dead son, she is unsure where his body has been laid to rest.

Back in Najah's house, while everyone was still in shock over the killing of Ammar, a quick decision needed to be taken about whether to stay in the camp or to flee. Um Muhammad wanted to leave the camp with her children. Sami's wife, Rania, was of the same opinion. The bombing of the bread truck had signaled to them that this conflict was being played by a different set of rules than previous ones. It was hard to interpret the truck bombing as anything other than a deliberate targeting of civilians. They feared for their lives and believed that they had no role to play in this fight. They viewed it as being between the Lebanese army and Fatah al-Islam, and they preferred not to be caught in its midst. They were encouraged by the great number of refugees who had begun to leave the camp. However, Fatima, who had just lost her son, and her sister Najah were too afraid of leaving the camp. They worried that they would not reach the outside of the camp alive and they wondered where they would go. Their fears were compounded when they heard that a man and a pregnant woman had been shot dead and others injured as their fleeing bus approached a Lebanese army checkpoint. Fatima and Najah decided to stay in the camp, while Um Muhammad and Rania decided to leave with their children.

Um Muhammad told her husband to go home, as she and her children were still wearing their sleeping clothes from the first day of the battle. Abu Muhammad brought back a big bag of garments, but upon opening the bag, Um Muhammad realized that he had brought back the clothing that was in the closet. These were old discarded clothes that were torn and that she kept aside for her husband and sons to use when working on construction sites. Their wearable clothing laid on her bed, unfolded; Abu Muhammad had forgotten that he had placed them there when he brought them down from the roof on the first day of the bombings. They would keep talking about this misfortune for years to come, as once their home destroyed they could simply not afford to buy any new outfits and had to keep on wearing their old, previously discarded ones.

The next morning, in a brief lull in the fighting, Um and Abu Muhammad and their three children left with Sami's wife and her three children, looking for a way out of the camp. Abu Muhammad spotted a car with the flag of the Lebanese Future movement, the party of the Hariri family. At first Um Muhammad refused to get in, but upon looking closer she realized that a Palestinian from the camp was in the car and the car was actually his, although the driver was from the Future movement. At that point they got in the car. Abu Muhammad sat in the front with the two other men, Um Muhammad, and her daughter, Sami's wife, and her three children sat in the back seat, and Mahmud and Ahmad sat in the open trunk. They soon realized that they had done well, as they went through the Lebanese Army's checkpoint without being stopped or searched. Instead, the man from the Future movement just waved at the soldiers and passed through while they watched other camp residents wait in a long line at the checkpoint. The car took them to a house outside the camp that had turned into a relief station for Nahr el-Bared residents. They were given juice boxes, and from there other cars took them to Beddawi camp. They were surprised at how well organized the evacuation was, and they started wondering: why was the Lebanese Future party helping them leave the camp? But there was no time to dwell on such thoughts; they first needed to find a refuge. Um Muhammad planned on going to Tyr, to her eldest son's home. However, when her other children saw that most of Nahr el-Bared, and therefore many of their friends, were now in Beddawi camp, they convinced her to stay at her relative's home in the camp. It was a few days later, and in that home, that I first met them in 2007.

. . .

Palestinian refugees in Lebanon live on the fringe of Lebanese society. For more than seven decades their experience has been one of constant pressure, crisis, and turmoil. Living with the Talal family gave me a glimpse into the survival mechanisms that Palestinian refugees adopt. Such a window is essential if we are to understand the continued relevance of Palestinian political factions in everyday life. Through this account we were able to identify different features of daily life, notions that we will go back to in the next chapters: the general disillusionment with Palestinian political factions; the importance of family and interpersonal trust; and the struggle, the daily and grinding struggle to make ends meet.

FIGURE 9. Woman cooking, Nahr el-Bared camp. Photograph: Ali Alloush.

3

"We Drank the *Jabha* with Our Mothers' Milk"

Joining Factions

"Rotten," "traitors," "thieves," "merchants of death" (*tujjār damm*)—those were just some of the names Palestinians used to describe Palestinian political factions in Lebanon. Others went further, saying "they should be burned" or "killed." However, factions were more often the subjects of jokes and ridicule than murderous fantasies. Khalil, a young man in Shatila camp, explained to me that his father once gave him a list of the factions in the camp and told him to go and give them a try to see if he liked any of them. Khalil explained that he attended several meetings, and upon hearing the different factions call each other "*wlād al kalb*" (sons of dogs), he concluded, with a poignant sarcasm, that "All Palestinians must be 'sons of dogs' then."[1] He stopped going. Another young Palestinian recounted how his grandmother warned him that political work was about the pursuit of personal ambitions rather than the general good: "The Palestinian people are like a bag of garlic, no matter which one you pick out you always end up with a head." Many young Palestinians recounted how their parents forbade them from approaching factions, often physically pulling them away from factional offices or activities when such associations were discovered. In the Talal household, such condemnations were also common, especially from Abu Muhammad: "They only care about their own interests," he often repeated.

The popular dissatisfaction of Palestinian refugees with Palestinian political factions has been highlighted in numerous studies (Frisch 2009; Kortam 2011; Peteet 1995; R. Sayigh 2001, 96; 2011; 2012; Suleiman 1999). They have been accused of factionalism (R. Sayigh 2012, 22), of corruption (Brynen 1995b, 25; R. Sayigh 2012, 22), and betrayal (Allan 2014; Khalili 2004; Peteet 1995). In light of such heavy criticisms, a question arises: are Palestinian factions in Lebanon able to attract new members? Nahr el-Bared camp had a popular committee comprised of sixteen members, one for every faction. It was notorious for its internal divisions and its subsequent inability to take decisions. Few Palestinians in the camp could actually list the different factions represented on the committee, which underscored the fact that many of these factions had little to no existence in the camp.[2] These factions were called "facades" (*wājhāt*) in the camp, and they were in fact the subjects of even greater mockery. Um Muhammad laughed as she told me that the PPP had two members in the camp, one of whom sat on the Popular Committee and acted as the "head of the PPP" in Nahr el-Bared camp.[3] The second member was his son-in-law. These "facades" often infuriated residents who felt that "the only ones who were sillier than those people were those who dealt with them"—referring to UNRWA, NGOs, and the Lebanese government, who sometimes considered the Popular Committee a counterpart and occasionally involved them in decision-making. However, it would be incorrect to assume that all factions were such shells. Of the fifty-one interviews I conducted with "close" Palestinians, forty-three individuals (twenty-two of the younger generation and twenty-one of the *thawra* generation) had contact with factions, while only eight Palestinians (six of the new generation and two of the *thawra* generation) had no relations with factions.[4]

How did the initial contact with a faction occur? How did Palestinians choose which faction to approach, whether for political, social, cultural, or economic reasons? How were factions able to attract young Palestinians in light of such heavy criticisms? Is there a difference in how the *thawra's* generation was mobilized versus today's generation? Were Palestinians ideologically motivated? Islamic factions in particular are often studied through their ideologies; their popularity is explained by the rise of Islamism, which is linked to the decline of secular nationalism (Israeli 2008; Rougier 2007). In short, Islamism is seen as "a useful tool that can be wielded to generate support from the Palestinian street" (Schanzer 2008, 10). Other works suggest that Palestinians act strategically in their dealings with factions in order to maximize the financial benefits of such relations. In other words, is economic patronage the main tool of mobilization? Moughrabi (1983) argued that Palestinian politics became "lebanonized" (212): "each Abu has his system of patronage and his own budget" (214).[5] Or, are there other factors at play? Investigating this line of questioning allowed me to walk down another avenue of inquiry about the actual mechanics involved in "joining factions." Was "joining a faction" a singular event? Could it be delineated in time and pointed to as the moment when a person crossed the line separating those "outside" a faction from those on the "inside"?

What my research suggests is that Palestinians approached factions based on interpersonal relations imbued with high levels of trust: family, friendship, and neighborhood ties were the main vehicle behind factional affiliation. In fifty-one interviews with close Palestinians of both generations, I found that only two people spoke of party ideology when they discussed their initial contact with a faction (one from the *thawra* generation and one from the younger generation).[6] While many spoke of the financial pressures they faced and the lack of stable employment, those economic predicaments rarely determined which factional door they knocked on. Rather, the picture that was drawn was of people coming together because of trust relations built on a local basis. This did not mean that ideology did not matter. It just means that the initial appeal of factions was not to be found in the political platforms which Palestinians were often quick to disavow. As the examples will show, people often criticized the factions' political platforms while maintaining contact with them, and it is impossible to explain this contradiction without looking at the personal relations that form the factions' very core.

My research also suggests that the importance of interpersonal relations in forging factional relationships was present for both the *thawra's* generation and today's. While the factions' appeal has vastly decreased since the *thawra*, the mechanism by which interpersonal relations are transformed into political relations remains the same. In fact scholars of the Palestinian resistance movement in Lebanon (Jalloul 1994, 52–53; Peteet 1991, 119–24; R. Sayigh 1994, 105–8) have noted that refugees in the 1960s and 1970s (the *thawra* generation) were most often mobilized through their kin ties. Rosemary Sayigh (1994, 119–24) mentions that "members of the same household usually joined or supported the same Resistance group, but this was not always the case." A more recent study conducted in the West Bank points out that a mixture of family and friendship ties can account for political mobilization (Sabella 2001, 44). This finding was corroborated by Jensen (2009, 71–74), whose ethnographic study of Hamas in the Gaza Strip highlights how players were drawn to the Hamas football club for non-ideological reasons such as its geographical proximity to their homes, as well as to satisfy their own sporting ambitions. This argument is also supported by social movement literature. Doug McAdam (1982, 44) affirms that "if there is anything approximating a consistent finding in the empirical literature, it is that movement participants are recruited along established lines of interaction." Gerlach and Hine (1970, 79) add that "no matter how a typical participant describes his reasons for joining the movement, or what motives may be suggested by a social scientist on the basis of deprivation, disorganization, or deviancy models, it is clear that the original decision to join required some contact with the movement."

Expanding on this argument, I want to unpack the actual process of mobilization. How is factional membership passed down within a family or through a friendship? Is it through a process of indoctrination and the inculcation of a party ideology? How did it operate during the *thawra* and how does it operate today, in the context of increasing dissatisfaction with existing factional structures? And finally, what are the implications of this finding for our understanding of the nature of factions and faction membership?

Bringing to light the process by which factions and families interacted could be seen as reinforcing the view that Arab politics is patrimonial (Bill and Springborg 2000, 112–29) which is seen as the blind following of kin ties. In its crudest form, patrimonialism is understood as people submitting "themselves as a flock unto a shepherd" (Hudson 1977, cited in Brynen 1995b, 24), where subordinates are not seen as officials with defined powers but rather as pawns who act according to the will of their leaders (Clapham 2004, 48). However, the life stories I collected point to the contrary. In this chapter I show how dynamic and diverse this process is. Far from resembling a sheep following a shepherd, "joining" was an unstable and non-linear process, which featured unexpected elements such as critical analyses of factions and the defiance of parental authority even when the person was inspired by family members to "join a faction." Additionally, "joining a faction" was not a singular event occurring at a particular moment in time. While some Palestinians could point to a particular moment when they officially became members of a faction, that moment seldom represented the beginning of their involvement with it.

There were two main reasons why Palestinians "joined factions:" family and friendship/neighborhood ties. Out of the forty-three interviews with close Palestinians whose life stories featured relations with factions, twenty had developed their initial contact through family ties, while twenty-two rested on friendship and neighborhood ties. Finally, one young Palestinian joined a faction based on a desire to maximize financial rewards. It is interesting to note that the propensity of family ties was higher for the *thawra* generation (thirteen out of twenty) while the importance of friendship and neighborhood ties was greater for the younger generation (fourteen out of twenty-two). My ethnographic methods revealed the importance of looking at life stories in order to better understand the dynamics that animated refugees' and factions' relations and whether we could even separate the two. The examples included below were chosen because they typified how initial contact with factions most often occurred.

FAMILY TIES

> My past, my upbringing, the passing of the years, my culture, my home environment, this is what contributed to my belonging to Hamas.
>
> —WISSAM, YOUNG GENERATION, BEIRUT, NOVEMBER 2, 2011

> I was born PFLP, I don't know why. What's the story? What's the issue? [Laugh] My siblings and parents were all PFLP, so I ended up PFLP.
>
> —NIDAL, *THAWRA* GENERATION, NAHR EL-BARED CAMP, DECEMBER 17, 2011

> I come from an original Fatah family.... My grandfather.... was a martyr for Fatah (*shahīd la fatah*) and my aunt was also [stops himself] a martyr for Palestine and for Fatah. We are an old Fatah family. But that's the issue, what should I believe in? If something was left, I would believe in it, but there is nothing left.
>
> —FARIS, YOUNG GENERATION, BEIRUT, OCTOBER 10, 2011

It was common for Palestinian refugees to associate entire families with a given faction. Similarly to how Faris introduced his family in the above quote, the name of the faction would be added as an adjective to characterize the family. For example, Palestinians would say ʿ*ayli fatḥāwiyyi*, "a Fatah family," or ʿ*ayli jabhawiyyi*, "a PFLP family." Additionally, the duration of the association was sometimes added: ʿ*ayli fatḥāwiyyi aṣīli*, "an original Fatah family." By adding this extra adjective the family emphasized that one of its ancestors was a founding member of that faction. I illustrate the process through which family and factions intersected through the example of the Hamdan family, whom I had known for over four years prior to this research. Focusing on one family, instead of including many short stories, allows me to explore the interactions of the *thawra* and the younger generations. The relationship of the father, Abu Ali, as well as two of his sons, Ali and Rabieh, with the PFLP typifies how factional affiliation, at times, was transmitted to the next generation. Indeed, Rabieh formed a deep association with the PFLP, becoming an armed guard for the faction, while his older brother Ali disassociated himself. This story gives us insight into several phenomena. First, it allows us to see what it meant to be in a factional family. How were children affected by their parents' political affiliation, and how was that influence experienced? Secondly, this story illustrates how factional reproduction occurred during the *thawra* as well as today in spite of the vast criticism targeting them. Finally, it permits us to start the conversation, expanded in the next chapter, about the nature of faction membership by examining what appeared to be its "beginnings."

The Hamdan Family

Abu Ali was a charismatic, kind and well-spoken man in his mid-fifties. He possessed a variety of skills and over the years worked in many trades. He was at times a welder whose job, as he put it, "was to look for a job," highlighting that he worked one day out of ten. On other occasions he was a fisherman, turning the camp's location by the Mediterranean Sea to his advantage. He was also an entrepreneur, who over the years operated a thrift shop and, more recently, a fresh-juice and grilled corn-on-the-cob stall next to the metal trailer he called home.[7] Finally, he was a playwright, a poet, and a chronicler of current affairs, constantly updating his Facebook page with stories, images, and information about the situation in the camp. The common feature throughout all of these experiences was his poise. Abu Ali always impressed me with the calm demeanor he kept in the face of adversity, whether it was the indiscriminate shelling of his community, the destruction of the home he spent thirty-five years to build, his grandchildren's fits and fights in small and overcrowded spaces, or his inability to pay the "satellite guy" knocking on his door to receive the 10 USD monthly fee.[8]

I initially met the Hamdan family in Beddawi camp, where they were sheltering during the Nahr el-Bared conflict in 2007. Throughout the years I kept a relationship with the family, visiting them whenever I was in the camp. Following their return to

Nahr el-Bared camp the family settled in UNRWA-provided metal trailers, locally known as the "Baracksat." These were made of corrugated steel panels. Apart from the windows on their long sides, the trailers resembled shipping containers. They were about three meters wide and seven meters long. A family of five people was allowed one container, while larger families could claim two. They were placed in stacks of two, six in line for about twenty-four rows. Initially about 240 families lived in the "Baracksat." These were meant to be temporary quarters, but up to the time of writing, six years later, the Hamdan family was still living in them. Inside the trailer there was, on one end, an aluminium counter equipped with a sink; above it was one wooden shelf and a water heater. The family later added a two-burner stove for cooking. This was supposed to be the "kitchen." Next to it stood the bathroom: a small one-meter-square stall with a sink, a squat toilet, and a shower. The rest of the trailer was an open space that the family filled with mattresses that were used as beds at night and as a sitting area in the day, as was common in the camps. I was never quite able to figure out how many trailers the Hamdan family as a whole had, because the family was quite large: many of Abu Ali's children were married and had offspring of their own. However, it seemed that one trailer was used as the common area for the extended family, and it was to this that I always directed myself. It was always packed with infants, toddlers, teenagers, and adults. In fact, I seldom knew the family relations between the different people present at any time.

At the time of my research UNRWA provided rent subsidies and strongly encouraged people to leave the "Baracksat," and I witnessed several visits from an UNRWA employee trying to convince the family to move out. However, the Hamdan family found that the rent subsidy was not enough to be able to find housing in Nahr el-Bared, which was in short supply and therefore more expensive. Additionally, water and electricity were available for free in the "Baracksat," while they would have to pay for them if they were to rent a home. But more importantly, the family's daily survival was predicated on living close to each other, with collective cooking, shared care of young children, and many other forms of joint work and solidarity. This form of communal living was unlikely to be replicated if they were to rent apartments, which would certainly not be neighboring each other even if they were lucky enough to find them in the first place. It was precisely in such environments that familial bonds were solidified, stories were shared, and new connections were made, as I learned from Abu Ali, Rabieh, and Ali.

The Thawra *Generation: Abu Ali*

"I drank the *Jabha* with my mother's milk," was Abu Ali's answer to my question of how his involvement with the PFLP began.[9] We were sitting in a metal trailer further away from the family commotion. He continued by explaining that his father, Ali,[10] had been an early member of the Arab Nationalist Movement (ANM), and later became part of the Revolutionary Youth Organization and then the PFLP (see Hasso 2005, 7–10). Abu Ali remembered how, as a young child, he used to stand guard outside his family's home during meetings there. It was the era of the Deuxième Bureau, when gatherings at homes were forbidden.[11] It was common to have children watch out, signalling to their parents when a patrol was passing by. Abu Ali emphasized that his association with the *Jabha* started from an early age and was something he was nurtured with. He remembered how as a teenager he used to go to the bakeries to collect donations for the fighters and women would sometimes give him their entire batch, stressing that, at the time, people trusted in each other and in the *thawra*.[12]

Abu Ali's father talked to him about Palestine, and taught him "to love it" and to fight for it. He insisted that he "drank the *nidal* (struggle)" from his father. He continued by explaining that "our household was all *Jabha*, we were raised in the *Jabha*." Abu Ali was replacing "family"—where a person is usually raised—with the "*Jabha*." This stressed that no clear line could be drawn between them: his family was the *Jabha* and the *Jabha* was his family. The *Jabha* was something very personal, and it was not just encountered in offices or in political events, but also and more importantly at home. For Abu Ali, the *Jabha* was first and foremost people, not a party ideology.

At school he became part of the PFLP student movement, and then in his first year of high school, he heard that the PFLP was organizing training sessions for future guerrilla fighters. He dropped out of school and registered. His mother and uncle were against his decision to stop his education. He said that at the time he understood their motives and that he was aware that, as a Palestinian, getting an education was paramount. He added that he actually enjoyed school, especially Arabic literature, of which he was still fond. He boasted of being one of the best students in his school in that particular subject. However, at that time, his love for Arabic literature and his belief in the importance of an education could not compete with the excitement of fighting for his country. Political protests were common in the camps and Abu Ali explained how he could never stay away from them. "Resistance was in my blood" (*al-nidāl bi dammī*), he explained.

In 1972 he went to the training camp, but within a few days Israeli warplanes bombed the camp early one morning, killing eleven people, including his friend, Ibrahim Rabieh, who was also from Nahr el-Bared camp, and injuring twenty seven others.[13] Abu Ali explained that the training camp had few defences; he remembered that they only had one heavy Soviet machine gun, which was useless against warplanes. He hid behind rocks. Following the destruction of the training camp the survivors returned to their homes. Abu Ali became a full-time member of the PFLP (*mutfarrigh*). Although Abu Ali's father had been placed in charge of armaments (*mas'ūl al-tislīh*) in Nahr el-Bared, he explained that he did not receive special treatment due to his father's position. He stressed that he started like any-one else as a member of a cell, and that due to his own merit he was elected and became a cadre. He was then put in charge of political guidance (*mas'ūl al-tawjīh al siyāsi*) for the PFLP in the north of Lebanon.

Abu Ali considered his participation in PFLP training to be the moment he officially joined the PFLP. He explained that it was at that time that he "filled out a form." However, if we recall how Abu Ali first spoke of the PFLP, as something he drank with his mother's milk, it seemed that Abu Ali's relationship with the PFLP did not really have a start date. The official moment when Abu Ali "filled out a form" did not correspond to the time when he moved from being "outside" the faction to being "inside" it; he appeared to have been "inside" all along. This is the first reason why I always put quotation marks around the phrase "joining factions," as that expression seems to imply an action delineated in time. (The second reason will be explored in the next chapter, where I recount the subsequent evolution of Abu Ali's relationship with the PFLP and examine the concept of political membership and the possibility of defining its end).

The Younger Generation: Rabieh and Ali

Rabieh was a sensitive young man, six years younger than Ali. During the 2007 Nahr el-Bared conflict he worked with an international NGO in Beddawi camp delivering relief aid. The NGO's emergency relief operations ended once the Lebanese military allowed the residents of Nahr el-Bared to return to the camp, and Rabieh was subsequently unable to find stable employment. Occasionally, he helped journalists and filmmakers make contacts in the camp, and in the process heard several Palestinians from the camp recount their stories of torture in Lebanese jails. He was profoundly affected by these accounts. His work with journalists later caused him trouble with Lebanese military intelligence, who began to question him. At the time of my research he was unemployed and had lost all hope of finding work. In his mid-twenties, he was significantly depressed and felt he had few prospects for his future. He explained:

Rabieh: When I go to cafés and I hear the guys, of course it is going to bother me, because they are living what I am living. There is no work, there isn't anything. There is no future; everything is lost. My ambitions are broken. We don't know how to dream; even dreaming we don't know how to do it anymore.

[He lights up a new cigarette]

. . .

[Prior to the war] there wasn't an hour of boredom. Now the whole day is like that. There isn't anything. A person like me should be doing something.

Perla: What was different?

Rabieh: Everything was different. I was studying. I would leave school and go home. Our home's atmosphere was nice. Our family is big. We were six apartments but we all shared one door. Our homes formed a circle; we were all next to each other. If you were bored you would go sit in the courtyard and you would forget the world. My time was full, I had a lot of work, I worked in the *shabibe* [the youth organization of the PFLP], I had workshops, scouting trips, and my guard duties. The *shabibe* was my second home (*al bayt al tāni*). I never felt any emptiness.

The interior courtyard that Rabieh described and the form of collective living that the Hamdan family worked hard to replicate in the "Baracksat" was central to how the different generations of the family interacted. Rabieh highlighted this point, and as we will see later on, so did Ali. In particular, Rabieh had strong memories of his grandfather, to whom he was very close. In fact, it was his grandfather's stories that affected Rabieh and made him want to "join the PFLP" and later become a fighter. Rabieh recalled:

Rabieh: We always used to sit and talk. I used to ask him, where did you go in the past? Where did you fight? Where did you serve? He would tell me: I would take them to the mountains, to Tyre, Saida. He would tell me which battles in Lebanon he'd taken part in. I was trying to figure out how nice the *Jabha* is, how much did it engage in resistance? I was still discovering, until today [I am discovering]. . . . I was liking it, I wanted to be in the *Jabha*, I was loving it, I wanted to be a fighter, that impacted me a lot, a whole lot, I wanted to go to Palestine to fight. And I told you I had a group of friends and we had a room in the [PFLP] office and we asked to have military training.

Perla: And did your father tell you stories too?

Rabieh: No just my grandfather. My dad and me, our relationship was of a father and son, not that of a friend. With my grandfather I would tell him everything, even if I liked a girl I used to tell him. I would tell him I like this girl, what do you think about her? And he would tell me, well, she's from a good family. [Laugh]. He was considerate of my age.

We can see how Rabieh's conversations about the PFLP with his grandfather were mixed with other casual discussions, such as Rabieh's affection for girls. The discussions were informal, non-ideological and interwoven with everyday life. They did not aim to indoctrinate or politicize Rabieh, but were tied up with everyday social and familial practices. Later in our conversation, Rabieh labelled his affinity to the PFLP as "hereditary." He highlighted that as a child it was very "natural" to him (*ṭabī'ī*) to say that he was part of the PFLP. However, when I asked Rabieh what the PFLP meant to him, this is what he had to say:

What makes me love the *Jabha* are the people, it is not because it is the *Jabha* and that my parents are *Jabha*. Of course if I had joined and didn't like what I saw, it would be different, I wouldn't be convinced. But what I liked was the people in the *Jabha*. The cadres. There is no hierarchy; it is not a leader and member's relationship, but a friendship. It is like a family.

It is revealing that when talking of the PFLP, Rabieh spoke of the people of the PFLP. In particular, Rabieh discussed the role of Faris, his mentor, who left a strong impression on him:

I would be in the youth center, [my supervisor] Faris would come and we would talk of things. I liked him a lot. I felt that he was the *Jabha*. I felt that he should be a leader. I often talk to him on Facebook and on email; I call him 'Sir.' I love him a lot. He is the one who pushed me to open up, to discover how much energy I had, what I am capable of. He wanted to make something out of me.

While family ties often drew young Palestinians to factions, it was personal relations developed with other members that kept Palestinians "inside" the factions. Rabieh equates Faris to the *Jabha*—"he was the *Jabha*"—to stress how the factions were first and foremost people and not an ideology. Rabieh went on to explain that his chance to become a fighter for the PFLP came in 2006 when, following the July war with Israel, the PFLP decided to organize training sessions for young fighters. Like his father, Rabieh halted his education and signed up. To be a "fighter" in the early 2000s, however, was a very different experience compared to the 1970s. Palestinian military operations from Lebanon against Israel had halted and following the end of the Lebanese civil war Palestinians could no longer carry arms outside of the camps. Being a "fighter" in Lebanon basically meant being an armed guard for the factions' offices. By the 2000s, arms within the camps had become controversial even amongst Palestinians themselves. While Palestinians continued to feel threatened and in need of armed defence, they also often saw guns in the camps as a source of insecurity (Abou-Zaki 2013). Rabieh highlighted to me that his family was opposed to his decision to carry arms for two reasons: they opposed his decision to forego an education and they worried about him getting involved in an armed confrontation in the camp. Abu Ali explained that he wanted Rabieh to continue his education, especially since he himself had been unable to go to university. He explained that he used to beg Rabieh to continue his education and after a long pause he continued:

Abu Ali: I used to dream when I was in school that I would go to university and study Arabic literature because I liked it, I was in love with it. This is why I write short stories or poems from time to time. I may not be good at it, but I like it and this used to be my ambition. If I could go back in time, I would study. At times I think of studying at home, even if I am fifty-six years old. I think of getting the baccalaureate books and studying on my own, but there is no time. . . . You feel that your youth was wasted, fifteen, twenty years went like that, you didn't do anything.

Perla: But you tried to do something.

Abu Ali: Yes, but if you see what it is being used for today, how it is being marketed and sold, in a very different way from what you believed in or wanted. You feel that your dream became smaller. Your dream used to be big, now it is just 8 percent of Palestine. If we knew that then, maybe all those martyrs wouldn't have had to die, and there would have been no need for all the injured and all the widows. Believe me, maybe no one would have sacrificed anything. What am I going to sacrifice anything for? If it is not for Nahf or Acre, which is where I am from, am I going to sacrifice myself for 8 percent of the West Bank? It is depressing.

Abu Ali's objection to Rabieh's military training was directly linked to his own experience as a fighter and his anger at the leadership's subsequent betrayal of the principles he fought for. He was highly critical of the current Palestinian political leaders and did not want his son to forego the possibility of forging a future for himself as self-sacrifice would lead nowhere. Additionally, his family also worried that he would get entangled in armed confrontations in the camp or that the PFLP might call on him in case of fighting. Abu Ali expressed his concern:

> There is a total loss of trust, in all these people, the sixteen factions.[14] I am not telling you that one is better than another. All of them are problematic. All of their lies have become apparent after forty years of the beginning of the *thawra*. When I used to see each day in Nahr el-Bared factions go on military alert against each other—for what? (*istinfār min tanzīm 'ala tanzīm, 'ala shū?*) This is what made us lose trust. I remember we used to run after the *fidā'ī* just to see his boots.[15] He was something amazing, a symbol, like an angel. We imagined him as an angel when we were children. Just say *fidā'ī*: a camouflage uniform and a pair of boots. We would follow him just to look at him. He represented something important to us. Unfortunately they erased this image from our mind with their politics and their actions.

Rabieh's father was highly critical of the Palestinian factions, not only in terms of their positions during negotiations with Israel and their abandonment of the ideals he fought for, but also in terms of their local behavior in the camp. In particular, he insisted that his criticism was directed at all factions, which therefore included the PFLP. He lamented how the higher cause of fighting Israel had given way to internal fighting in the camps. In 2007, when Rabieh became a guard for the PFLP, there were two armed incidents in the camp involving Fatah al-Islam. On those two occasions, his parents sent Rabieh's oldest brother, Ali, to bring him home from the PFLP center. Rabieh explained that he had refused to leave and that Ali had had to drag him home on both occasions. Rabieh explained that when there was a situation of heightened military alert in the camp he would wonder if this was what his father and grandfather used to experience. He explained:

> I wanted to live something of what I was hearing. You know when there were military maneuvers I would wonder, is this what used to happen with my grandfather or with my dad? I was longing for this experience.

After a pause he continued:

Rabieh: I like my tea strong because of that, because the revolutionaries (*thuwwār*) liked it strong.

Perla: Really?

Rabieh: In the training camps, you can't go to the kitchen all the time to get tea. The kitchen has a guard, so you can't keep going asking for tea. You can go once a day to get tea, and they put it in the pot and boil it all day long, so it turns black. [He laughed and then sipped his tea.]

Rabieh's desire to be a fighter was directly linked to what he perceived to be the experiences of his father and grandfather in particular and of the revolutionary generation in general. His detailed knowledge of their mundane practices, such as how they prepared and drank tea, reiterates that the process of the transmission of factional affiliation is not an overtly political or ideological process intended to indoctrinate or inculcate. Rather, it was the natural product of daily interactions with family members and was mixed with discussion of girls and tea-drinking habits.

Rabieh was not the only one influenced by the tight-knit family environment in which he grew up. Ali also remembered his grandfather's accounts, but explained that he was a lot more interested in the tales his great-grandmother used to tell. He reminisced how he, as a child, would gather with his siblings, cousins, and sometimes even the neighbors' children, and sit on the ground in their interior courtyard, while the adults formed a semicircle around them. He explained that the tales would last three days, "like a television series." Similar to the tactics used by modern-day television editors, his great-grandmother would interrupt her stories just before the climax and tell the children that it was time to go to bed. Screams, and sometimes even tears, would follow and his great-grandmother's response was always the same: "it's for tomorrow (*labukra*)." This left Ali with a strong sense of anticipation for the next evening. He added that he could barely sleep those nights, waiting for the next day to pass in order to hear the remainder of the story. Ali emphasized that she was the one who taught him the meaning of *turāth* (cultural heritage), as she often accompanied her chronicles with real artefacts, such as old keys and pictures from Palestine. It was in that same spirit that he later formed a *dabka* group.

Ali's interest in cultural productions did not mean that he was not interested in experiencing the *thawra*, like his younger brother had been. However, Ali's friends had a greater influence on him. At the age of fifteen he joined his friends in attending political meetings with Jabhat al Nidal, another faction in Nahr el-Bared camp. His involvement did not last long once his father became aware of his association: he physically pulled him out of a meeting and forbade him to return. Ali then began going to the PFLP youth center but he soon lost interest, explaining that he did not feel a strong sense of belonging (*mish zyādi*). He highlighted that by the time he was an adult the situation of Palestinian factions was different from that during the *thawra*; he had lost trust in them. He also explained that most of his friends were "outside" the PFLP and that he preferred to form a *dabka* group with them. He added that one of his friends was in a leadership position in a local NGO, and the organization ended up adopting the troupe and provided them with costumes and musical instruments, as well as the opportunity to travel around Lebanon performing at different events. His friend soon left the NGO over a dispute with the new director and the entire troupe left the organization in solidarity with their friend.[16] This example highlighted the power of friendships and how Palestinians valued personal solidarity over institutional fidelity.

Ali soon married and started to concentrate on income-generating activities. At the time of my research, Ali had two young sons and an infant daughter. He was working as a driver for a vegetable wholesaler, transporting fresh produce from the fields of Akkar to Tripoli. His pay was minimal but he rejoiced over the fact that he was often given fresh fruit for his family, which, as I explained in the previous chapter, was a luxury many families could not afford. Ali's younger son soon joined us in the trailer; he had just showered and was ready to be put to bed. Ali took the opportunity to explain that he used to send his children to the Ghassan Kanafani kindergarten. The kindergarten was run by Annie Kanafani, the wife of the late Ghassan Kanafani, a famous Palestinian writer, artist and one of the founders of the PFLP.[17] He explained that he liked their style of teaching, as it was closer to his "home environment" (*jaw al bayt*). However the nursery was too far away from the "Baracksat" and Ali could not afford the 10 USD monthly bus fees, so he sent his two sons to the closest nursery, an Islamic facility run by a local mosque.

Recounting Ali and Rabieh's stories in conjunction is valuable both for contrast and similarity. Ali and Rabieh were raised in the same environment, yet their political trajectory was different: Rabieh felt a deep association with the PFLP while Ali did not. Both stories, nonetheless, show that personal relations based on trust—and not a set of political ideas and beliefs—determined how Palestinian refugees interacted with factions. This was true for Rabieh, who was inspired by his grandfather, as well as Ali, who was influenced by his friends. This, however, did not mean that Ali and Rabieh blindly followed their friends or family members. On the contrary, Ali attempted to disassociate himself from the PFLP and Rabieh defied his father's desires. Indeed Rabieh's desire to become a fighter with the PFLP was challenged by his father, and Rabieh believed that his grandfather—who had initially inspired him—would have probably opposed him too if he had still been alive. These stories showed that trust relations, developed on a local basis, exemplified by Rabieh's relations with his mentor and Ali's relations with his *dabka* friends, determined the strength of their relations with organizations, whether factions or NGOs. Finally, Rabieh helps us understand how "illegitimate" and "unpopular" factions continue to exist and reproduce regardless of the condemnations directed at them, while Ali's choice of daycare gave us a glimpse of how geographical proximity helps establish new ties and connections, a theme I turn to next.

FRIENDSHIPS, NEIGHBORHOODS, AND SPACE

> I joined because of a girl, I was ten years old and I used to pass by the [DFLP] hall on my way back from school and I was looking at the girls singing with kids. I saw a beautiful girl and I thought I should join. I didn't want to go to Fatah [where my father was], the girls were not pretty in

> Fatah [laughter]. . . . I used to always go and watch them. At the end I was
> convinced of the idea, I needed to enter. So I entered this organization and
> I liked it so I continued with them.
>
> —SAMI, YOUNG GENERATION, SAIDA, DECEMBER 6, 2011

> [The PFLP youth center] was a very nice center [prior to its destruction in
> the 2007 conflict]. There were a lot of activities; there was football, music,
> the scouts, and theatrical plays. The center was always full; it would never
> be empty, not like now. Now the center is sometimes closed, there isn't any-
> one. The center in the past wouldn't close; it was open twenty-four hours
> a day. If we were inside preparing something we would lock it so no one
> would come in, if we were preparing for a summer camp or an activity.
> People loved us.
>
> —RABIEH, YOUNG GENERATION, NAHR EL-BARED CAMP, OCTOBER 13, 2011

Just as particular families came to be associated with political factions, so too did particular quarters of the camp. During the *thawra* it was common to refer to neighbourhoods as *Iqlīm Fatah* (Fatah quarter) or *Iqlīm al-dimuqrātiyyi* (DFLP quarter) (R. Sayigh 1994, 92). However, this was not always the case. When Palestinians first settled in the refugee camps in Lebanon they organized themselves according to their village ties, with camp quarters taking on the names of villages in Palestine (Peteet 2005, 110–24; R. Sayigh 1994, 59). These village bonds were a system of support and survival in difficult and daunting circumstances (R. Sayigh 2007, 109). It has been pointed out that these village ties gave way during the *thawra* to an organization based on factional affiliation, with each faction "controlling" a part of the camp (Khalili 2004, 13–14; R. Sayigh 1994, 92).

In this section I reveal how neighborhoods came to be associated with a specific faction by outlining how neighborhood ties helped develop friendships, which in turn led to factional associations. This phenomenon was clear for both the *thawra* generation as well as the younger generation. However, before I begin my exposition, it is important to note that my choice of Nahr el-Bared camp as the site of my fieldwork affected how I conducted my research into the importance of space in understanding factional affiliation. The destruction of the camp in 2007 meant that I could not witness those dynamics first hand. The majority of its residents were no longer living in their original homes and factional offices and centers had been destroyed. While some factions were able to rent new spaces to act as offices and youth centers, not all were able to. The interplay between neighborhoods, friendships, and factions was to be found in the stories that Palestinians told about themselves and about their involvement with factions.

The physical location of factional offices, centers, or NGOs mattered for the simple reason that Palestinians often developed friendship ties with their neighbors and the physical closeness of these centers made them more convenient for parents to send their children. Ahmad, the youngest son of the Talal family with whom I lived, began his association with the Islamic Jihad in a similar fashion. His mother explained to me that when Ahmad was young they lived next door to Abu Fayez. Abu Fayez was a member of Fatah in his youth who left the party during the internal fighting of 1983 because he refused to participate in the battle.[18] He stayed away from politics until he met Dr. Fathi Shaqaqi, the founder of Islamic Jihad, who was visiting Nahr el-Bared after he was exiled from Gaza. After their meeting, Abu Fayez decided to start a scouting group for children in Nahr el-Bared camp. Um Muhammad explained that she sent her three boys to the scouting group, which basically consisted of religious classes and occasional outings to a nearby river. However, Ahmad was the only one who enjoyed the group and made several friends there. Ahmad continued to participate in their activities over the years and once he began his studies he became a member of the student group al-Rabita al-Islamiyya, which was referred to as just al-Rabita. Ahmad went to al-Rabita's center every day. He had the key and was responsible for opening and closing the center, which had a computer and a television set. This was Ahmad's only social outlet outside the family home, except for visiting other relatives in the camp.

One of the reasons why young Palestinians joined their friends in going to factional spaces was to partake in the activities that were offered to, and created by, them in those spaces. I often heard about the old PFLP center by the sea from Palestinians in the camp. Muhammad, the son of the head of Islamic Jihad in Nahr el-Bared, told me that he used to go to the PFLP center to use their library, as it was one of the few quiet places in the camp where he could study. Herein lies the importance of these spaces in the camp: their rarity. Young Palestinians had a limited number of locations in the camp where they could gather and take part in activities such as *dabka* practice or singing, or just hang out. The available places usually belonged to either factions or NGOs. They provided a breathing space for many young Palestinians, a place to go to during the day or in the evening.

These spaces were not always to be found in faction offices, but were sometimes located in people's homes, especially during the time of the *thawra*. Um Nabil, who was a young child when the revolution started, remembered how her affiliation with Fatah started when she and her friends started going to their neighbors' home. Her neighbor, Jamileh, was affiliated with Fatah and had turned her house into a youth center. There were political meetings, sports activities, English classes and, sometimes, trips. "I really miss those times, it was great," she said. They were about twenty to twenty-five girls, all from the neighborhood, and she "started to get attached to Fatah." She explained that she felt that she was discovering herself through Jamileh. Factions often had student centers close to universities with computers where students could meet to talk, play games, or surf the Internet. For many Palestinians who lived in the camps, going to university was the first time that they had actually left the camp and lived in a Lebanese neighborhood. This moment was often scary and stressful to them. A student center offered them a space where they could meet fellow Palestinians, discuss their problems, find solutions, and feel more at home. Some factions even had dormitories for students, where they rented out beds for the semester for a fraction of the market price.

The factions also organized outings several times a year. It was rare for many Palestinians who lived in the camp to leave. While no legal restrictions limited their exit from the camp, financial pressures kept them inside. It was common to meet young girls in their twenties who had left the camp only a few times in their lives, generally on outings to the sea or the river. The situation was different for the camps in Beirut, but for the camps further away from the Lebanese capital this situation was rather common. Therefore outings organized by factions or their associated NGOs were welcomed by the youth. They often spoke about them for several days before and for a long time after. Factions also often organized summer camps where youth gathered for several days and attended speeches by the leadership of the factions. But what these summer camps were more known for was the long nights where the youth gathered, smoked narghile, chatted, danced, and had fun together, far away from the suffocating confines of the camps.

It is important to point out that what often determined the strength of the relationship with a faction was the strength of the friendships developed in these spaces. Fouad, the PFLP football coach, was a good example of this. Fouad's father, a falafel salesman, was a prominent Fatah military figure. In fact I had heard about his father from several different people in the camp. He was well-respected as he had remained in Lebanon following the departure of the Fatah forces from the north of Lebanon in 1983. He therefore lived under the constant threat of being arrested and detained by the Syrian authorities. He had passed away a year prior to the 2007 conflict and Fouad highlighted that his only comfort was that his father did not live to see the camp bombed into annihilation. He showed me a short video on his cell phone of his father in military fatigues walking along with other colleagues. He was very proud and grateful that he still had this video, as all of his other possessions had been destroyed in the war.

When I asked Fouad how his relation with the PFLP began, considering that his father was such an important Fatah figure in Nahr el-Bared, he answered that he had liked the PFLP since he was twelve years old. They had a big center close to his home in Hay al-Madāris where he and his friends used to go.[19] He explained that most of his friends were from his neighborhood and that they all used to go to the PLFP center to play games, work on the computer or just enjoy each other's company. His friends would talk about George Habash, the founder and Secretary-General of the PFLP from 1967–2000, who sometimes visited the homes of his neighbors. He explained that they would later show him where Habash sat.

As Fouad was talking to me about his links to the PFLP, he immediately and without prompting started to talk to me about Shadi, his best friend for over ten years. Fouad recounted how, in the war that destroyed Nahr el-Bared, he had left the camp on day fifteen, leaving behind Shadi, who remained until day twenty-five. He told me that those ten days apart were the only time they had ever been separated from each other. He blamed himself for what he saw as the abandonment of his best friend and remembered how he had cried when he saw Shadi again, even though his friend was alive and well. For Fouad, his friendship with Shadi was integral to his sense of belonging to the PFLP, and once Shadi faced problems with the PFLP leadership, Fouad's own links with the PFLP were strained.[20]

For Ahmad, Um Nabil, and Fouad, friendship ties, neighborhood ties and factional ties were all linked together. The physical location of these centers played an important role in determining which factional space a young Palestinian went to. However, I am not arguing that if a Palestinian lived next to a faction's office then he or she would necessarily become affiliated with that particular faction. Instead, I aim to show how factional ties always begin with personal ties involving family members, friends or neighbours. Indeed, when looking at how Palestinians "join factions" we see that the factions no longer appear as structures defined by their respective ideologies, but as a group of people coming together on the basis of personal relations.

"REVOLUTION UNTIL THE END OF THE MONTH"

A very common joke in the Palestinian camps was that Fatah's new motto was *thawra ḥatta ākhir al-shahr* (revolution until the end of the month). This referred to the payroll that came at the end of the month, insinuating that people "joined Fatah" for the money, and played on Fatah's actual motto, *thawra ḥatta al-nasr* (revolution until victory).[21] This joke was employed as a criticism addressed not only against Fatah but against all factions. Another common condemnation was to point out that in the past *individuals* used to pay membership fees to the factions—people, in other words, used to contribute to the factions—while, at the time of my research, the *factions* had to pay people for them to "join." While being part of a faction could have financial benefits, my research suggests that financial incentives alone were not enough to explain how Palestinians chose which faction to "join." If money was the major reason behind factional affiliation then we should expect Palestinians to "join" the richest factions, which was not the case for the vast majority of the Palestinians I interviewed (forty-two out of forty-three).

Being part of a faction could have several benefits. It increased the person's network in the camp, it could lead to a job opportunity in one of the faction's NGOs, youth or women's organizations,[22] and it meant that they were eligible for aid in case the faction was distributing any.[23] While this could explain why people "joined factions," it did not explain how they chose which one to "join." Fatah often appeared to be the richest faction. For example, at the time of my research a university student who was part of Fatah received 40 USD a month, while a DFLP student received 200 USD a year (which breaks down to a little less than 17 USD a month) and a PFLP student didn't receive any compensation. A socioeconomic survey conducted by a team of AUB researchers found that 66.4 percent of Palestinian refugees in Lebanon were defined as "poor" in 2010 and 6.6 percent as "extremely poor" (Chaaban et al. 2010, 27).[24] Consumption expenditure was found to be on average about 170 USD per refugee per month (28). By this measure, the

Fatah contribution of 40 USD a month for a university student was substantial, representing about 23 percent of the average monthly expenditure. Yet, as shown in this chapter, many Palestinians created links with other factions. In some of these cases Palestinians did reap benefits from their association with a faction, but their choice of which faction to approach was not based on a calculation that sought to maximize it.

This point can be further illustrated through the example of Ahmad's relationship with the Islamic Jihad. Ahmad was the youngest son of the Talal family with whom I lived. As I elaborated in the previous chapter, the family faced severe financial hardships, which made them vulnerable to food insecurity. There was no doubt that Ahmad benefited financially from his relationship with the Islamic Jihad and that this assistance was vital to the family. They provided him with a monthly stipend and contributed to his tuition fees. Um Muhammad often said that if it were not for the Islamic Jihad, Ahmad would not have been able to go to college. However, it would be wrong to assume that Ahmad initiated a relationship with the Islamic Jihad in order to obtain such assistance. In actuality, the financial benefits that Ahmad received were the reflection of his longstanding relation with them. As we saw in the previous section, Ahmad's relation with the Islamic Jihad was based on neighborhood ties. At the age of twelve his mother sent him to their scouting group, which was led by their neighbor. This relationship continued over the years and was entering its eleventh year at the time of my research. When Ahmad was young there were few monetary incentives to this relationship. The stipend and tuition help that the Islamic Jihad provided only began once Ahmad attended college. This financial assistance can only be seen in context; it could not explain why the relationship was initiated. Other members of the Islamic Jihad received different stipends. Um Muhammad always reiterated the fact that Ahmad had been with the Islamic Jihad for eleven years and that the relationship was therefore superior to other members. I further examine the process by which Ahmad obtained the aid in chapter 5 when I inquire into the aid distribution process in the camp. What is important to realize for now is that while Ahmad no doubt benefited from his association with a faction, these benefits could not explain his choice of faction.

Furthermore, the role that Islamic Jihad played in Ahmad's life exceeded just a financial transaction. As highlighted in the previous section, Ahmad's participation in the Islamic Jihad's student group provided him with a crucial social outlet. Ahmad went to the youth center every day. He often returned in the evening with many stories of the latest news in the camp, which his mother always listened to attentively. I would therefore be wrong to qualify Ahmad's relation with the Islamic Jihad as being purely financially motivated.

· · ·

Rabieh described to me the official method of joining a faction. He explained that once he had decided that he wanted to be part of the faction, he had to fill out a form, which he believed was sent to Palestine, where it had to be approved. It was only after that process that he was considered a full-fledged member, was allowed to participate in factional meetings, and became a member of a cell. It was this process that was characterized as *dakhalit tanẓīm* by Palestinians, loosely translated to "I entered an organization." Three points can be inferred from this two-word expression. First, it evokes the image of crossing a line as the person moved from the "outside" to the "inside" of the faction, signalled by Rabieh's ability to now attend party meetings. Second, it implies that this crossing of borders occurs in a moment delimited in time, in this case the moment when Rabieh's application was approved in Palestine. Third, it confers order; it classifies people by giving them an organizational rank: Rabieh was now a member of a particular cell in Nahr el-Bared camp. These three points all work to build the appearance that factions are structures that organize people.

However, by examining the stories of how and why Palestinians "joined factions" we realize that Palestinians encountered factions in the form of people and not in the form of a party ideology; those individuals could be parents, grandparents, uncles, aunts, friends, or neighbors. It was no accident that kin and neighborhood ties formed the backbone of factions, as those two networks formed the basis of Palestinian endurance and survival since the *Nakba* (Rosenfeld 2004; R. Sayigh 1994, 2007; Taraki 2006). This is not to say that a person's kin ties and geographical location in the camp would solely determine his or her political affiliation; this was generally not the case. Rather, that process was non-linear, non-ideological, and interwoven in everyday practices, such as hearing grandparents' stories or joining friends to play games on the computer. This process also featured instances of opposition to parental authority, as illustrated by the case of Rabieh, as well as volatility, as shown by the different trajectories followed by Rabieh and Ali, two brothers raised in the same environment.

Further, "joining a faction" is not an action that can be delineated in time. It is not a matter of entering a structure defined by its ideology; it is about connecting with family and friends. Indeed, if we stop looking at factions as structures that a person enteres or leaves, as a bounded entity with lines separating those on the "inside" from those on the "outside," but instead as a group of people coming together because of trust relations, we realize that a person's affiliation with a faction cannot be understood as "affiliated" or "independent." Instead we notice that such a relationship is much more complex, as it is a continuously unfolding story of human relations. It is to the examination of such relationships that I now turn.

FIGURE 10. Protest in Beddawi camp demanding to return to Nahr el-Bared, June 29, 2007. Photographs: Ismael Sheikh Hassan.

4

———

"We Are the Factions"

Political Faction Membership

> *Perla:* During the [2007 Nahr el-Bared] conflict you were with the PFLP-GC?
>
> *Um Jihad:* Yes. No, no!
>
> *Abu Jihad:* We were taking aid from the PFLP-GC.
>
> *Um Jihad:* We had a sort of superficial relation (*kunna hayk ya'nī innu fī 'ilāqa sathiyyi*).
>
> *Abu Jihad:* A relation, a relation.
>
> *Um Jihad:* I used to be in the "progressive women association" [the PFLP-GC women's union].
>
> *The sister of Um Jihad:* It was a belonging [to a political organization] (*intimā'*). You know how everyone has a political belonging? Each person had to have a belonging.
>
> *Perla:* I can't keep up with the three of you!
>
> —Conversation between the author and Um Jihad, her husband, and her sister, all members of the *thawra* generation, Beddawi camp, July 20, 2011

> You say you are independent but really you are with the DFLP!
> —Half-serious, half-joking accusation hurled at Dr. Salah, who smiled in return as he was signing up as an "independent" for the media committee of the May 15, 2011 march to the southern Lebanese border, Beirut, April 10, 2011

When I first asked Mahmud, the youngest son of the Talal family, about his political affiliation, he answered that he was "in theory" (*mabda'iyyan*) with the DFLP. His choice of words seemed to imply that there was potentially a different "in practice" answer. Yet when I inquired further in an attempt to obtain the "real" answer, I was left dissatisfied; Mahmud just recounted how he had volunteered with the Najdeh NGO during the 2007 Nahr el-Bared conflict.[1] He explained that he then found himself invited to meetings and "became DFLP." It seemed that

71

Mahmud was not willing to self-identify as a DFLP member, but was just telling me that "officially" he was a member.

It was rare for Palestinians to declare a clear and direct affiliation to factions. Of the fifty-one close Palestinians with whom I had in-depth conversations, only eleven refugees openly claimed an affiliation to a faction (six of twenty-three members of the *thawra* generation and five out of twenty-eight of the younger generation), and eight claimed no contact with factions (two of the *thawra* generation and six of the younger generation). The rest seemed to fill a grey area that did not fit any conventional definition of factional membership. Some maintained that they were not affiliated with factions, but I would later see them at faction events and offices, which seemed to cast doubt on their earlier statements. Others used vague language to define their relationship, such as "superficial" or "not deep." Or, similarly to Mahmud, they would qualify it as "theoretical." A few would describe their affiliation as a form of "coloring" (*sabgha*).

In her study of women's involvement in the *thawra* in Lebanon in the 1970s and the early 80s, Peteet (1991) identified three different levels of mobilization within the factions. Palestinians could either be "organized" (*munazzam*) or "friends." "Organized" Palestinians were considered members of factions and were divided into two other categories: cadres (*mutafarrigh*) and members (*anāsir*). Cadres were usually employed by the faction on a full-time basis. They could be active in the political, military, social or administrative sectors of the faction. Regular members were Palestinians who paid their dues. These were expected to attend party meetings, carry out assignments, and had an organizational rank within the faction (143). Peteet highlighted that "there is no affiliation without action" (146), implying that the key to factional membership is active participation. Finally, "friends" were considered supporters but not official members. They might identify with the factions and attend factional events but did not participate in factional meetings (145). This classification became the conventional way of looking at factional membership in the literature and was adopted by numerous scholars (Brynen 1995a; Hasso 2005; Roy 2011). It implied that it was possible to separate factionalized Palestinians from independents, as highlighted in studies of "independent" and "grassroots" initiatives in Palestinian camps in Lebanon (Abou-Zaki 2012; Kortam 2011; R. Sayigh 2011).

The formal classification of factional commitment in terms of cadres, members, friends, and independents did little to help me navigate the confusing terrain of factional affiliation that I found myself in. However, I soon noticed that this inability to clearly define a person's relationship with a faction was not just something I experienced; Palestinians themselves often had discussions regarding their political affiliations. I experienced many such discussions, especially in meetings where popular actions were being organized, such as the planning of the 2011 march to the southern Lebanese border where people needed to openly declare their associations, as quoted in the epigraph to this chapter.

The difficulty in defining Palestinians' relationships with factions was only resolved once I began to question some of the assumptions that underlie conventional thinking about faction membership. The official classification of friend, member, and cadre implied that the relationship between a Palestinian and a faction was a relationship between a person and a structure with different degrees of commitment. It drew faction membership as a person's relative position vis-à-vis the *faction* seen as an entity. Palestinians often used this classification to characterize their relationship with factions as it reflected their official position. However, as the first part of this chapter will demonstrate, through my immersion in daily home life it became apparent that this classification missed the complexity and ambiguity of the actual relationship. Factional affiliation should not be seen as a snapshot of a person's present position in relation to a structure; rather it should be seen as a continuously unfolding story of human interactions.

It is these stories, in all their diversity and intricacies, that I seek to highlight in this chapter. Through them we realize two important points. First, factional membership should not be looked at as the fulfillment of a contractual agreement, but rather carries with it an important dimension of self-identification, which was independent of whether a person was meeting their obligations within the faction or not. I highlight this point by contrasting the stories of two young Palestinians: Shadi, who deeply identified with the PFLP while his official membership was in doubt, and Lina, who did not consider herself factionalized even though DFLP regulations indicated the contrary. Second, through an examination of what it meant to end factional associations, I demonstrate that the relationship of a Palestinian to a faction was not a relationship of a person to a structure that he or she "entered" or "left," but a relationship between people. As we have already seen, Palestinians' initial contact with factions was mediated through personal relations, and it is an extension of that same argument that the relationship between a person and a faction was a relationship between people. It was about personal associations, and those carry different grades of closeness and distance that could change according to time and context. This cannot be accounted for if we expect factional membership to fit into ready-made categories. This point also clarifies how refugees made sense of the seeming contradiction of partaking in the reproduction of Palestinian political factions while openly critiquing them.

A LATERAL APPROACH

The story of Mahmud's relationship with the DFLP was the initial impetus that led me to rethink the nature of political membership. Living with the Talal family I was privy to the mundane micro-interactions that textured political membership. My interactions with him over the course of several months were instrumental in helping me better understand people's relations with Palestinian political factions.

As we have already seen, Mahmud initially characterized his relationship with the DFLP as "theoretical." About a month later I referred to him as a DFLP member, at which point he burst out: "I already told you I am not with anyone, I am with my own interests" (*maslaḥtī*). This sudden burst of dissent surprised me. I wondered whether I had misunderstood him earlier. Mahmud was responding to the common criticism of the factions in the camp: that they worked for their own interests rather than the people's general good. Mahmud was underscoring that he was not a fool and he knew that he had to protect himself. It was early evening. Mahmud had just returned from working in the old camp and had to shower and eat quickly before heading out again to DJ a bachelor party on the rooftop of the house across from us. His cousin soon came over and helped him carry his four speakers down the three flights of our building and back up the three flights of stairs of the building across from us. There was no time to continue our conversation, and Um Muhammad and I took two of the kitchen chairs out onto the balcony to watch the party.

It took me about a week to be able to catch Mahmud and learn the details of the incident that had infuriated him that evening. He was home for his lunch break, and after eating the daily meal of *muhammara*[2] he took a longer than usual break and sat down to enjoy a midday *narghile*. He explained to me then that the DFLP's yearly anniversary was approaching and they were planning, like every year, to have a celebration, which consisted of a series of speeches by its leadership and some Lebanese politicians in a hall in the camp. Mahmud's immediate supervisor in the DFLP, Abu Mustapha, had asked him to provide the sound system for the event and told him that they would pay him 70,000LB, about 47 US dollars. Mahmud refused and handed in his resignation through a text message to Abu Mustapha: *kul ʿām wa antum bikhayr wa laʾilkun ghayr*. The closest, but still inadequate translation, as the Arabic sentence actually rhymed, would be: "Happy Anniversary and you better find someone else." When I asked Mahmud why he refused the job, he told me that he knew that the previous year they had paid 100 US dollars for the sound system. He thought this was unfair: they should pay him as much as anyone else—or even more, as he was starting up his DJ business and could use their support. He said that he wanted to leave the DFLP, that he didn't like the factions anyways. His mother agreed: "They are no good." He then got up and went back to work.

About a month later, as we were riding back together from Beirut to Nahr el-Bared, Mahmud told me of a romantic relationship he was having with a girl in the camp. He explained that he had met her in one of his NGO activities and they were sending each other text messages. As the conversation proceeded, I learned that the girl's father was Abu Mustapha. I was taken aback; his ex-supervisor in the DFLP, the person to whom he had sent his daring text message a month earlier, was now the father of the girl he liked. It seemed his relation with Abu Mustapha was entering a whole new level. However, the story did not end there. Several months later, at the beginning of the school year, Mahmud decided to go back to technical college to complete his degree in hotel management. He told me that he had seen Abu Mustapha and they had agreed that the DFLP would give him the yearly stipend of 200 USD that they usually gave their students.

Mahmud's tumultuous story made me begin to question the way we imagine faction membership. Trying to define Mahmud's position as being "inside" or "outside" the DFLP would have not only been impossible, but would have also missed a lot of the complexity of this relationship. This story underscored the importance of following an ethnographic approach to the study of factional membership. Faction interactions such as "joining" or "leaving" might merely consist of sending a text message or having a conversation. They were informal practices, not confined to offices or political events, but interwoven with everyday activities such as meeting girls or deciding whether to continue an education. By following Mahmud's relationship with the DFLP over several months I realized that faction membership was not about determining a person's present classification as a faction member or not; rather, faction membership represented an evolving story of personal interactions. To properly understand faction membership, we therefore need to investigate people's life histories.

Mahmud's story also highlights the two main points I make in the next two sections of this chapter. To begin with, it revealed that there was a difference between a contractual understanding of factional membership and a personal sense of belonging that was fostered (or not) in trusting environments. Indeed, it was Mahmud's direct experience of corruption in the form of reduced pay which made him eager to distance himself from the DFLP. Additionally, it illustrated with forceful clarity that the relationship between a person and a faction is mediated through interactions between people who likely also have non-political relations. Factional and personal relations intermix; it is difficult to separate the two. This is not only highlighted by the fact that Mahmud's supervisor in the DFLP was also the father of a girl he had an interest in, but also by the fact that once Mahmud needed the DFLP again—in this case to help him finance his education—he was able to get that help, no matter how minimal it was. This meant that his relationship with them was not over, as "leaving a faction" would imply. Although Mahmud's "return" to the DFLP was financially motivated, it was obvious that it was more complicated than that as he could have gone to Fatah who paid their students twice the amount the DFLP did.[3] Choosing not to go to Fatah but to "return" to the DFLP showed that the relationship was still ongoing even if he had "left" them.

"EACH PERSON HAD TO HAVE A BELONGING"

> I can't see myself in a *tanzim* other than Fatah, but I cannot go back to Fatah, therefore I stay outside.
>
> —FATIMA, *THAWRA* GENERATION, SAIDA, DECEMBER 3, 2011

Young Palestinians often explained to me that being part of a faction's youth club did not necessarily entail membership in the faction. In particular, they highlighted that they could not attend party meetings, as those were confidential and only fully-fledged members could participate in them. However, upon looking at people's own understanding of factional affiliation we get a different picture. Factional affiliation could not be limited to an evaluation of whether a person was officially a member or a friend; it was also about how people identified themselves and how other people perceived their political affiliation. It was in that sense that Palestinians sometimes referred to their adherence to factions as a sort of belonging, an *intimā'*. This was a self-assigned label which some chose to take on while others, like Mahmud, did not. I explore this process by recounting my interaction with Shadi, one of the rare young Palestinians who openly self-identified with a faction. It is ironic that it would take a committed young Palestinian, whose factional belonging was not in question, to highlight how official ways of looking at factional membership are lacking. I then recount the story of Lina who, as opposed to Shadi, did not consider herself a member of a faction—even though she attended closed party meetings.

Shadi

A young man in his thirties, Shadi was a well-known PFLP figure in the camp, which was rare for his age and for any Palestinian faction. Trained as a nurse, his notoriety increased during the 2007 conflict when he remained in the camp, along with a doctor, for several weeks. Shadi became an important mediator for the Red Cross as well as a main contact for the media. Reflecting upon that time he once explained to me that he felt he "was living life and death at the same time." Shadi was highlighting that this new phase in his life, when he began to play a more prominent role in his community, was ushered in as destruction and death had befallen them. Shadi also linked his activism and his interest in community work to both his parents. His father was a prominent PFLP figure, and his mother a much-loved nurse who had inspired him to take up nursing himself. Following the refugees' return to Nahr el-Bared, Shadi was recognized by the local PFLP leadership for his organizational and mobilization abilities and was asked to lead their efforts in establishing a new NGO in Nahr el-Bared camp.

Throughout the next few years I often visited the NGO and always found it bustling with children and young adults. The NGO lacked any sense of visible hierarchy. It occupied a one-floor house with a caged-in dirt strip that was used as a football training ground. The center had a kitchen, four rooms, and a large open hall at the entrance of the house. Shadi's office door was always open, but I seldom found him there; instead, young Palestinians would sit at his desk and use his computer. The couch and armchair, situated across from the desk, were often overcrowded with other young people jostling to fit more people on them. The rest of the rooms were used in a variety of ways. There were tutorials, *dabka* practice, musical rehearsals, photography and film workshops, as well as football training.

The many tables and chairs were constantly moved around to create the spatial layout desired by the participants. There was also a large terrace that looked onto the football strip, which was also always full of children and teenagers chatting, doing homework, or playing games. In the summer, European activist groups would come and participate in events, and over the years Shadi developed an important network of international support and funding.

It was therefore with great surprise that I heard in the summer of 2011 that the administrative committee of the NGO had relieved Shadi of his responsibilities and brought a different person to head it. Shadi believed that the leadership wanted to control the funding he was bringing in, while the official version was that he was no longer following orders and acting too independently. It seemed that the two versions corroborated one another. Subsequently, I went to see Shadi to discuss the situation with him and see how this had affected his relationship with the PFLP. I asked him whether he was thinking of leaving the PFLP. Below is an extract from our discussion. While it is long, it is useful to relate in its entirety as it shows how Shadi and I had two different understandings of what faction membership was; consequently, we had difficulty understanding each other.

Perla: You didn't think of leaving the PFLP?

Shadi: No.

Perla: Why?

Shadi: If there is something wrong, we should not ignore it but fix it.

. . .

Perla: So you want to fix the PFLP like you want.

Shadi: You can say not my way, but the *Jabha* way, but not with these people. Before, the leaders of the *Jabha* were role models for the people, and Ahmad Saadat is still a good example for leaders inside the *Jabha*. If we look at the *thawra*, of course many factions gave a lot, but if we look at the *Jabha*—Leila Khaled, Ghassan Kanafani, Wadih Haddad, Che Guevara Gaza—it has many people who left an important legacy, so I am proud of these people and I would like people in the *Jabha* today to be like them.[4] So I am disappointed when I see people in the *Jabha* who are not like that.

Perla: You are attached to the *Jabha*.

Shadi: Yes, of course.

Perla: You wouldn't accept an alternative?

Shadi: Of course I would, I am with anyone who works right. Now if Hamas proposes something new, something good, of course I would support them. I would stand with them.

Perla: And you would leave the *Jabha*?

Shadi: What? No! Why would I leave the *Jabha*? If Hamas wants to do something good, something that is to the benefit of the people, will they refuse the help of someone because he is with the *Jabha*? For example.

Perla: No, of course you can help, but I mean if you want to join them.

Shadi: I can work with them even if I am with the *Jabha*.

Perla: Forget about Hamas. Suppose a new group forms and wants to do military work. If you want to work with them you need to join them, you need to leave the *Jabha* and join this new group.

Shadi: Why?

Perla: You can't remain *Jabha* in the new faction.

Shadi: I remain *ibn Jabha* [the son of the *Jabha*] and I [would] do everything in the new faction, but as *ibn Jabha*.

Perla: But the logic of a faction is that you become part of it.

Shadi: No.

Perla: Can you be Fatah in the PFLP?

Shadi: I can do something with Fatah.

Perla: But you can't be leading a military operation in Fatah if you are with the PFLP.

Shadi: You are correct.

Perla: So forget about Fatah or Hamas, something new is starting and you figure out that they are working right and in the way you like.

Shadi: I would go along with them.

Perla: But you need to leave the *Jabha*.

Shadi: Who needs to leave the *Jabha*? Me?

Perla: Yes.

Shadi: OK, I accept that I would stop going to *Jabha* meetings and not to participate in their events or anything factional. But I can't leave the *Jabha* as *Jabha* because I will remain *ibn Jabha*. I will participate in the new faction, and go to their meetings and I will become a member and do everything that is required, to work, but I would still be known as *ibn Jabha*.

Shadi's last sentence is quite revealing. Shadi was laying out a scenario in which he would no longer be a member of the PFLP according to any official criteria. He would no longer attend meetings nor participate in their events, and would basically "leave" the PFLP. But he still insisted that even in that case he would remain *ibn Jabha* (the son of the *Jabha*). Shadi simply could not envision a situation where he would not be linked to the *Jabha*, regardless of what the official membership regulations specified. I could not initially understand this point, insisting on envisioning a situation where he would have to leave the *Jabha*, for example if he had to lead a military action with another faction. But Shadi was always surprised at my assertion that he would then need to disassociate himself: "What? No! Why would I leave the *Jabha*?" While he could not understand why I was implying that he needed to quit the PFLP to join another faction, I could not understand how that precise implication was not obvious to him. The reason for our mutual puzzlement was that we each had a different understanding of factional affiliation. For me it was about being a member according to the official regulations of the faction, while for Shadi it was something personal and was not related to whether he was an official member or not.

My conversation with Shadi also highlighted the use of the word "son" ("*ibn*") or "daughter" ("*bint*") in reference to a person's relationship with a faction. Shadi was not the only Palestinian I met who chose to use those terms. Shadi's use of the word *ibn* highlighted that he considered the *Jabha* family, that membership in a faction resembled membership in a family. Recall Rabieh, the young Palestinian who liked his tea dark because it brought him closer to the *thuwar's* experience. Just like Rabieh, Shadi was also born into a PFLP family; his father, Mustapha, was a prominent PFLP figure in Nahr el-Bared camp. When I asked Mustapha whether he believed he had influenced his son in choosing a path similar to his, he did not seem sure. "God knows!" was his immediate answer as he waved his hand in the air. He continued: "I used to encourage [my children] to do the right things, but then they stopped listening to me!"

We were in Mustapha's home at the time, sitting in his living room, and he pointed to a rather uncommon red Bob Marley poster hanging on the wall. "Who is this?" he asked with obvious disapproval. This seemed like an attempt to illustrate to me that not only had his son stopped listening to him, but that he, the father, could no longer even control what hung on the walls of his own home. Shadi answered, laughing, "Doesn't he look like me? It's my picture"—pointing at his own curly long hair. His father brushed off his answer: "No really, who is he?" "We got used to having Che Guevara as a symbol of the left, this person also sang for freedom," Shadi replied. His father seemed unconvinced, at which point Shadi asked me to back him up. I answered that it was Bob Marley, that he did sing for freedom, and that Mustapha would probably like his music. "I see, so like Sheikh Imam then!," Mustapha exclaimed, which made Shadi and I laugh. Shadi's father realized that he had unintentionally made a joke and laughed with us.[5]

Shadi added that his father was rarely home when he was a child; he was either travelling or residing in different bases around Lebanon. While he used to be afraid of Mustapha, he was also proud of him, as "at that time a fighter was a good thing, I was proud, it was about sacrifice." Shadi mostly saw him in the PFLP summer camps that he attended as a child. "A small organized army (*jaysh mnaẓẓam ṣghīr*)" was what he felt they were. He added that the camps were quite rigorous and that punishments "actually meant something." They had to crawl bare-chested on thorns as a form of reprimand. He liked it though, as he could then brag about his scratches to his friends. I later realised that his early fear of his father was linked to the severe punishments that he used to deliver to his children. Shadi added that they also used to sing revolutionary songs, learn about Palestine, and perform plays. "We used to see the *fidā'ī*, he was the main picture, so whatever we could do to be like him made us happy," he explained. Shadi's childhood was typical of young Palestinians who were raised in a faction family. However, his self-identification with the PFLP was unusual for Palestinians of his age. I asked him to elaborate:

Perla: It's incredible how attached you are to the *Jabha*.

Shadi: Yes of course, I am proud of being in the *Jabha*. For its principles, for its history, for its ideas. . . . It is great! Honestly, it educated me. It is one of the factions that made me hold on to the cause and made me love Palestine more than anything else.

Here lies the double meaning of "*ibn*." For Shadi the PFLP was not just a family, something that was personal and close to him, but it was also a learning center that taught and educated him. He was in a sense the "offspring" of the PFLP, its descendant. Shadi later explained to me that his involvement in the PFLP increased in high school as he participated in a sit-in with many of his friends in Beirut, aimed at pressuring UNRWA to open a secondary school for Palestinians in Tripoli.[6] Once the sit-in succeeded, Shadi became active in developing a PFLP scout troop and youth group in Nahr el-Bared. He explained that he had begun by enlisting his close friends who were from PFLP families as well as non-factional families. With time their activities increased: they had summer camps, musical groups, and political meetings with Palestinians of the *thawra* generation who would discuss their experiences. They started visiting the martyrs' cemetery, commemorating national events, and organizing traditional Palestinian weddings. The PFLP youth center had a computer room, a library, and an exhibition of Palestinian heritage. It was these activities and the human relations that they fostered that cultivated in Shadi a sense of belonging and a feeling of being forever related to the PFLP. His association with it could not be described as the satisfaction of internal regulations. It was an identification as strong as any family identification.

Identifying oneself as a son or daughter of a faction was rare among young Palestinians. For the older generation it was more common, as during the *thawra* the factions were much more active and people often felt a deep and close association with them. For many, their identification with a faction was so strong that they felt they would betray it by joining another faction. Such was the case with Fatima, quoted at the beginning of this section. Fatima left Fatah after experiencing firsthand the corruption of officials stationed in Beirut; but she felt she could never affiliate to another faction and as a result she remained "outside." This behavior contrasted with the younger generation, whose sense of belonging was less deep. This was also the case with Lina, to whose story I turn to next.

Lina

Lina was a university graduate in her late twenties with an infectious smile. I quickly formed an affinity for her as she was highly inquisitive and always keen on partaking in group discussions but would, nevertheless, always second-guess herself. As I got to know her more I realized that she had vast experience working in the camp and was highly knowledgeable about community affairs. However, she remained humble and held other people's opinions in high regard. She was a good listener. I first met her, and would regularly see her, in the Nahr el-Bared Reconstruction Commission compound where she worked.[7] Located next to the Lebanese Army checkpoint that marked the entrance to the old camp, its premises consisted of several air-conditioned metal trailers painted in white. Lina and her colleague Rania usually sat in an inner room lined with filling cabinets, while colleagues would come in and out handling different tasks.

Lina often stated that politics was a "headache" in which she was neither interested nor involved. She added that her dislike of factions, which for her were synonymous with "politics," did not mean that she was indifferent to the Palestinian cause. On the contrary, she just "didn't care about being in a faction." Her co-worker Rania, sitting with us, interjected that Palestinians needed to be part of a faction to have a "back" (*dahir*), evoking the image of factions as edifices that encompassed and protected their members. However, later in our conversation Lina explained that she was in the DFLP student union. This came as a surprise to both Rania and me. She explained, "I entered the DFLP student union because it was the closest to me, and I knew the most people in it; they are in the same area where I live and my friends are there too." Rania voiced her surprise: "I didn't know this and I don't like these things at all." Lina continued, explaining, "I am [still] in the union, but I don't consider myself to be politically affiliated (*munazzami siyāsiyyan*)." Confused about how she did not consider herself a member if she was technically a member, I asked her to elaborate.

Lina: Each faction has a student union. They say that this is separate from politics when you first join, so you imagine yourself getting into something that works for students, for student goals . . . and it is supposedly separate from politics, and I don't like politics. . . . [But] when I started to learn more, I started to see that things are not separate at all. It is true that their main goals are the students and the universities and when we want to mobilize about a topic it is all about scholarships and university matters . . . but there is still a link to their political ideology that you may not believe in. . . .

I support their general political demands, the right of return and the refusal of naturalization in Lebanon (*tawṭīn*). These are not just slogans, they really work on this. They have meetings and they go see members of parliament and ministers. They are not silent. But I am not with their internal political goals.

Perla: Which are?

Lina: Now *I* am talking about these things? [Laughter]

Perla: Please continue.

Lina: I am not with their internal politics, which is secularism, political secularism. They separate religion from politics. Now I studied social science and I read a bit of philosophy, so I know how those people they talk about think, they follow

> Lenin and I am not too convinced of these things. I am wary of them. But on matters related to students and Palestine I am with them.

This discussion was revealing. Lina believed that the DFLP student union was actively and effectively trying to improve the situation of students. She later told me about a new project they were working on: establishing a Palestinian university in Lebanon. She enjoyed attending those meetings as the topic interested her and she "liked to know what was going on." However, Lina was not convinced by the stated ideology of the DFLP and was uneasy at how the DFLP student union had attempted to disguise that connection in order to get her to participate in their meetings. This increased her general dislike for factions, which was always somewhat "suspicious" (*mashbūh*). She explained:

> I feel like [politics] is confusing and a lot of talk and talk and talk, and now politics is more like problems and the goal is no longer the country, or the people, but the goal is to destroy someone or someone take authority. So I don't spend my time on this, I don't care who is in charge or who his deputy is or who is in control. I really don't care. I think that they [the factions] are all the same.

Lina's dislike of factions was related to her lack of trust in "politics" in general. It was related to how factions were perceived in the Palestinian camps, and she worried about how her participation might be viewed by the community. She explained: "as soon as you talk to someone, people consider you to be affiliated with this someone. And I told you I don't like political factions and I will be considered a member of them." Her personal involvement in local meetings was not enough for her to counter the general feeling of distrust she felt. She therefore did not want to appear to be affiliated, which explained why her close friend and colleague did not know of her involvement. Additionally, she did not feel a sense of belonging to the organization, although according to the DFLP's internal regulations she was a member. This raises the question: was Lina a member or not? We may want to say that she was, since the DFLP considered her to be so. However, if she did not see herself as a member, should we still count her as one?

The official membership regulations were about drawing lines, lines that separated those on the "outside" from those on the "inside." However, a closer examination revealed that it was impossible to draw that line in practice. Looking at how individuals spoke of their own involvement in factions added another layer of complexity. Political membership cannot be seen as the fulfilment of a contractual agreement, as it was also about a sense of belonging that was nurtured over time through personal and trusting relations with other faction members. The examples of Shadi and Lina were constructive in their opposition. Shadi felt he belonged to a faction to the point where he identified himself as its offspring, regardless of whether he was technically a member or not, while Lina, who believed in the work that the DFLP student union was doing and attended their meetings, did not feel she was politically affiliated. Lina expressed her desire to leave the DFLP, as she felt she could not be with them "one-hundred percent." I asked her if she could simply stop attending meetings. She explained that that was not enough, she needed to make sure that her name was "crossed out," otherwise they would always consider her one of their own. It is to a discussion of ending factional affiliations that I turn to next.

"TERMINATING" FACTIONAL AFFILIATIONS

> Being part of a faction has become a crime!
> —GHASSAN, YOUNG PALESTINIAN, BEIRUT, OCTOBER 12, 2011

Investigating the process of ending factional membership is particularly interesting in light of the current premium attached to "independent" and "grassroots" initiatives. Many of the ills in the Palestinian camps in Lebanon were attributed to the incompetence and disunity of Palestinian factions. It was in light of such criticisms that being factionalized became an indictment, and many scholars point to "grassroots" organizations as being in opposition to factions (Kortam 2011; R. Sayigh 2011; Suleiman 1999). In this section I look at one such grassroots initiative whose rise and fall I witnessed during the Nahr el-Bared battle of 2007. Rajiin ("We will return") was a group of young Palestinians from Nahr el-Bared camp who regrouped in Beddawi camp, where they were taking shelter.[8] They attempted to make their voices heard to the Lebanese government and to their leadership. It was through their activities that I initially came to meet the Hamdan family, whom I introduced in the previous chapter. I explore this initiative to highlight how difficult it was to draw a distinction between "factionalized" Palestinians and "independents." This section examines my own understandings of and reactions to Abu Ali and Rabieh's involvement with *Rajiin* and their subsequent rapprochement with the PFLP upon their return to Nahr el-Bared camp. This example will also help us understand how Palestinians made sense of their involvement with factions while openly opposing them.

Rajiin

Walking into the garden of the Ghassan Kanafani nursery of Beddawi camp, I saw a group of young Palestinians sitting and chatting together. Several plastic chairs had been brought outside and everyone was seated in the shade underneath a vineyard facing a deserted children's playground painted in blue. It was the second week of the Nahr el-Bared battle and many Palestinians had sought shelter in Beddawi camp. A friend introduced me to the group, which went by the name Rajiin. Compelled by the ongoing destruction of their camp, they wanted "to do something." A discussion was in progress about the need to organize a sit-in in the school's courtyard to demand the end of the fighting. Having escaped from Nahr el-Bared a week earlier, the only form of mobilization they had witnessed from different organizations, whether the factions, UNRWA, or local and international NGOs, was the distribution of food, blankets and T-shirts. While relief assistance was needed, they worried that everyone's focus rested solely on delivering immediate relief aid and not on halting the destruction of their homes. They wanted to make clear that what they needed was not cardboard boxes (*karātīn*), which epitomized relief, but a return to their homes. Ali was one of the more vocal activists in the group and following several meetings he introduced me to his family, who were living at the time in the corridors of the UNRWA school.

Ali explained to me that after fleeing from Nahr el-Bared camp they had first sought shelter with friends, and only came to the school several days later. By this point the school had already been occupied, with at least three different families in each classroom. He noticed that they could claim the space that extended from the end of the hallway, which was lined with windows, to the first classroom door, without interfering with anyone else's private space. The family marked their space by hanging a blue tarpaulin across the corridor next to the classroom door, which gave them a personal space of about five by eight meters. Our discussions during those days revolved around what Fatah al-Islam was, the fear that the onslaught on Nahr el-Bared was a pre-planned campaign to destroy the camp and render its residents permanently homeless, and the role that factions played (or, more accurately, did not play) during the battle.[9] In particular, Ali's younger brother Rabieh was highly critical of the factions, arguing that they should have intervened militarily to disarm Fatah al-Islam: "What's the point of having arms if we do not use them to protect our camp?," he often repeated. He explained that he was a trained fighter in the PFLP and was on guard duty during the beginning of the battle, but he had left the PFLP and handed in his weapon when his supervisor told him on the third day of the battle that "the battle does not concern us" (*mā ilna bi hal ḥarb*). He felt betrayed, and departed from the camp with the first wave of refugees.

Rabieh was not the only one disappointed by the inaction of Palestinian political factions. A general sense of frustration could easily be felt, and this was what contributed to the making of Rajiin. While the group began to organize sit-ins they soon decided that they needed to increase their visibility and called for a protest on June 29, about six weeks after the fighting in Nahr el-Bared broke out. That day the school courtyard filled with thousands of refugees, well beyond the expectations of the young organizers. Soon the march started out along Beddawi's main road. As the leading group turned left into one of the camp's alleys, other protesters continued along the main road and exited the camp. They were marching towards Nahr el-Bared, which was still fifteen kilometers away, when they encountered a Lebanese military roadblock. From eyewitness reports that I gathered that same day, I learned that the people in the front sat on the ground, implicitly indicating to the army that they neither aimed to storm the roadblock nor were they willing to go back to Beddawi camp. However, after firing warning shots in the air, the army began shooting at the protesters.[10] As a result, two young Palestinian men were killed and several were injured. This experience was particularly traumatic because protesters were not only attacked by the army but also by local residents who wielded knives and sticks, attacking fleeing protesters who had sought refuge in the hallways of buildings adjacent to the protest.

Following the march and the death of the two protesters, the Palestinian ambassador to Lebanon, Abbas Zaki, condemned the protest and declared that Palestinians should respect the army and should not "cause disruptions" or "cause any further strain on the army" (Ghazal 2007). In another statement Zaki referred to the protesters as "*fawdawiyyn*," loosely translated as "anarchists" (Nahrelbared 2007). Abbas Zaki's statement became famous among the young men and women of Rajiin. To them it reflected the distance that existed between them and their leadership, as they were risking their lives to return home and their official political representative was calling them "anarchists." But more importantly, they feared that these statements were a signal to the Lebanese army that the Palestinian leadership would not object to their arrest. A few days later Fatah released a statement referring to the organizers as "reckless young men" (*shabāb ṭāyshīn*) who sought to destroy Beddawi camp. At that point the young refugees felt that they not only had to worry about the Lebanese army, but also had to fear the political factions. They continued to meet with each other, and to assist activists and journalists visiting the camp, but they refrained from organizing further direct action. These events clearly situated the Rajiin initiative as an "independent" grassroots initiative and positioned its organizers as being "outside" the factions. However, as we will see upon closer inspection, no such line could be drawn.

"It Was Not Your Average Friendship"

When I first met Abu Ali, as part of the Rajiin activities, he explained that he was a "friend" of the PFLP. This meant that he was not an official member of the faction but a supporter who attended events periodically. A few years later, I heard the entire story that had led to his resignation in the early 1990s. His decision related to the revamping of the Soviet Union exit visa policies, as a result of the perestroika reforms, which favoured mass emigration of Jews to Israel (see Al-Haj 2004, 83–84). He believed that the leaders of the Soviet Union, and subsequently of Russia, were encouraging this mass immigration to Israel. He went on to explain that at a meeting to discuss the issue he had voiced his opposition. In his words:

> In the meetings we had, I was against the perestroika; I was the only one against it. I registered my opposition and my reaction was nervous (*aṣabi*). In one of the meetings in the office, there was a Lenin statue on the table; from my anger and frustration I hit it with my shoe.[11]
> [Laughter]

> What infuriated me; what made my blood boil, was that, I adopted your [the Soviet Union's] ideas, I, as a Palestinian with a rightful cause. And now I see the Soviet Jews immigrating to Palestine and you [Russia] are allowing them and providing them with the means to go to my country that was stolen from me and that I am fighting to return to. Look at the contradiction! . . . Honestly my mind could not handle it. Maybe my actions cannot be understood, maybe my colleagues could not accept them but in my opinion they were justified. I have a cause (*sāḥib qadiyyi*) and to see those who considered themselves my allies [help my enemies]. . . . So yes my reaction was strong, maybe I should not have acted like that, maybe I should have communicated my position in a more civilized way.

After hitting the bronze Lenin statue with his shoe, Abu Ali was sent to the PFLP correctional committee and then demoted. At that point he decided to leave the organization. He explained that he handed in his resignation, which was discussed and accepted. He then returned his weapon, became a civilian, and opened a thrift shop. This was a decade and a half prior to the Nahr el-Bared conflict in 2007.

Upon the Hamdan family's return to Nahr el-Bared camp, after the end of combat, Abu Ali starting working with the head of the PFLP in Lebanon on increasing the media coverage of the camp. By that time the head of the PFLP in Lebanon was also the official liaison between the Palestinian Embassy and the Lebanese government on the reconstruction of Nahr el-Bared camp. Abu Ali was highly qualified for this position. He was a seasoned writer, an active member of his community, and a person with substantial relationships with journalists in Lebanon. However, this job opportunity made me wonder if he had "returned" to the PFLP. When I inquired, he answered that no, he was not a member of the PFLP, and that the position was not with the PFLP but with the PLO. This was technically correct. However, others in the camp pointed out to me that it was the PFLP who provided him with a computer and an Internet connection, which seemed to implicate him in the "internal" workings of the faction.

Around that same time I began seeing Rabieh at the PFLP youth centre. When I asked him whether he had returned to the PFLP, he explained that while he was still upset at the leadership's decision to stand idle during the battle, it was impossible for him "to deny his origins" (*yinkur aslu*). This was a surprising statement following the scathing denunciations he had directed at the PFLP leadership just a few months earlier. He expanded:

> It is difficult, I would be upset at them, I witnessed a lot of things that I was unhappy with and I say that I don't want to be [with them], but after that, without even realizing it, I go back, I return and I enter the *markaz* (center).

At first glance, by using the word "origins" it seemed that Rabieh was implying that what he described as an almost involuntary return to the PFLP youth center was the result of a longstanding family association with the faction. However, upon further discussion it became clear that "origin" did not refer to his family but rather to the strong personal ties he had built with other people in the faction. In his words:

> Most of my friends are in the *Jabha*. I met [my brother in-law] when he was very young in the *Jabha*, through him I met other people. I was the oldest among them and they respected me. I felt we were friends, like I am their older brother. We would think together; work together; do things together. . . .
>
> We were friends not just in the *Jabha*. We would sleep over at each other's homes at night; we would decide today we are all staying at Muhammad's; tomorrow we stay with Ali. We spent our nights and days together. For example, my friends called my mother, mother, and I called their mothers, mother.

We have already seen that the strength of a person's relation with a faction really reflected the strength of that person's link with other comrades. In this case, we see how those personal ties should also alter the way we look at "ending" factional memberships. What Rabieh was highlighting was that even if he disagreed with a particular political position of the PFLP, in this case their stand during the 2007 conflict, it did not mean that he could or would cut his links with his friends. Trying to determine whether Rabieh was "factionalized" or not was simply impossible. It was this precise point that I had missed in my earlier understanding of Abu Ali's new work opportunity. Abu Ali's association with the head of the PFLP was not the reflection of a "covert membership" in the PFLP; it was quite simply the reflection of a long-term trusted friendship, the strength of which was eloquently related to me by Abu Ali himself:

> [I am still friends] with everyone [in the PFLP]; we visit each other, things are normal between us. What joined us together was something big, not a small cookie (*Yalli kān yirbutna shi kbīr, mish ḥabbi*). It was not your average friendship. We were comrades in struggle, comrades in arms (*rafīq nidāl, rafīq silāḥ*). We ate together; we slept together in the cold and in winter. We guarded together. We did a lot of things together. You can't forget that. We shared one tent, one blanket.

Abu Ali's description of his relationship with his comrades suggests the strong ties that he developed with his peers. What linked Abu Ali to his comrades was a lifetime of shared experiences in what were sometimes life-threatening circumstances. These ties were not going to end just because he had "left" the PFLP. This did not mean that he could "infiltrate" the PFLP by having a close friendship with its leadership. This assumption could only be based on looking at factions as bounded structures where only members were allowed "inside." But Abu Ali's story highlights how difficult it was to separate the "faction," seen as an entity with a life of its own, from the personal relations that were its basis. It also explained how Abu Ali made sense of his opposition to the PFLP's political program while appearing to personally engage with them. This was not a contradiction. When the head of the PFLP chose Abu Ali as his media consultant he was not only looking for someone with proper qualifications; more importantly, he was looking for someone he could trust. After all, mutual trust was paramount when working on raising the visibility of a camp that was declared a military zone and that required journalists to obtain special military permits to access it.

Examining the process of ending factional membership was fruitful for me, as it showed how Palestinian refugees made sense of the seeming contradiction of partaking in the reproduction of political factions while openly critiquing them. Interpersonal trust, between Rabieh and his mentor or between Abu Ali and his comrades, helped maintain a relationship with the PFLP even as they clearly distrusted it. In other words trust and mistrust coexisted within the same relationship. While Palestinians may oppose a faction's *political stance* and openly voice their opposition, this did not mean that they would sever their ties with the *people* who had been their trusted friends for many years. Palestinians' relationship with a faction was not just a relationship with an impersonal framework defined by its stated ideology; it was also a relationship between people. In that sense attempting to classify Palestinians as being "factionalized" or "independent" was not appropriate if I wanted to properly understand the dynamics that animated factional politics in Palestinian camps. Factional affiliation could not be separated from the personal relationships that brought it into being; it was impossible to delineate the political associations from personal ones.

"WE ARE THE FACTIONS"

The stories of Palestinians' relations with factions did not all feature deep friendship ties like those experienced by Abu Ali and Rabieh. While some did, others included personal disputes over non-political issues, such as a disagreement over the location of a new cafeteria, which then was a cause to terminate factional affiliation. Individuals implicated in such behavior would label it as "tribal" (*ashāʾirī*). This indicates that Palestinians themselves viewed the intermixing of political and personal relations as undesirable and reflecting, in their view, a "backward" form of political behavior that should be eradicated in "modern" times. However, what these stories really point to is the importance of trust in building political associations. Indeed, if individuals had personal disagreements and felt wronged by each other, it was unlikely that they would then collaborate in political work, regardless of whether they espoused a similar worldview or not.

In the context of repeated forced expulsions, wars, and severe political oppression, as well as social and legal discrimination, it was not surprising that Palestinians placed a high value on interpersonal trust. The image we get of factions from examining people's life histories is that of a network of people coming together with varying degrees of cohesion, which could change with time. Viewed laterally in this way, factions lost the appearance of bounded entities defined by party ideology. A friend made this point to me early on in my fieldwork, but I could not grasp it as

I was still looking at Palestinian political factions as entities with boundaries. I was sitting in his home, asking him how factions could destroy so many "grassroots" initiatives. He answered that the factions were not something outside this community; rather, "we are the factions."

Reinscribing the agency of Palestinian refugees into accounts of factional (re)production means that factional membership should not be looked at as the evaluation of a person's position in a present moment vis-à-vis a structure, but rather needs to be seen as an evolving story of human interaction. Factional adherence was not about the respect of internal regulations but was about how Palestinians identified themselves. Additionally, we saw how the relationship between a person and a faction should not be imagined as the relationship between a person and a building that a person "entered" or "left." Rather, it was about personal relations, which carried a lot more complexity and ambiguity that went unaccounted for if we expected them to fit into ready-made categories. Factions had no independent existence; they were quite simply people coming together with varying degrees of trust and cohesion that changed with time.

The alternative view I have presented was precipitated by the different methodological approach I took, which consisted of approaching factions not from the top or bottom but laterally, through immersion in daily home life. In light of these conclusions, a new line of questioning arises. The Palestinian refugees I spoke with were well aware that personal relations underlay factional relations; however, the everyday terminology they used still reflected an imagination of factions as buildings with "walls" and "ceilings" that they "entered" and "left." Could a lateral view help me elucidate this puzzling observation? In the next two chapters I look at the practices of aid distribution, physical representation, and factionalism and show how they served to inscribe distance between people and factions— the very distance that disappeared by looking into people's life stories. The central question that the next two chapters seek to answer is: how do people coming together appear to create the effect of a structure with a life of its own?

FIGURE 11. Jars of red pepper paste distributed by an NGO in Nahr el-Bared. Photograph: Perla Issa.

5

———

"Factions Are Like Shops"

Aid, Discipline, and the Structural Effect

Now [the factions] are all *dakākīn* [shops]. Meaning now a student gets 43,000LB [30 USD]. He doesn't give the money to his parents anymore; he goes and buys cigarettes. They bring him to the protests, it's not that he goes of his own will; no, they bring him. If he doesn't come to the protest, he doesn't get paid the next day. Payday is always after the protest. And when they started giving him 100 USD he stopped working or trying to get an education. He just goes and guards the offices for a couple hours. He lives by night and sleeps in the day, smoking all the time.

—ABU RASHID, *THAWRA* GENERATION, SHATILA CAMP, DECEMBER 7, 2010

"Al-faṣā'il zay al-dakākīn" ("factions are like shops") was a common expression in the camps in Lebanon. While it seemed initially puzzling, with time I came to see the points of similarity. A *dukkāni* was not just an average shop; it alluded to a hole-in-the-wall, small, broken-down, dusty, and old shop—just the image that Palestinians want to associate with factions nowadays. But there was more to the metaphor. Shops carried advertisements marketing their goods; factions carried posters publicizing their martyrs (*shuhadā'*). Shops were sometimes deceptive about the quality of their products; factions' self-proclaimed martyrs were sometimes people dying of old age. Shops engaged in fierce contests with their competitors; factions engaged in heated confrontations with their opponents. Shops had owners; factions had leaders. Shop owners unilaterally directed business; faction leaders unilaterally decided on policy. Shop owners controlled finances; faction leaders controlled funding.

The likeness, however, seemed to have its limits. In particular, I felt there was one glaring contradiction: the type of relations assumed to govern both entities. Shops were impersonal; customers could enter one, not find what they wanted, and then move on to the next. Yet, as we saw in the previous two chapters, those were not the type of relations that seemed to take place "inside" factions. Indeed

91

we saw how Palestinians had contact with factions based on *personal* relations, which stands in sharp contrast to a customer's relation to a shop. Additionally, the image of shops conferred an edifice with walls and a ceiling that a person "entered" or "left." Again we saw how that imagery did not correspond to people's relations with factions.

Can these two images, of an impersonal building and a personalized network, be reconciled? Looking for an answer, I found my first clue in Abu Rashid's description of factional "shops," quoted above. The clue also helped me answer another pressing question I had: what did factions sell? That was, after all, a shop's defining activity: trade. The answer seemed to be "money." What factions were selling, according to Abu Rashid, was dollar bills. This may seem counterintuitive, as usually a customer pays money to receive a good; in this case, it seemed individuals "paid" with their presence at protests in order to receive financial benefits. While I did not initially give this metaphor much attention, I later realized its sharp insight into how practices of aid distribution served to draw factions as impersonal structures with particular spatial characteristics, those of a perimeter and a ceiling.

This chapter examines how factions transmute from personal networks to disembodied edifices through the provision of care. I elucidate this mutation through an ethnographic examination of how Palestinian refugees obtained aid in the camps of Lebanon. Palestinian political factions, along with local and international NGOs, as well as UNRWA, provided a wide range of services whose central concern was the welfare of the population. These included health, educational, relief, development, economic, and cultural programs. These activities illustrate well how the goal of political power in the Palestinian camps in Lebanon was the administration of life in all its details, or governmentality, as Foucault (2006) termed this modern form of government.

In this chapter I look at practices of aid distribution from the perspective of aid receivers, not aid providers, through my immersion in daily home life as opposed to being embedded in the bureaucratic apparatus of factions or NGOs. In particular I examine the efforts the Talal family exerted in order to cover the tuition fees of their second son, Ahmad. This endeavor exemplifies how Palestinians navigated the web of factions and NGOs in a desire to better their lives. While there are significant differences in the capacity, power, and funding of Palestinian political factions, local and international NGOs, and UNRWA, the ways in which aid is distributed in the camp on a day-to-day basis—the ways Palestinian refugees experience the dissemination of aid—remains largely the same.

Through the many examples outlined in the present chapter I make four interrelated points. First, I show how in the name of distributing aid fairly, a whole series of surveillance and monitoring techniques have been brought to bear on the population. I draw parallels between these methods and what Foucault (1991) calls discipline, and highlight how aid distribution processes worked in a similar way, generating a form of productive power. I also show how these practices served to embody a hierarchy with an "above" that was in control and a "below" that lacked it. Second, building upon Ferguson and Gupta's (2002) notion of the "spatialization of the state," I examine how these disciplinary practices imbued factions with particular topographical dimensions. Factions lost the appearance of networks and took on the cloak of an overarching and encompassing reality, which existed "above" and "surrounded" the people it cared for. Third, I argue that it would be wrong to end our analysis with a description of factions as a hierarchical organization, with a "top" that had power and control over those "below." Following Mitchell (1988, 1990, 1991), I show how these particular practices served to establish factions as impersonal entities, containers that existed prior to and separately from the very people and practices that brought them into being. Finally, I underline how this very process also created the conditions under which the provision of services increased mistrust in the community, breaking it down and hindering collective political action.

"AHMAD *BIRAKKID*"

My day started with hot, delicious homemade *za'tar*-and-cheese *mana'ish*.[1] It was a ritual: every week or two all the young girls of the family, sisters and cousins, would congregate for an all-girl sleepover at the house of Mariam, Um Muhammad's unmarried sister. The most eagerly anticipated moment was, however, the morning, when Mariam would sit on the floor with a gas-powered oven to her left, a large green plastic basin brimming with risen dough to her right, and a small wooden table between her legs. Taking a lump of dough between her hands, she would roll it into a compact ball and then flatten it into a perfect circle. She would then top it with either cheese, a mixture of *za'tar* and olive oil, or upon request she would make a "cocktail," as they called a mixed cheese-and-*za'tar man'ushi*. When several had been made she would place them in the oven, piercing the dough from time to time to prevent them from puffing in the heat. The rest of us would anxiously wait, teacup in hands, while the sweet scent of freshly baked bread worked our appetite to unbearable levels. Mariam was always the last one to eat, as she was determined to make enough *mana'ish* for herself and her three married sisters, as well as their entire families; everyone, present or absent, was accounted for.

Congregated around Mariam that morning, her sisters were engaged in a conversation comparing their children's daily expenses. Who was willing to take a homemade sandwich to school or college with them instead of purchasing one? How many teas did they consume from the cafeteria? How much did they spend on cigarettes and on tobacco for the *narghile*? Fatima, Um Muhammad's younger sister, was the driver of the conversation, as she seemed to be frustrated the most about her youngest son's expenses. After accounting for transportation, cafeteria expenses and smoking habits he appeared to be the highest spender by about 2,000 LBP per day (1.33 USD). In contrast, Ahmad, Um Muhammad's son, seemed to be the role model. He was not only a careful spender but also, and much more importantly, he had honed a vital skill. Um Muhammad explained: "Ahmad *birakkid*." "*Birakkid*" literally means "runs around." In this context it referred to the unending labor involved in applying to different organizations for aid. That labor was time-consuming and took a lot of effort from Ahmad, as well as his family. It involved a lot of physical displacement to different NGOs, factional offices, government bureaus, embassies and UN agencies, which was required at all levels of the process from obtaining information to applying to following up.

I had experienced this "running around" from my first days living with the family, especially as it pertained to securing aid to cover Ahmad's tuition fees. This aid was obtained from a Palestinian political faction, the Palestinian embassy, and an international NGO. However, at no point in time did the family know how much each party would be paying so that they could know how much would be left over for them to cover.

The uncertainty around how the family was to cover Ahmad's tuition fees dominated daily conversations. My attention was first drawn to it on my second week with the family. Ahmad had just returned from a workshop on "youth empowerment" with an international NGO.[2] He and his mother began discussing how much aid the NGO would probably give him as a form of help towards his tuition fees. Ahmad had just heard from the workshop leader that the minimum would be 250 USD, but he was hoping that he would receive at least 350 USD as the college he was attending was more expensive than the public Lebanese university where most of the other workshop participants were studying. Ahmad was majoring in Business Administration in a technical college, and his tuition was two million Lebanese pounds (about 1,334 USD). This was a considerable sum, the equivalent of almost nine months of expenditure for an individual refugee.[3]

Ahmad was significantly distressed, as his exams were two weeks away and the family needed to pay an upcoming tuition installment without which Ahmad would not be allowed to take the assessments. He explained that on examination day he had to present a receipt to be able to enter the classroom. He had highlighted the urgency of the matter to his workshop leader, a fellow young Palestinian from Beddawi camp who was a recent graduate from the Beirut Arab University, but the man had responded that "the matter was not in his hands" and that usually these things "take time." Time was a luxury the family did not have. They began weighing their options.

Ahmad had also applied to the Palestinian embassy for financial assistance, but had not received an answer. The embassy had recently started a new fund for students, the President Mahmud Abbas Fund. However, the fund's mandate was unclear. Ahmad believed it only helped first-year students and it had, indeed, helped fund his education the previous year. He heard from other students in the camp that it wouldn't fund his second year, but his parents had insisted that he should apply anyway. When Ahmad's father had handed in the application several months ago, the embassy's employee did not provide him with a clear answer as to whether the application would be accepted or not. He explained that "the decisions come from Palestine." Um Muhammad added that the prior year the embassy's contribution did not even cover the entire sum and that the family had had to pay an additional 600,000 LB (400 USD), which was raised with the help of Ahmad's brother Mahmud.

Another source of assistance was Islamic Jihad. Ahmad was part of their student group and they usually contributed to his education (see chapter 3). I already knew that Ahmad received a monthly stipend that was slightly higher than the other students, as he also had more responsibilities. He was entrusted with opening and closing the apartment they used as a youth center, distributing salaries to the other members of *al-Rabita*, and sometimes paying the bills. Ahmad had already asked his supervisor if they could provide him with their contribution but he too had replied that "matters were not in his hands" as the decision about how much aid would be given and when "came from Palestine."

Having exhausted all options, Um Muhammad tried to reassure her son that "everything will work out in the end" since "everyone knows our situation." This seemed to calm him for the moment and he brought his books out to study. Ahmad was a serious young man interested in any opportunity to increase his knowledge and skills. He had attended a vast number of workshops in the different NGOs in the camp, ranging from English classes to courses on computers and conflict resolution. His mother once showed me with pride all the different certificates he had accumulated over the years. While he was studying business administration, his real passion was politics and he acted like the official news broadcaster to the family, always entertaining his mother with the latest developments. He spent many hours on the Internet, on Facebook and browsing through different websites and blogs pertaining to Nahr el-Bared camp and other camps in Lebanon, and was also constantly informed of what was happening in Palestine, where the latest Palestinian protests were and where the Israeli bombings, incursions, arrests, demolitions, or assassinations were.

The following day Ahmad returned from his college even more frustrated. He had gone to the administration to explain his dilemma: that three different parties were offering him help (an international NGO, the Palestinian embassy, and a Palestinian faction) but that he did not know when the assistance would be provided. The administrator just shook his head and said there was nothing that he could do; Ahmad needed to pay the current installment to be able to take the exams. That night a heated discussion occurred between Ahmad and his father. Ahmad was anxious and worried, which at the time translated into anger towards his father who had not been able to find a solution to his problem. When his father told him to concentrate on studying and that he would take care of the situation, it only inflamed Ahmad more. He wondered why should he care about studying when all his efforts would be thrown away if he could not take his exams.

Mahmud, present at the time, looked at his mother and sarcastically asked her if she still wanted him to stop working and continue his education.

The next day Abu Muhammad called his contact in the Palestinian embassy, which was an expensive endeavor, to explain to him the bind that the family found itself in.[4] Again the employee answered that "matters were not in his hands" as the decision "came from Palestine" and that he did not know how much the aid would be for, nor when it would be disbursed. The situation was getting desperate. After several nightly discussions that went nowhere, Abu Muhammad finally decided that he would go personally to the embassy to have a face-to-face conversation. Travelling to Beirut was not only time-consuming, as it took on average two to three hours to get to Beirut and another two or three hours to get back, but it was also costly. In addition to paying for transportation to reach Beirut and back, Abu Muhammad had to forgo the possibility of earning money that day. He explained that he would use this opportunity to pass by UNRWA's headquarters to try to convince them to update the file of his daughter-in-law, Latifa, to reflect her marriage to his oldest son. It should have been a routine bureaucratic procedure, but up to that point UNRWA had been unwilling to make the change because the relevant Lebanese government ministries were refusing to legalize his son's marriage certificate due to the fact that Muhammad was a non-ID (see chapter 2).

Abu Muhammad returned that night with one promising and one bad piece of news. The promising news was that he was one step closer to finding a solution to Ahmad's conundrum. He had been able to convince his contact in the embassy to provide a verbal guarantee to Ahmad's school certifying that they would be covering Ahmad's tuition fees. However, the embassy's employee refused to call the school himself, insisting that the school needed to call him. The bad news was that UNRWA had again refused to recognize his son's marriage certificate and to change Latifa's personal status from "single" to "married." This was a sore point, as Latifa was six months pregnant. The rejection of this one-word amendment meant that she not only had to face disapproving looks whenever she went to health clinics and had to present her UNRWA card, which then had to be followed by a long explanation of her situation, but that she was also often denied free health services based on the fact that she was legally "single."

The next morning, Abu Muhammad went to Ahmad's college in Tripoli and was finally successful in convincing the administration to accept the embassy's verbal guarantee. He then called the embassy himself, using Ahmad's cell phone which he had borrowed for the day, and had the school administrator speak directly with the embassy. At this point the college gave Abu Muhammad the most precious receipt. From now on, Ahmad could concentrate on studying and passing his exams—that is, until the next installment would be due.

The above example is just one small glimpse into the never-ending process of qualifying for, applying for, and obtaining aid. I recount this story not only to highlight the anxiety and uncertainty that the process added to refugees' chronically insecure lives but to make a point about how individuals experienced aid distribution and how it created a particular imagination of what factions were. The family's lack of knowledge of how much and when the aid would be given altered the way they viewed factions and NGOs, turning them from personal networks to powerful impersonal structures.

HIERARCHICAL OBSERVATION

Um Muhammad's assertion that "everyone knows our situation" was very accurate, and an important part of how the aid distribution process was experienced and practiced. Indeed, aid providers needed to obtain information about the economic situation of camp residents. The impetus for this was the principle that aid needed to be distributed fairly. Camp residents needed to be ranked according to their respective miseries in order to be able to distinguish between them. Therefore Ahmad and his family's financial precariousness needed to be rendered visible for Islamic Jihad, the Palestinian embassy, and the international NGO. However, that transparency into the family's situation was not translated into an equivalent transparency into the aid distribution process. It was unidirectional. This unequal access to information seemed to embody a hierarchy with an "above" that was in control and a "below" that lacked it.

Islamic Jihad's ability to examine Ahmad and his family's lives was rooted in personal and neighborhood ties. As we have already seen in chapter 3, Ahmad's family's former neighbor was Abu Fayez, the head of Islamic Jihad in Nahr el-Bared camp. At the age of twelve Ahmad started participating in their scouting activities and over the years became part of their student group. Um Muhammad used to emphasize the length of their relationship, which spanned eleven years. However, the closeness of the relationship was revealed to me when I met Fayez. Fayez had been living in Beirut for several years, yet he knew the details of the family's life. He had been a schoolmate of Muhammad, Ahmad's oldest brother. He knew that Abu Muhammad was a day laborer; he was familiar with his past political engagement and with the fact that the Talals were non-IDs. While he was not living in Nahr el-Bared any more he was up to date on the more current news that Mahmud was working to help support the family. He further explained to me that "they"—that is, Islamic Jihad—were sensitive to Ahmad's situation, revealing that he knew that Ahmad received a higher salary than other members. It was quite obvious that if Fayez, who lived in Beirut, knew this much, that his father, the "head of Islamic Jihad" in Nahr el-Bared, would know at least as much.

The nature of the Talal family's relation to the Palestinian embassy was less personal than their relationship with the Islamic Jihad, as it was based on an official application with supporting documents. However, it was nonetheless not entirely impersonal. It was in fact the embassy that issued Abu Muhammad and his children (and later grandchildren) the only piece of identification they possessed. This was an A4 sized letter with the PLO letterhead that stated the person's name, as well as the father and mother's names, date of birth, place of birth, sex, and place of origin in Palestine (*al-balad al-aṣlī*).[5] The embassy was therefore well aware of the family's situation and Abu Muhammad often joked with them that they could obtain a copy of the ID themselves, since they were the ones who had provided it to him; he should not have to travel to Beirut to hand it in as part of the application process.

Finally, the evaluation and selection of Ahmad as a self-motivated and disadvantaged young student in the "youth empowerment workshop" was also based on personal ties rather than an impersonal selection process. The international NGO had operated through a local Palestinian NGO, using their offices and asking them to select participants for the workshop. The Palestinian NGO, in turn, asked other local NGOs to each select two participants for the workshop, and one of these had selected Ahmad. Ahmad's two brothers, Muhammad and Mahmud, had in fact both worked for this particular NGO, and the person in charge of selecting the candidates was a close friend of the family, often visiting them. She therefore had intimate knowledge of the family's situation and of the level of commitment that Ahmad usually exhibited in group activities.

Information about the lives of aid recipients was gathered in all cases of aid distribution. People's relative levels of misery needed to be calculated and measured. While in Ahmad's case this was accomplished through personal ties, surprise home visits were also common. Through visiting families unannounced social workers, drawn from the local community, could literally see the financial situation of residents by looking at the size of the home compared to the number of people living in it, the family's possessions, and the quality of the furniture. As we saw in chapter 2, UNRWA had two social workers who conducted surprise visits to the Talal family's home, examining every room in the house. One worked for the special hardship cases department while the other was employed by the rent subsidy division. There were many additional examples. Um Muhammad's sister Mariam explained to me that when she applied for an electric heater from an international NGO she received a surprise home visit from one of the organization's employees. The social worker, a camp resident herself, went through all the different rooms in the house to make sure that Mariam did not already own an electric heater. Mariam added that she even knocked on the neighbor's door to confirm the information. She also recounted how another organization, this time a local one, wanted to compensate women who had run businesses prior to the war. Mariam was a seamstress who had owned two sewing machines prior to the destruction of her home. She therefore applied for the aid. Again she received a surprise home visit from an employee making sure that Mariam had indeed lost her sewing machines in the war and had not recovered them.

This capacity to demand the visibility of people's lives and homes was justified in the name of distributing aid fairly. However, the total visibility that was expected from aid receivers was not matched by a reciprocal transparency of the aid distribution process. Ahmad did not know who decided on how much aid would be dispensed, when the decisions would be made, or on what criteria these would be based. Similarly, Mariam did not know how many electric heaters the international NGO had or how it decided to whom they would go. Nor did she know how much funding the local NGO had to compensate self-employed women or how they would divide it between all those who qualified. It was as if a beam of light was illuminating their lives, uncovering every detail, and simultaneously blinding them and preventing them from looking "up." This one-way visibility established and demonstrated hierarchy. Um Muhammad highlighted this point when she referred to the UNRWA employee who refused to abide by local custom and remove her shoes prior to walking around the house as a person who liked her job "to be able to control people" (*tatithakkam bilnās*).[6]

Foucault (1991, 171) referred to this ability of seeing without being seen as a "hierarchical observation," and argued that this surveillance technique was used as a disciplinary tool to gently alter behavior. Its function was not to repress but to train, to reduce gaps. In that sense it was "essentially corrective" (179) and sought to produce a certain type of behavior. Indeed, several months after the workshop on "youth empowerment" had begun the organizers contacted Ahmad and told him that he had applied too late to receive financial aid. Ahmad was upset. He protested that they were incorrect and he was then told by the workshop leaders to be patient. With no alternative, he was. It was not until the end of the school year that Ahmad was finally granted the aid, but only after he was reprimanded yet again for not respecting the deadline. Ahmad was categorical that he had applied on time, pointing out that other participants had submitted their paperwork after him. Both Ahmad and his mother were furious about how the international NGO had treated him, but the lesson learned was that it was better to always apply early. This exemplified what Um Muhammad meant when she told her sisters that "Ahmad *birakkid*." She didn't say it with a sense of pride; rather her statement underlined that Ahmad had developed the type of behavior deemed to be appropriate for securing aid. He had the capacity, and willingness, to follow any and all leads to potential sources of aid and to spend the time needed for gathering the required documentation, applying, and following up. He was also willing to live with the uncertainty that came with the process. In contrast, his brother Mahmud did not develop that same capacity. He chose to forgo an education, being unwilling to chase after political factions and NGOs to cover his tuition fees. He preferred living with the uncertainly of a daily wage.

SPATIALIZING FACTIONS

Ferguson and Gupta (2002, 982) added to Foucault's study of discipline by pointing out that practices of surveillance did not just work to discipline individuals but also created "a taken-for-granted spatial and scalar image of the state that both sits above and contains its localities, regions, and communities." This is what they referred to as the "spatialization of the state." The "spatialization of the state" should not be confused with the social construction of space, with the way that states act to structure space and influence the social experiences and relations that unfold within them. Rather it refers to how states themselves are spatialized, how individuals come to perceive that states are imbued with particular topographical characteristics. In particular Ferguson and Gupta examined the everyday workings of a child's development project in India. They related how social workers experienced the state as an overarching organization through surveillance techniques such as the keeping of registers and surprise visits by project officers who travelled to local centers. The project officers' mobility across Indian territory, their "sudden swooping 'down'" (987) into the social workers' spaces, established their control over the geographical area and enacted a hierarchy. Echoing Foucault, Ferguson and Gupta argued that it "was a demonstration of the inequality of spaces" (987) where officers "higher-up" in the hierarchy could enter "local spaces" at will while social workers could only visit supervising officers at prescribed times.

Indeed we have seen how in Nahr el-Bared local social workers could enter a home at any time and look into any room they wished. On the other hand, aid receivers could not go to the offices of the NGOs, factions, or UNRWA and wander around their workplaces. Whenever they did visit offices, they were confined to specific areas where they were allowed at predetermined times. This unequal access to space exemplified how those "higher up" seemed to encompass the people below them. Social workers' mobility around the camp and inside people's homes produced an imagination that they engulfed the geographical area under their control. In other words, this system of surveillance not only created the imagination of an "above" that was in command but also an "above" that enveloped those below it, that surrounded them like the walls of a building.

Ferguson and Gupta further argued that the state's encompassment was achieved through positioning social workers as "locals" who were then associated with particular communities and interests. They explained that the "localization of the [social] worker is precisely what enabled those overarching institutions [the Indian state and the multilateral aid agencies] to disavow the particular, and to claim to represent the 'greater' good for the 'larger' dominion of the nation and the world" (988). Similarly, by acting as caregivers, providing tuition aid, electric heaters, and compensation for destroyed property, factions and NGOs positioned themselves as looking out for the well-being of the entire community, surrounding the population within their reach through their care. While the claim to represent the greater good was strongly contested, with camp residents continuously critiquing factions for looking out for "their own" rather than the overall community, the idea of encompassment itself was not. By highlighting how factions just helped "their own" rather than all camp residents, Palestinians were just restricting the area that a faction appeared to encompass, from that of the entire community to the people it considered its "members."[7] This observation brings me to my last point, about how factions now appeared to have a boundary that separated "members" from those on the "outside."

As we saw in the previous chapter, the question of whether an individual was part of a faction or not did not have a simple answer. Through looking at people's life stories and the way they spoke of their relation with factions, we realized that factional membership was better understood as a continuously unfolding story of human interactions and self-identification. There was no clear line that separated faction members from non-members. Yet the provision of care was redrawing that very line. Palestinian refugees obtained a personal identification number from factions when they would be receiving monetary contributions. This "financial number" (*raqm mālī*) was needed for logistical reasons, as the disbursement of funds needed to be recorded and accounted for. However, this number had an additional effect: it could be pointed to as a marker of factional membership. Adherence to a faction could now be understood as having one's name on the list of aid recipients. This transformed the relationship between a person and faction from a complex and dynamic relation to one defined by a financial transaction. In short, it helped build the impression that factions did not only have a "top" but also a "perimeter."

THE STRUCTURAL EFFECT

Nonetheless, it would be wrong to stop our analysis with an image of factions as an organization controlled by those "on top." Firstly, "those on top" often had other people above them. This was clearly visible when the Palestinian embassy employee told Abu Muhammad that he did not know when Ahmad's aid would be dispensed as "the decisions came from Palestine." We can imagine that "the people in Palestine" themselves were not in complete control either, and were dependent upon others, such as their funders. Similarly, heads of factions and of NGOs also had to answer back to their funders.[8]

Secondly, the positions in the hierarchy were interchangeable. As we saw from the previous examples, factions, local and international NGOs, and UNRWA relied on local camp residents for the dissemination of aid as it reflected what was deemed to be a participatory approach. It is easy to understand why that view prevailed: aid workers drawn from among the community were inherently more knowledgeable about its residents since they belonged to multiple community-based networks (see Rempell 2010; Svoboda, Barbelet, and Mosel 2018). In other words Palestinian refugees were both aid recipients and aid providers, since the aid workers assigned to the monitoring tasks were also Palestinian refugees from the same camp. Aid workers were monitoring others while being monitored, visiting each other's homes and using their knowledge of the local community in making assessments as to who was more deserving of the aid. This meant that an individual's position would change from sometimes being on "bottom" to being on "top." This point was brought home to me during a visit to the Talal family in the winter of 2014.

The oldest son, Muhammad, had recently started working for an international NGO as an aid worker in their relief program for Syrian refugees. He was in charge of verifying the information given by Syrian women who had been displaced to Lebanon as a result of Syria's descent into civil war following the 2011 popular uprising against the regime and who claimed to be either widows or to have lost touch with their husbands. As I sat chatting with Muhammad he recounted story after story of how he had "caught" women lying and how he would lay traps for them to fall into. One story involved him looking through a woman's hanging laundry and finding what he deemed to be "sexy" underwear—in his mind, a sure sign that her husband was present.

The irony of his newfound position was not lost on his mother, who stated "he has become one of them" as Muhammad continued to brag about his accomplishments. She was clearly referring to the fact that he was now acting like the UNRWA worker who had walked in on him and his wife in the privacy of their own bedroom. Roles had indeed been switched. This lack of a discernible "top" and constantly changing hierarchy transformed a process which depended on personalized and close relations for its day to day operations into a disembodied machine that controlled people's lives. It made the highly personal aid distribution process impersonal. Going back to Foucault's (1991, 177) analysis of disciplinary practices can illuminate this point:

> Although surveillance rests on individuals, its functioning is that of a network of relations from top to bottom, but also to a certain extend from bottom to top and laterally; this network 'holds' the whole together and traverses it in its entirety with effects of power that derive from one another: supervisors perpetually supervised. The power in the hierarchized surveillance of the disciplines is not possessed as a thing, or transformed as a property; it functions like a piece of machinery. And, although it is true that its pyramidal organization gives it a 'head,' it is the apparatus as a whole that produces 'power' and distributes individuals in this permanent and continuous field.

The functioning of disciplinary practices in the camp did not rely on a specific person for its functioning; it was the whole apparatus that was responsible for its effect. Every person was interchangeable and this made the entire process very impersonal. Additionally, it was impossible for the family to identify the person responsible for the decisions about how much or when aid was dispensed. The family could only say that it was Islamic Jihad, or the Palestinian embassy, or the international NGO dispensing the money. It was impossible to say it in any other way. The lack of visibility back into the aid arbitration process meant that it could not be attributed to a specific person; it could only be associated to a structure that was called by its own name. I was bound by the same logic while writing this chapter: I could not write in any other way. I had to say, for example, that "Islamic Jihad contributed to Ahmad's education." By virtue of dispensing money, decided in unknown places by unknown people, using unknown criteria, at unknown times the faction gained a sense of separation and remoteness compared to the family and it became an entity that had to be called by its name.

This disconnection between the social relations that underpinned the factions and the opaque and secretive dissemination of aid served to create the appearance that factions existed as containers, as buildings independent from the personal relations that formed its core. This is what Mitchell (1991) refers to as the structural effect. Building upon Foucault, Mitchell contends that modern disciplinary practices served to create the appearance of a framework, of a container that appeared to exist separately from its content. He explains:

> The precise specification of space and function that characterize modern institutions, the coordination of these functions into hierarchical arrangements, the organization of supervision and surveillance, and the marking out of time into schedules and programs all contribute to constructing a world that appears to consist not of a complex of social practices but of a binary order: on the one hand individuals and their activities, on the other an inert structure that somehow stands apart from individuals, precedes them, and contains and gives a framework to their lives (94).

As we have seen, knowledge about the lives of aid recipients was achieved through either personal relations or through surprise visits carried out by local camp residents. In both cases a high degree of visibility was expected and achieved. However, the distribution of aid was anything but transparent; it seemed to operate by a different set of rules. It was opaque, inaccessible, and evaded scrutiny. In that sense the logic of the aid distribution seemed disconnected from the social relations that underpinned its everyday workings. For example, the international NGO had delegated the selection process for its "youth empowerment" workshop to a local NGO, and Ahmad was selected due to a long-term relationship with a social worker who knew the family and their situation well. However, this local knowledge was deemed irrelevant once Ahmad was accused of applying too late. In order to get the aid, Ahmad had to be judged based on an impersonal application process, with its own rules and deadlines.

The same process was also at work with Islamic Jihad. Ahmad had initiated his relation with the Islamic Jihad through neighborhood ties and it was clear that his own understanding of his relation with the faction was based on personal fidelity, which was seen to increase as the number of years went by. However, when requesting tuition aid Ahmad was again treated like an anonymous applicant whose fate would be decided upon in Palestine by people to whom he had no relations. The disembodiment of the distribution aid from the personal relations that determined its very eligibility created the impression of a container that was separate from its content. The "faction" seen as an entity was now the one responsible for the distribution of the aid, not the personal relations that had joined its people together.

The strangeness of these taken-for-granted methods and the effects to which they give rise can be brought to light through an examination of an alternative, and much more widespread, model of aid distribution that was present in the camp: the way that family members helped each other. The crucial role that family played in sustaining everyday life in the camps has been highlighted in many studies (Rosenfeld 2004; R. Sayigh 1994, 2007; Taraki 2006). I illustrate this process through the most common and by far the largest enterprise that any family in the camp ever undertook: the construction of a home. It required a concerted effort from everyone: time, labor, and financial resources. I will examine this process through the example of Nesreen, a young woman in her late twenties who was a social worker for a local NGO in Nahr el-Bared camp. One day, while I was visiting her in her half-demolished home, she explained to me how she, along with her family, had initially built it.

When she was growing up, Nesreen's family shared a two-floor house with her uncle's family. The ground floor consisted of a kitchen, a bathroom, and a single room, which her parents along with her younger siblings occupied at night. The second floor had two rooms. Her uncle, along with his wife and younger children, slept in one of the rooms, while the grandmother and the older children of both families used the second one. This meant that Nesreen shared one room with her siblings as well as her cousins. As she grew up this arrangement began to trouble her, as she slept in the same room as her male cousins and she felt that she was not therefore a "real *muḥajjaba.*" Employing the term for "veiled," she indicated that she was not abiding by her own understanding of what Islam required of her.

Nesreen went on to study nursing and, unable to find employment upon graduation, she worked in her uncle's clothing store in the camp making 100,000 LBP (about 67 USD) a month. She told her parents then that she wanted to use her salary to start renting a home of their own. They thought she was crazy but she insisted. Her younger brother, who was still in school, also began working, and he contributed an additional 50,000 LBP. Their joint efforts allowed the family for the first time to rent a two-room apartment. Over the next four years she changed employment over four times, each time earning a slightly higher salary, which culminated at 300,000 LBP (200 USD). Her brother had also completed his schooling and began working on different construction jobs in the camp. While his earnings were a lot more irregular, Nesreen explained that he too saved money, and after four years of renting they were able to buy a small parcel of land in the new camp. Her brother then began the physical labor of constructing the house, often offering his services for free to different workers in the camp, such as masons, painters, and tile layers, who would then reciprocate and help him build the family home.

Throughout her narration of the story Nesreen was careful to specify how her situation and her brother's were changing with time and how that affected their respective contributions. This clarity and transparency was a feature of many narratives I heard in the camp. When people would tell me how other family members had helped them attain a certain goal, whether securing an education, obtaining medical help, immigrating, or building a home, there was always a description of the "giver" too. The helper's personal situation was always described and it served to qualify how much his or her contributions could be. A sister could help raise her nieces and nephews until she started a family of her own, an uncle working in the Gulf helped pay tuition fees until he lost his job, brothers working in Germany helped pay for the pouring of a concrete roof in an amount according with their respective jobs. Information was a two-way street: aid receivers knew as much about the economic situation of aid givers as the other way around. Certainly, all family members did not help each other: there were numerous examples of "rich uncles" who did not care about a sick young niece. However, my point is to highlight that regardless of whether a family member helped or not, information was flowing in both directions—allowing the "uncles" themselves to be blamed in this case. There was nothing that stood outside of those relations. This was in stark contrast with aid from factions, which appeared as immaterial entities, as stores that people entered to shop for aid.

OPEN POCKETS

> During the [2007] war, some people got richer and some got poorer. The factions and NGOs made money off of our misery. They get funding because of our situation. They give twenty-five percent and they take seventy-five percent.
>
> —UM NABIL, *THAWRA* GENERATION, NAHR EL-BARED, NOVEMBER 29, 2011

It is impossible to end this discussion of aid distribution practices without also pointing out what should be obvious at this point, which is that the lack of control and transparency into the decision-making process created unequal relations of power and built mistrust between what now appeared as the refugees on one hand and factions and NGOs on the other. With so little visibility into the aid distribution process, recipients could never be certain whether providers were distributing aid fairly, or worse, whether the aid at their disposal was even distributed in its entirety. It was therefore possible to distrust factions and NGOs, seen as entities that existed separately from the local trust relations that kept them together. The same way that personal relations became impersonal, so did trust relations became distrustful. This did not dissuade Palestinians from attempting to obtain the aid that they saw as their right, but it did make them reticent about joining any type of mobilization organized by those "entities."

Palestinians were well aware that factions and NGOs were receiving funding from third/outside parties and knew that they were merely intermediaries between the donors and themselves. However, being kept in the dark about how much aid was available and how it was disseminated, they could only wonder if indeed the aid was being distributed fairly. Lina, whom I introduced in the previous chapter, told me about an NGO project she worked on. It was called "Money for Work" and was implemented in partnership between a local NGO and an international NGO and funded by a European agency.[9] Lina described the project she worked on for three months as a surveyor, registering project participants. She recounted her story in the presence of Abu Ziad, who worked as an office clerk for UNRWA and who lived in the metal barracks, and of Rania, her friend and colleague.

> *Lina:* There was funding coming. Honestly, I don't know what its goal was. Was this funding destined for a project, or was it intended for direct distribution [as cash] to the people, which they turned into a project? I really don't know. What I know is that there was an idea. I am not sure if this was their idea or the funder's, but the idea was that instead of giving a person cash and getting them used to receiving money and being lazy, we would give them the money in exchange for work, so that they feel that they are received cash in exchange for work, that it isn't just charity—so they would get used to working to get the money.

> *Abu Ziad interjects:* I'll tell you what is going on! These are funds that are meant for the people. We make the people work a little, and we put some in our pockets a little.

> *Lina:* Now the issue of pockets! Pockets are open everywhere.

> *Rania:* Well, I didn't dare say that, but turns out it's true.

> *Abu Ziad:* No, I will say it! What kind of work is this? What did I gain from this work? What do I gain from trees? Am I going to sit under a tree? They got pickles to give to people.

> . . .

> *Lina:* Now how the money came, how it got distributed, I don't know. But the idea was to start making up projects for the people to work on. They took into consideration that there were women and men, some with a formal education and others without. So they created different projects for the different categories of people: for the women without formal education they created cooking projects. They would get them to prepare different types of pickled vegetables.. . . They made projects just to make the people work, not to provide real work opportunities.

> *Rania:* I wish they made real projects so that people could work for the long term.

Lina continued to explain that the pickled vegetables produced in the project were not sold, but distributed free to camp residents. I remembered at that point that I had seen one of these jars at the Talals' home. It was a plastic jar with a label featuring the local and international NGOs' logos as well as the funder's. Lina continued to list the different projects. They had made the men without formal education plant trees to create small "parks" in the camp, but as Abu Ziad pointed out this was considered of little value to locals. I often passed one such "park" with a broken bench; it was right on the edge of the camp, facing barbed wire and a military post. They asked the men and women with formal education to tutor young children, when their involvement in the program was limited to a single month. The tutoring program was therefore of limited use to students, who "didn't have time to start learning before their tutor changed." Lina finished the story by saying that "of course connections were active. Those who 'knew people' worked for more than a month, and those who didn't did not get to work."

The mistrust induced by the lack of visibility into the aid distribution process explained why camp residents, whether or not they worked for NGOs or were part of factions, often declared that these organizations "profited from their misery." Such statements reflected the frustration they felt, which was well expressed by Abu Ziad. The funding was meant to reach the people; however, they could never be certain if they had indeed received it, even if they themselves were working on a given project. Nevertheless, they pursued their attempts to obtain aid from organizations they distrusted, in part because they understood this as a way to fight corruption.

A further example illustrates this idea. In March, news went around the camp that Hamas was paying the application fee for the baccalaureate exam for all high school students in Nahr el-Bared. However, Um Muhammad and her sister Fatima feared that it was going to Hamas "members" only, as both had children taking the matriculation exam and they were not contacted. One day Um Muhammad came back home from her afternoon visit to her sisters and proudly told me that she and Fatima saw a "Hamas guy" in the street and reprimanded him for only helping their own rather than caring about all Palestinians. The next day Ahmad received a call from the same individual to arrange for paying the examination fees. Um Muhammad and her sister were very proud of themselves, recounting this story to their friends. They explained that they were proud not because they were able to get 50,000 LB (33 US dollars) each from Hamas to pay for the exam fee, although that certainly helped. Rather, they had openly challenged Hamas and had gotten what they perceived was their right and in the process minimized the corruption of Hamas. They added that if they had not claimed the aid, then it would have gone to the "official's pockets."

Looking at aid distribution from the perspective of a recipient, it was better to get aid from a corrupt entity, because doing so prevented the organization from being even more corrupt. This explained why refugees would still deal with NGOs and factions while continuing to criticize them. It was made clear to me again and again that refugees saw the aid distributed as their right and it was their duty to make sure they received it even if it meant dealing with what they perceived to be corrupt entities. However, these undemocratic aid distribution processes greatly diminished the NGOs' and political factions' ability to mobilize refugees in times of crisis. This created a situation in which refugees continued to solicit aid and social services from NGOs and the relief arms of the factions in order to get what they perceived to be their fair share while ignoring their calls for action. That is why certain individuals referred to the people of Nahr el-Bared as *sha'ab al-karateen*, the people of the cartons. Viewed from the perspective of that denigrating description, residents appeared to be solely interested in getting "free" aid and not in working towards the betterment of their situation or that of the camp. In reality, theirs was a rational response to a system of power that stripped them of autonomy, dehumanized them, and deprived them of their right to have a say over aid distribution processes undertaken in their name. By insisting on obtaining the aid available, camp residents believed they were getting what was rightfully theirs and preventing factions and NGOs from profiting even more from their misery.

Lastly, it is important to note that this effect of mistrust did not necessarily happen in every instance. It depended on the level of knowledge or transparency into the aid distribution mechanism. Many camp residents knew certain heads of factions or NGOs personally and could see for themselves how they lived and infer their income level. While this did not always mean that they were familiar with the details of the aid distribution process, they could at least evaluate whether these people were profiting at their expense or not. Through personal relations, then, individuals could get some visibility back into the fairness of the aid decision-making process, infusing trust back into the relationship and breaking down the appearance of structure.

. . .

> My daughter needed an operation and we needed 1,000 USD. I asked an NGO for help and the social worker told me 'Is it worth it to ask for 1,000 USD?' [Implying that I should be able to cover the cost.] I told him, 'those who make 300,000 LBP [200 USD] a month and have young children, can they save 1,000 USD?' Anyways I wished that God may preserve his health and left while carrying my daughter in a cast. I did not enter another organization. I had expected something different. I thought that once I told them [about my daughter's condition] they would say, come on in.
> —UM FATHI, *THAWRA GENERATION*, BUSS CAMP, DECEMBER 9, 2011

Two main topics dominated the Talal family's everyday discussions: their lack of legal documentation in Lebanon and Ahmad's tuition fees. While the former was particular to non-ID families, the latter was generalized across camp residents. The process for obtaining aid from factions and NGOs was pervasive in nature, not only in its penetrating gaze into the lives and homes of people but also in the amount of time it took camp residents to acquire it. While factions and NGOs had numerous aid programs, they were always minimal in impact, barely making a dent in people's lives, but constantly keeping them busy with the qualification, application and following up processes. The lack of NGO coordination only worsened the problem and turned a process that was supposed to be of assistance into an aggravating one that was particularly painful and humiliating for families searching for medical assistance.

My aim in this chapter was not only to highlight the frustration and insecurity of the aid distribution process but to also show how it turned networks built upon close, personal ties into impersonal and suspicious bureaucracies, how the provision of services which depended on highly personalized and intimate relations for its day-to-day operations suddenly metamorphosed into a disembodied machine that controlled people's lives and sowed mistrust in the community. In the name of distributing aid fairly a pervasive system of surveillance was put in place to monitor, evaluate, and compare refugees' different levels of misery. This system of surveillance served to establish and demonstrate a hierarchy with a "top" that could see below it and a "bottom" that was blind. This sense of hierarchy, the impersonal and secretive nature of the decision-making process and the redrawing of the line between "faction members" and "independents" through the dispensing of aid, led to the creation of an imagination where factions appeared as structures that are not to be trusted. They appeared as a container that stood outside and separately from the people contained inside of them. And although there was a head, like the head of the faction, of the NGO, or of the PLO, the structure and the functioning of the aid distribution process did not depend solely on them. The factions resembled a building that existed separately from the very people that they contained, demarcating them from those outside, and while trust sometimes thrived through personal relations on a local and individual basis, there was a great level of mistrust about these "entities."

In the next chapter I look at two other sets of practices, of factionalism and of the physical representation of factions through emblems, flags, and anniversary celebrations. I show how these practices served to give life to factions through the creation of a novel position, the position of an observer. This serves to highlight that practices that produce the effect of structure do not only work from what appears to be the "inside" of factions, through aid receivers and givers, but also from what appears to be the "outside."

FIGURE 12. Watching a faction's parade. Photograph: Perla Issa.

"Factions Are Forced Husbands"

Physical Representations, Factionalism, and Party Ideology

[Following the beginning of the *thawra*] the splits started. So a faction became four. The Arab front, the PFLP became some ten fronts. Even once we joked: What is this? They should give them birth control pills. They became too many. [Laughter]. They don't know how to stop. Each day they give birth. [Laughter]. Fatah also became several Fatahs.

—UM JIHAD, *THAWRA* GENERATION, BEDDAWI CAMP, JULY 12, 2011

Don't you hear the expression "your husband is chosen from God'? . . . The factions are forced husbands (*ghasbin 'an al-dunia*). . . . The international community recognizes [the PLO], it's not me who recognizes it.

—ABU FIRAS, *THAWRA* GENERATION, NAHR EL-BARED CAMP, JULY 26, 2011

Imagining factions as living beings was a common feature of how Palestinians spoke of factions. The PLO was sometimes referred to as a "sick child" and factions as "forced husbands." These images highlighted two important points. First, factions appeared to have a life of their own. They were pictured as actors, sometimes gendered ones, that could have a particular medical condition and could even spawn other beings. Second, refugees felt they had little choice in their representatives, as if these were forced upon them by some greater power.

This chapter examines how the existence of factions becomes naturalized not only to those considered on the "inside" of factions, but more importantly to those who appear to be on the "outside." In the previous chapter we saw how the provision of care created the effect of structure, of an impersonal edifice that stood outside and independently of the personal relations that formed its backbone. In this chapter I highlight how the appearance of structure comes into being not only through what may appear as "internal" practices, such as the distribution of aid, but how it creates an "outside," how it brings into being a position from where we appear to be able to observe, judge, study, and critique factions.

I do so through the examination of two sets of practices, that of physical representation and factionalism. I first examine how the abstract idea of factions take material form through the process of representation. Emblems, flags, posters, pins, stamps, and letterheads: all became the physical embodiment of factions. In particular I look at anniversary celebrations and underline how they enacted a distance between people and factions, a distance that was vital in creating the position of "spectator." As we will see, anniversary celebrations were criticised and few people ever participated in them. They were rather pathetic displays of the demise of factions, rather than of their health. However, to dismiss them would be to ignore the powerful way in which they consolidated the image of factions as autonomous entities. I then look at factionalism—the way factions compete with each other, at times violently—through the testimony of Um Fadi, a veteran of the PFLP and one of the few Palestinians who told me that she joined the faction based on its stated ideology rather than because of personal ties. Through an examination of how she spoke of the death of her husband at the hands of Fatah and of her relationship with the PFLP I reveal how joining through personal ties or through ideology were not opposites. Rather, they only appeared to be so due to a particular modern rendering of subjectivity where a person is believed to exist outside and prior to power relations. This in turn exposes how our modern understanding of subjectivity as autonomous agents was vital in creating the effect where factions appeared to be structures defined by their ideologies.

PHYSICAL REPRESENTATIONS

We wrote a statement. I remember, we read it in a shelter. We declared that we [Fatah al-Intifada] made a Women's Union of our own. . . . The shelter was the only place we had available and we used to be afraid of the army. That day journalists came and they published it in newspapers. From that day on we had our own union.

—HANAA, *THAWRA* GENERATION, SAIDA, DECEMBER 3, 2011

This is an invitation, an invitation from the PFLP. They gave it to us a few days ago. [It states] 'The lighting of the torch (*ish'al al-shu'li*). The forty-fourth anniversary of its great launching! The PFLP is proud to invite you to the annual commemoration of the martyrs who fell defending the Palestinian people and cause. Rashidiyeh camp, *Dayr al-qāsi* hall, Friday 3 p.m. Transportation is provided.' If we went to these people and told them that someone is sick and needs an operation and it costs 5,000 USD and we need your help, they would tell you we don't have the means. But here it says that transportation is provided. How are you paying for transportation? They provide transportation so that the 'responsible' can make a speech and scream. And it's actual screaming.

—ABU AHMAD, *THAWRA* GENERATION, RASHIDIYEH CAMP, DECEMBER 8, 2011

Palestinian political factions all have a foundation date. In Arabic, this date was referred to as the *inṭilāqa*, "the launching." A faction launched itself by declaring its own birth in a public statement. The *inṭilāqa* of each faction was then commemorated every year to mark the number of years the faction had existed, its age. In the Palestinian camps of Lebanon these celebrations took the form of marches or rallies and featured political speeches, Palestinian music, and sometimes *dabka*, Palestinian dance. These celebrations were often the subject of criticism from camp residents, who viewed them as unnecessary spending. While it is easy to dismiss such actions as an additional indication of the corruptness of factions, I argue that these practices played a vital role in bringing factions to life.

At first glance, the process by which factions came into being through anniversary celebrations appears to be straightforward. After all, an anniversary by definition is the celebration of a birth. Birthdays denote life. Having and celebrating a birthday annually is a practice associated with living beings. When I celebrate a friend's birthday, I am celebrating the number of years my friend has been alive. My friend exists and is breathing regardless of the practice of celebrating his or her birthday. He or she exists outside and prior to the ceremony. Indeed, the practice of the birthday celebration only exists because my friend is alive in the first place. Associating that practice with Palestinian political factions was one way to imbue them with life, with an existence that could be calculated in a precise number of years. Additionally, this life appeared to exist outside and prior to the anniversary celebrations, just like my friend's life was. However, I contend that anniversary celebrations worked in a much more subtle way, by creating the very position of an "outside," a position from which a person could even criticize factions and appear to be in opposition to them. Beyond being pathetic displays of the irrelevance of factions, the practice of anniversary commemoration perpetuated and guaranteed the imagination that factions were entities with a life of their own, the crucial technique through which they came to represent "the people" regardless of "the people's" desires.

Marches

I attended several marches commemorating the birth of factions during my stay in Nahr el-Bared camp. The first one I experienced was the twenty-ninth anniversary of the Palestinian People's Party (PPP).[1] It was established on February 10, 1982 when it split from the Jordan Communist Party (JCP) by publishing its "Founding Statement and the Provisional Internal Statutes of the Palestinian Communist Party" (Y. Sayigh 1997, 477). On Sunday February 6, 2011, the Nahr el-Bared branch of the PPP commemorated its anniversary with a march through the camp that ended in the martyrs' cemetery.

It was a sunny Sunday. I mostly stayed home that day, as Sunday was the only day of the week when all family members would be home at the same time. After a joyful family lunch, Mahmud left to prepare for the march. At the time he was the head of the DFLP scouts, and he said that this was a good opportunity for the youngsters to practice being in a marching band in preparation for the DFLP's own anniversary, some twenty days away. Ahmad, who was also planning on joining the march, stayed a little longer at home with us, leaving just a few minutes before the march's starting time.

While I was trying to decide if I should join the march myself, Um Muhammad convinced me to watch it from the kitchen balcony. She told me that they would start the march on the street right below us and then walk towards the camp's martyrs' cemetery. When I asked her how she knew the route, she explained that they always went the same way. The third floor balcony did indeed give me a perfect view of the march from above. Um and Abu Muhammad decided to join me, so I took three of the kitchen plastic chairs onto the balcony while Um Muhammad made tea and Abu Muhammad prepared his usual Sunday afternoon *narghile*.

Mahmud soon appeared, walking down the main street with his marching band. Um Muhammad explained that the marching band was coming to join the rest of the participants, who had started to gather below our building. The band was already in formation. Three young girls, probably around eight or nine years old, led the band holding up the Palestinian and the DFLP flags. Following them were about five children, slightly older, probably in their early teens, playing drums, and two girls holding clash cymbals. Behind them were three young boys, again holding a combination of the Palestinian and DFLP flags. Most of the children, whether boys or girls, veiled or unveiled, were wearing black berets. With the exception of the head attire there was little resemblance in their clothing. Mahmud walked between the children, trying to get them to walk in three straight lines, stopping every few minutes to give them a chance to get back in formation. They walked in this fashion until they reached our building, at which point they stopped. Ahmad soon joined them with a group of about five young men. Another group of about ten men also walked towards the meeting point. Um Muhammad mentioned that these men "are Fatah." And soon the march was in formation.

The DFLP scouts led the march. Next came two young men holding a banner with the PPP emblem reproduced in triplicate. Behind them were a group of about twenty young children holding a mixture of the Palestinian and the PPP flags. Following them were two young men holding another banner stating on top, in red, "29th anniversary of the establishment of the Palestinian People's Party"; below this, in black, was the phrase "National unity is the way to liberation, independence and return." Finally it was signed by the Palestinian People's Party, again in red. The youth in this initial portion of the march were well separated from each other, making this section of the march the longest, about twenty meters. The second portion of the procession was the adults. About forty men stood behind the young children. The men at the forefront of the group stood in a well-formed line. The rest of the men followed, with the younger men grouped towards the back. About twenty women were a few meters behind. Some were carrying infant children in their arms, others were holding their toddlers by their hands, and two women were carrying the PPP flag. Finally, behind the women were two young men, holding another banner with the PPP emblem reproduced in triplicate. That completed the procession. They soon started marching and we could hear the beating of the drums. The march then took a right turn towards the martyrs' cemetery, at which point I could no longer see them. Ahmad came back home not long after that. I looked at my watch; forty minutes had elapsed from the time he left the house to the time he returned.

In total about one hundred people participated in the march, a third of whom were young children, even though at least four different factions were present: the DFLP, Islamic Jihad, and Fatah, in addition to the PPP. Few people watched the march from their balconies or windows, and people in the street paid little attention, sometimes stopping for a few minutes to watch but not joining in. I thought that the whole event was indicative of the PPP's inability to mobilize people. Um Muhammad and Abu Muhammad, sitting next to me, did not give the march much attention either, other than pointing to their children when they first appeared on the street on their way to join the march. They were more interested in speaking about their fears for their children. In particular, Abu Muhammad expressed his fear that his children would make the same mistakes as him. I could feel a mixture of pride but also regret about his previous life choice of joining the *thawra*. He explained that his siblings who had not followed his path were in a much better legal and financial situation. He concluded by saying that "factions were worthless."

Rallies

The other form taken by the annual commemoration of the establishment of factions is a political gathering marked by speeches. On Friday February 25, 2011, I was in Nahr el-Bared camp when a car with loudspeakers drove through the camp announcing the celebration of the DFLP anniversary in the Jal al-Amar hall that same evening. I decided to attend.

Palestinian camps typically have several halls, which are privately owned and run as a business. The primary use of these halls is wedding celebrations, but political factions also rent them to conduct rallies and conferences. After Nahr el-Bared's destruction in the 2007 war, all of the halls were damaged; the Jal al-Amar hall was one of the first to be rebuilt after the refugees' return to the camp. Jal al-Amar was an area of Nahr el-Bared camp situated to the west of the old camp and the Bared River. However, the Lebanese military had restricted access to the old camp. Therefore, like any resident of Nahr el-Bared wanting to cross from the Eastern side of the camp to its Western side, I had to walk around the old camp, instead of through it.

It was a dark, rainy day as I set out to walk from the home of the Talal family to the Jal al-Amar hall. I did not know the exact location of the hall but decided to walk to Jal al-Amar and to ask for directions once there. I walked along the main road of Nahr el-Bared until I reached the army checkpoint blocking the entrance of the old camp. A couple of soldiers in rain gear were standing by the metal gate that had been painted red and white, the colours of the Lebanese flag. I turned left and walked past a huge sign advertising all the donors contributing to the reconstruction of the old camp. I kept going until I reached the southern edge of the old camp, at which point I turned right into an alley. The alley was deserted, as few people had returned to this street and most of the buildings were still partially destroyed, with collapsed roofs and perforated walls. Little light reached this narrow alley, making it dark and eerie. As I reached the end of it, I turned right onto the dirt road that ran along the Bared river. I was back in daylight. I had reached the southwest end of the old camp and I was walking north along the river to reach the main road again. To the right was a series of fully collapsed buildings, still untouched. To left was the Bared river, swollen by the rains, and surrounded by wild green vegetation. This was a sharp contrast to the narrow and dark alley I had just walked through. Large parts of this road had turned into puddles with the rain pouring down. As I was making my way, trying my best to stay on dry land, a car passed by and slowed down. Two young men asked me if I would like a ride. I gladly accepted the offer.

Upon reaching the hall I saw the head of Najdeh (a DFLP NGO) in Nahr el-Bared camp and another man, whom I did not know, standing at the door. They were greeting people coming into the hall. I said hello quickly and walked into the hall. Loudspeakers were playing nationalist songs that made discussion with people difficult. To the left of the entrance was a group of highly energetic young men holding a large number of DFLP flags and congregating around a loudspeaker. They would raise their voices above the sound of the songs and chant about Palestine, freedom, return, and the DFLP.

At about forty by twenty meters, the hall was bigger than I had expected. The walls, which were painted with different landscape scenes, such as birds flying in a blue sky, or a sunset, had been covered with red banners proclaiming different slogans calling for national unity and the reconstruction of Nahr el-Bared. Across from the entrance was the podium, decorated with a banner of what appeared to be DFLP martyrs, a combination of Palestinian and DFLP flags, as well as a large picture of Nayif Hawatma, the chairman of the DFLP. Plastic chairs had been lined up in two separate columns and were filling up with women and children on the left and men and a few children on the right.

I saw many of the women I had met at Najdeh and decided to sit next to them. Soon the proceedings started. The first speaker, a former member of Parliament from Akkar, was introduced. The speaker began by saluting the audience and congratulating the DFLP on its anniversary, but I soon lost track of the content of the speech, of the actual sentences being said. He was speaking in formal Arabic and in such an elevated voice that I found it hard to focus on the speech. Rather, my attention was diverted to watching the audience. A man was holding his young daughter in his arms and poking her nose, which amused her greatly; an Najdeh employee was videotaping the ceremony; a woman was standing by the entrance greeting latecomers; and the woman sitting next to me was silent, looking at the speaker with an expressionless face.

Nevertheless certain words rang in my ears as the speaker elevated his voice, stressing them: the inalienable right of return, the fight for liberation, the illegal occupation, the heroism of political prisoners, the expansion of illegal settlements, the sacredness of Jerusalem, the need for national unity and PLO reform, the condemnations of American policies (especially the practice of vetoing UN Security Council resolution condemning Israeli aggression), the demand for civil rights for Palestinians in Lebanon, the rejection of naturalization (*tawṭīn*), and the need for a quick reconstruction of Nahr el-Bared camp. The group of young men by the entrance would sometimes interrupt the speaker by chanting "Freedom! Freedom! We want freedom!" At this point the speaker took a moment and then continued his speech in an even louder voice, raised above the chants. This continued for about ten minutes and then the next speaker was introduced, this time a member of the Lebanese Communist Party. The same scenario was repeated with what seemed to be a reiteration of the same topics. The group of young men burst out in chants: "Justice! Freedom! DFLP!"[2]

In total, four different speakers took turns on the podium in a replay of the above-described scenario until the last speaker was introduced, but this time over music. He was the head of the DFLP in Northern Lebanon, Arkan Bader. While the other speakers appeared to be speaking at the top of their voices, Arkan Bader was literally screaming. I remembered a friend who had told me that he always had his mouth open; I now understood what she meant. Arkan Bader shouted for about twenty minutes, double the time of the previous speakers but repeating the same key words. At the end, after a long list of salutations, as he was uttering the words "may peace be upon you" (*al-salām ʿalaykum*), everyone got up and began to leave. The sudden ending of the ceremony took me by total surprise. I was still in a daze induced by the series of loud speeches. The swiftness of the audience in getting up and heading for the exit startled me. I soon got up and followed some of the participants to the nearby cemetery, where we visited tombs under the watchful eyes of Lebanese soldiers. We did not remain long, as it started raining, at which point everyone went their own way. I began to walk back home, but when a car pulled up next to me and asked me if I wanted a ride, I again gladly accepted.

While more people participated in the DFLP rally than the PPP march, the staged nature of the ceremony was very clear. The group of young men clapping and chanting intermittently was meant to remedy the audience's general lack of interest in the proceedings. The loud voices of the speakers were meant to dissuade people from chatting. The silence of the audience did not indicate any interest on their part as their faces remained expressionless, even though the topics of the speeches, the return to Palestine and self-determination, were certainly of interest to them. Finally, the speed of the exit led me to believe that most participants preferred to be somewhere else than this rally. This was a disappointing performance for what was supposed to be a strong faction of Nahr el-Bared. Najdeh, the DFLP's NGO, was one of the largest in the camp, if not the largest, with four different offices in Nahr el-Bared alone. It was also one of the first NGOs to come back to the camp after its destruction and had fought hard with the army in order to get access to different areas in the camp. But still, what was clear from this forty-third anniversary celebration was that the DFLP was unable to mobilize people.

These ceremonies were also the target of criticism by camp residents. They were seen as unnecessary spending when money, if available, would be better spent on meeting people's needs. People would point to the money spent on hall rentals and transportation (often factions provide buses to take people from different camps to the celebration hall) and argued that this would be better used on more essential needs such as providing medical help for the sick. A friend even pointed out that, at the PFLP anniversary, they had served food. He specified that there were fruits of all kinds, such as apples, bananas, and even kiwis. He insisted that there were also two huge cakes, each being one and half meters by one meter, with the PFLP slogan written on one of the cakes and the PLO slogan written on the other. Fresh fruits were out of reach for most camp residents; therefore a display of such fruits, not to mention large cakes, aroused his indignation.

Others would criticise these events by pointing out that young Palestinians often participated in these proceedings in order to obtain financial assistance from the factions. They argued that the heads of factions noticed an absence and penalized the absentee at the end of the month. However, trying to determine whether people's participation in these ceremonies was genuine, instrumental, or a combination can distract us from looking at what these proceedings actually accomplished. Building upon the work of Timothy Mitchell, I suggest that the proceedings, while failing in terms of a popularity test, succeeded in constructing Palestinian political factions as entities with a life of their own, separate from the very people and the very practices that brought them into being. The rituals employ three crucial techniques: creating the position of an "outside observer"; drawing the line between the "inside" and the "outside"; and finally giving life to factions through a process of representation.

Drawing Lines: The Creation of an "Outside"

One of the crucial features of these celebrations was that they were public. Indeed anniversary celebrations were not conducted behind closed doors among party members; rather they were meant to be watched. Sitting on a balcony, peering out of a window, stopping in the street, hearing the sound of the drums, or of the advertisement for a rally, were all positions that seemed to put the authors of such actions "outside" the practice of anniversary commemoration. They seemed innocent in themselves. However, it was precisely this innocuous position that enacted a distance between "spectators" and "factions." The physical distance that existed between the balcony and the procession represented my own separation from the PPP in particular and from factions in general. I felt I was standing outside, looking at the physical embodiment of factions go by.

Being on the "outside" also allowed Palestinians to criticize factions, as Abu Muhammad did. While this position may have seemed to be in opposition to factions, it actually served to reify them. Writing about corruption in India, Gupta (1995, 376) highlights how "the discourse of corruption turns out to be a key arena through which the state, citizens and other organizations and aggregations come to be imagined." He adds that "instead of treating corruption as a dysfunctional aspect of state organizations" he sees it as "a mechanism through which "the state" itself is discursively constituted." By stating that "factions are worthless," Abu Muhammad was distancing himself from the factions but in the process acknowledging their existence as entities. Two of his sons were in fact participating in the proceedings that he was criticising. He was therefore entangled in the network of relations that factions were. Yet through his criticism, Abu Muhammad placed himself on the "outside," which in turn helped create the image that factions were bounded structures instead of loose networks brought together by personal relations.

Just as watching or hearing a parade go by placed the individual outside the factions, so too did walking in the parade, attending a rally, hearing the speeches, or otherwise directly participating in the proceedings located the person as a faction member. A simple example can illustrate this process. When I was sitting on the third floor balcony watching Mahmud participate in the parade, I spontaneously thought that Mahmud was in fact a member of the DFLP. I registered this note in my head, in juxtaposition to the previous confusion I felt when he told me that he was only "in principle" with the DFLP. At the time I found his choice of word of "in principle" to be confusing, but when I saw him walking in that parade as the head of the DFLP scouts I settled the matter in my head: Mahmud was in fact part of the DFLP. Positioning myself "outside" the practice of anniversary commemoration, I pictured factions as edifices and positioned Mahmud inside of its walls. However, as I spent more time in Nahr el-Bared and saw the development of Mahmud's relationship with the DFLP I realized that that relationship was more complicated (chapter 4). As we have seen, faction membership is better understood as a relationship between individuals than a relationship between an individual and a building that a person entered or left. Whereas a person must necessarily be either inside or outside an edifice, a relationship with an individual carried with it ambiguity and varying degrees of cohesion. Therefore, attempting to define that relationship in terms of being inside or outside the faction failed to take into account the complexity of that connection. Yet, from the vantage point of the balcony that ambiguity disappeared, factions appeared as bounded structures, and Mahmud seemed to be clearly positioned on the "inside."

Physical Representations

Mahmud did not only appear to be "inside" factions but, along with his fellow comrades, appeared to represent those factions. Mitchell (1988, 60) argued that "the techniques of enframing, of fixing an interior and exterior, and of positioning the observing subject, are what create an appearance of order, an order that works by appearance. The world is set up before an observing subject as though it were the picture of something." Sitting on the balcony we were made to believe that the children, men, and women walking down the street were the representation of factions instead of just a particular instance of people marching. The refugees who were present in the procession and those who spoke in the rally no longer represented just themselves, but appeared to be representative of the immaterial abstract idea of factions.

Additionally, Mitchell (1988, 7–10) argued that the practice of representation created the effect of a reality that existed prior and outside of that very representation. For example, if I accepted the idea that Mahmud was a representative of the DFLP, that means that I accepted the idea that the DFLP existed, and in turn the DFLP's existence seemed independent of Mahmud, and of my acceptance of him as a representative of the faction. Once we accepted the concept of representation, we accepted the idea that there were two separate entities: the "thing" and the representations of the "thing." The "thing" is never in itself visible, it is just represented, but we remain certain that it exists precisely because it is represented. These material forms appeared to be "giving a visible exterior to the invisible 'inner structure'" (59). The representations of the "inner structure" were material; we could see them and touch them; however, the "inner structure" of the faction in itself was immaterial. In other words, once we accepted that something stood for something else, we took for granted that this something else existed.

Representations could only work if they had an audience that seemed to be positioned outside of them and that recognized them. Hence the importance of positioning those watching the parade as being "outside" factions became apparent. Watching anniversary celebrations and acknowledging them as representations was imbuing life to factions. Yet we did not realize that it was our acceptance of the idea of representation that created them. When I saw a PPP flag, I thought that I was seeing a representation of the PPP. I believed that the PPP existed and that this flag represented it. Yet in actuality, it was the practice of representation that was actually effecting the appearance of a reality underneath, of a life prior to and outside of the representation. Similarly, when the Lebanese government, UN agencies, or the media treated factions as entities, as representative bodies, they were involved in the very process of erecting a structure. By accepting to treat certain individuals as "representative" of factions, they were bringing factions to life. This was the paradoxical nature of the method of representation: factions acquired the appearance of a life outside and separate from their representations when it was those very representations that brought them into being. In other words, factions appeared as a framework that existed separately from the particular people and practices it enframed.

However, it is important to realize that the power of these methods did not lie in making us believe that these representations were accurate. Indeed, the claim that factions were representative of the Palestinian people was highly contested, with numerous individuals, campaigns, publications, and studies demanding "real" or "true" representation.[3] But the ability to represent was never in itself contested and the particular methods used to enact such effects were never questioned.

We grasp the importance of these practices when we realize that factions participated in each other's anniversary commemorations, yet they seldom joined in advocacy campaigns or protests. Anniversary collaborations crossed ideological lines, with Islamic Jihad, nationalist Fatah, and the Marxist DFLP joining the communist PPP in its commemoration. It also cut across political positioning; Fatah and the PPP advocated a two-state solution and the continuation of negotiations with Israel, while the Islamic Jihad called for the establishment of a single state through resistance. Palestinians often referred to the factions' mutual participation in each other's anniversary celebrations as "social visits" (*ziyārāt 'ijtimā'iyya*). This appellation stressed the fact that a given faction attended the celebrations of another faction expecting that in turn the other factions would participate in its own anniversary. While this cooperation failed to translate into a mobilization of a significant number of people, it succeeded in effecting the appearance of a structure, an entity that existed outside and prior to the very practice that brought it into being. It underlined that all factions had a stake in maintaining this system as it allowed them to act as the representatives of the "people."

It is hard to end this discussion without also pointing out that anniversary celebrations did not only appear to be material representations of factions, but they also served to portray what proper politics was about. The marches or rallies were carried out in specific, almost scientific ways. Children in black berets walked in straight lines separated into three columns, men formed a straight line, women were several meters back, the procession started and ended with young men holding flags, and the same route ending at the martyrs' cemetery was taken year after year. The rallies also followed a specific script. First, speakers who were not part of the birthday faction addressed the audience; their names and positions were explained. They each had ten minutes to give their speeches, interrupted from time to time by chants. Finally, a representative of the DFLP addressed the audience for double the time. The timing and number of the speakers might vary from rally to rally, but the pattern remained the same. Additionally, watching the DFLP rally, I felt a need to write down the names of the speakers and their positions, as if knowing that information would allow me to better understand the DFLP. The third speaker I noted was the lawyer Abdel Nasser al-Masri of the Organization of the Lebanese People. I had never heard before of this organization and wondered who they were. This missing piece of information made me feel ignorant, unknowledgeable in the proper conduct of politics. I felt compelled to conduct research on that organization to become politically educated. When I missed the name of the fourth speaker due to the high volume of the chants, I was even more upset.

The form and content of the speeches also projected an image of the appropriate way of conducting politics. They all followed the same format and highlighted the same topics. The exact content of the speech seemed less important than the form and the manner in which they were delivered, with high volume interrupted by energetic chants. What these proceedings did was project an image of the proper way of doing politics. Politics became a specific field of knowledge and practices separated from the everyday practices of Palestinians. Knowledge of party ideology, literature, and platforms defined what "political knowledge" was. It became disassociated from other forms of knowledge, or other ways of learning. "Political knowledge" became something that certain people grasped while others may "know nothing about it." As factions became separated from people, so did politics become separated from everyday life through the development of a particular expertise. Next, I expand on this idea and look at how party ideology opened up a space of separation between factions and people, which, similarly to anniversary celebrations, brought about a position that appeared to be on the "outside" of factions. Additionally, I show how our conventional understanding of factions as structures defined by a particular ideology relies on a certain modern rendering of personhood as existing outside and prior to power relations.

FACTIONALISM AND PARTY IDEOLOGY

> The nature of Palestinian society is tribal. To live in the camp you need to be supported by a faction. This is essential, you understand? You have to have a back (a protection)—(*ilik ḍahir*)—if you get into a problem, if you need a university scholarship. [By being in a faction] you have a following (*imtidād*). Additionally, your parents before you [may be affiliated]. The nature of Palestinian society is factional. . . . It is rare to go into a home and not find it following a faction.
>
> —RANIA, YOUNG GENERATION, NAHR EL-BARED CAMP, JULY 28, 2011

Comments like Rania's were common in Nahr el-Bared. Indeed, the fact that Palestinians joined factions due to personal relations, instead of choosing an ideology, sometimes created a sense that Palestinians joined factions for the "wrong reasons." Following personal ties (most often kin ties) instead of relying on a personal evaluation of the different ideologies of the factions was seen as "tribal" or "backward." Writing about the beginning of the *thawra*, Rosemary Sayigh (2007, 13) underlines how political ideology and consciousness were considered "the supreme good." She explains how the *thawra* generation believed "they had to be guided by a correct political ideology, which could only be the product of consciousness."[4]

In this section I ask: Is joining political factions through personal ties, rather than through a personal evaluation of the ideologies of the factions, a tribal, backward, or un-modern behavior? In doing so I investigate the role of party ideology in appearing to define factions and in creating a position on the "outside" of factions, a position from where a person is able to study and choose factions "freely." We have already seen how joining factions through personal ties did not mean that Palestinian refugees were blindly following their relatives, friends or neighbors (chapters 3 and 4). It was clear in several examples, like that of Abu Ali who hit the Lenin statue with his shoe over a dispute of Russian politics, and his son Rabieh who disagreed with the PFLP leadership over their stand in the Nahr el-Bared conflict of 2007. Palestinian refugees were not putting their faculty of reason on hold. Rather, they were actively engaged in thinking about and debating different policies and events and their ramifications on the Palestinian struggle and their lives.

However, I argue that this provides only a partial picture of the interplay between personal relations and party ideology. I explore the intricacies of this relationship through the example of Um Fadi, a veteran of the PFLP and one of only two Palestinians who told me that she joined the *Jabha* based on its stated ideology and not due to personal ties.

Um Fadi

Um Fadi was in her late fifties and hid a mixture of stubbornness and resilience underneath a frail body and a wrinkled face. "What type of circus is this?" was how she referred to the chaotic weekly organizational meetings for the May 15, 2011 march to the southern Lebanese border, which she never missed, travelling two hours from her home in Beddawi camp to Beirut in each direction. Meeting her in her home several months later, I had the chance to discuss her longstanding relationship with the PFLP, which helped me understand how death and party ideology interplay to give life to factions. Here, I recount the major events in her life, to give the context through which we can better understand the relation between party ideology and personal relations.

Directing me to her house in Beddawi camp, Um Fadi explained that I should go to the commercial street behind the UNRWA school and ask "anyone" for directions to her home. Sure enough, once I arrived I went into a grocery store where the owner took me a few meters down the street and introduced me to her son Fadi, who was sitting outside the PFLP office. Fadi was in his early twenties, and did not ask what I wanted or who I was; he just led me through the narrow alleys of the camp to his family's home. It seemed he had done this before. Lying on a hill, Beddawi camp was a dizzying labyrinth of concrete alleys and staircases, which Fadi guided me through until we reached his home. This was situated on the first floor of a corner two-story building. We went up an open-air concrete staircase to reach the apartment door. Fadi slipped off his shoes in a seemingly effortless motion, went through the cracked-open door, and called his mother.

Um Fadi came to the door and welcomed me into the house. I stepped into what appeared to be a hallway turned into a sitting area, but she did not motion me to sit there. Instead, she went straight into another room with more stylish couches and invited me to sit. This room had couches on three sides and a bookcase on the fourth. I sat in the corner of a sofa facing the only window in the room. The window gave onto the alley I had just walked up. The wall of the adjacent house was a mere two meters away, which allowed little light to come into the room. It was the end of July, the weather was hot and humid, and we spent the next few hours alternating between opening and closing the window in a desperate attempt to determine what was more bearable: the stifling heat, or the incessant noises coming from the alley. A fan turned from side to side, giving us some momentary relief from the heat.

The bookcase to the right of me contained a number of books and papers. On the top right shelf stood an old black and white picture of a young man in a silver frame. Um Fadi explained that this was her father. The picture, she added, was taken three months before he was killed by an Israeli commando operation in Beddawi camp. Below it was a picture of Che Guevara and to the left a picture of Nasrallah, the current Secretary-General of the Lebanese political party Hezbollah.

Um Fadi sat next to me and began almost without prompting to recount her life story. She was born in the mid-1950s and was exposed from a very young age to both the Lebanese government's repression of Palestinians and Palestinians' resistance against that repression. She began our discussion by telling me that her father had been working in the Palestinian resistance underground before the official start of the *thawra* in 1965. She remembered her father being imprisoned for six months by the Lebanese government, during which time she visited him and saw him performing hard labor. She attributed her later resistance activities to this early moment in her life. "That created something in my unconscious that I only felt later when the revolution started," she said. At the age of eleven she started going to the *ashbāl* of Fatah.[5] Although her father was socially conservative, he nonetheless encouraged her. She explained that she participated in Fatah events but did not become a member.

Um Fadi later married a member of the PFLP, but explained that she "kept an independent personality." She insisted that she did not join the PFLP just because her husband was a member. She further highlighted that point, and her husband's acceptance of her decision, by telling me that her oldest daughter went to the Fatah *ashbal* and that her husband would take her in his PFLP jeep whenever it rained. Um Fadi's perceived "independence" from her husband and the PFLP is a point I will come back to later.

Um Fadi went on to tell me that in 1978 her husband was killed "at the hands of Fatah." She explained:

> At that time Nayif Hawatma [the Chairman of the DFLP] proposed the idea of a state [in any part of Palestine] and Fatah adopted it.[6] The PFLP then formed the

rejection front,[7] supported by Iraq, so of course Fatah does not accept this, it wants to impose its project. So they hit their main location in the north and my husband was martyred.[8]

. . .

It was a political decision [by Fatah to close the PFLP office]. . . . Now my husband was the one responsible for military affairs. He sent a letter to the *Hakim* [the Chairman of the PFLP George Habash] because the PFLP has a rule that says that the blood of a Palestinian is sacred, it is forbidden [to fight a Palestinian] under any circumstances. They told him that the mood is not normal; that the camp is in a state of military alert that is unusual with the rental of over seventy-five offices just in this camp. I was very distressed at the time; my family is Fatah and my husband PFLP. I was very tired. He came and showed me the reply from the *Hakim*, he told me, look: self-defense is allowed just inside the office. Anyone who goes out of the office area and fights will get prosecuted in a civilian court. It is forbidden to fire a gun in the camp, even if the office gets demolished. He [the *Hakim*] sent another letter stating, this is our people, that we get killed is not a problem but the important thing is that nothing happens to the camp. So they stayed in that office. And at that time, there were three girls and thirteen guys in the office; the battle lasted from seven at night until seven in the morning.

Following the killing of her husband, Um Fadi, twenty-four years old and mother of four, secluded herself. After confining herself to her parents' home for a year and a half, she decided to visit Palestine for the first time. Her uncles had remained in their original village of Shafa 'Amr in Palestine after the 1948 *Nakba* and were able to get a permit for her and her four children to visit them for three months. Her trip to Palestine reinvigorated her, she explained:

I returned [to Lebanon from Palestine] energized and replenished. I was more attached to the *thawra*. At the beginning I entered because of the mood of the house, but when I went and came back I returned with a full awareness/consciousness (*wa'ī kāmil*) of the importance of Palestine, of how they live in it and outside it and that the return must happen. We should all be convinced of it.

Um Fadi explained that it was at this time that she joined the PFLP and started working full time in the PFLP radio communications department. She was proud to be working and providing for her children. In the 1980s her responsibilities increased and she took charge of the PFLP's "women's affairs" in Beddawi camp. She was a highly energetic woman who worked, along with other women, to provide food and vital supplies to the many fighters who were in the camp. (The number of fighters substantially increased in 1982 due to the Israeli invasion of Lebanon).

This work caused her to be well known in the camp, which explained how I could walk into any store on a busy commercial street and ask for directions to her home. She was also involved in creating economic opportunities for women. She once organized an exhibition to sell women's homemade products such as thyme mixtures (*za'tar*), pickles, dried cheese (*kishik*), and herbal teas (*zuhūrāt*). She explained that when the PFLP leadership refused to provide money for the exhibition, a sum of 250,000 Lebanese pounds (about 167 US dollars), she borrowed the amount from a friend, carried through her idea on her own, and with the sale of the products made enough money to pay back her friend. Throughout our conversation Um Fadi was highly critical of the leadership of the PFLP and of her comrades in Beddawi camp. She was particularly upset at the financial crisis that the faction was facing which meant that she could not implement any projects or help those in need. In light of her heavy criticism of the leadership and her comrades in the PFLP, I asked her to describe her relationship to it. I quote her answer at length, as it reveals the complexity of her affiliation with the faction and drives my analysis.

Perla: What do you feel towards the PFLP? How would you describe your relationship with it?

Um Fadi: I told you the organization (*tanẓim*), I respect it and I entered it out of conviction, without pressure and after a long time. And I don't forget that there are people who invested a lot in me, who helped me get the skills I have, who trained me, in the PFLP. People who were martyred. And this is what makes it hard. I feel it is a heavy load on me.

Perla: That they gave this much.

Um Fadi: Yes, and that we have to continue regardless of the problems and obstacles.

Perla: And they were from the PFLP?

Um Fadi: Yes, they were like a father or a brother to me. In the time when I was secluding myself, they were the family that took me in, at the height of my crisis. I remember mostly one person. I consider him like a father to me, Abu Mustapha Rashid of Nahr el-Bared; he was martyred in the internal killing.[9] Damn it!

Perla: In 1983?

Um Fadi: Yes, he was taking food to people or taking people to a shelter. He was killed in the street, a bomb killed him. When I used to go out in the morning, leaving my kids behind—you know they were young, it was a big responsibility, I had to work and leave them at home—I would be worried and upset. I would find him standing outside. When he would see me—his hair was greyish—he would ask me: What is wrong today? Why are you upset? I felt he was like my father, I felt he *was* my father. . . . I started bringing books to read, I wanted to read the books of the PFLP. One of the first things I read was the proceedings of the fourth conference of the PFLP. [Abu Mustapha Rashid] saw me, he told me, anything you need I am willing to help. I started discussing things with him; you know the person who is inside something is not like the person who is about to enter. I felt like he encouraged me, like he protected me, he gave me back the confidence I had lost. . . . Once a young man was martyred. I was very upset about it, I was with [Abu Mustapha Rashid] in a car going to Tripoli—he had many friends there—to get donations. He put the recorder on a PFLP song: 'It is not important if we are alive, it is not important if we die in the cry of war, if we find someone who carries the gun and continues the struggle.' He would say, when you are upset, listen to this recording. So this affected me the most. . . . What keeps me attached [to the PFLP] is that there are people who were martyred knowing that there are people behind them continuing the journey. They were martyred for convictions and principles that *made* the PFLP. So I have to continue with the same principles that they died for, even if the whole community wants to outcast me I don't care, because people gave their blood for this.

This passage is very powerful and reveals several important points. It highlights how sacrifice gave life to the PFLP by associating it with the ideals that people had died for. It shows how through these ideals the faction became an immaterial conceptual structure that we learn about through studying its stated ideology and became separated from the very people and practices that brought it into being and from Um Fadi, who positioned herself "outside" of the PFLP, looking at it, studying it and then deciding to "join" it. However, we will see that this position was ultimately untenable, as by her own words it became apparent that trying to place Um Fadi as "outside" or "inside" the PFLP did not properly describe her relationship to it.

Giving Life to Factions

When Um Fadi recounted the story of her husband's killing and when she spoke of Abu Mustapha Rashid, she stressed the fact that both men gave their lives for the principles of the PFLP. This was very clear in the way she recounted the story of her husband's death. In particular she highlighted the two letters that the Chairman of the PFLP George Habash wrote to her husband, explaining that the PFLP did not engage in internal fighting and forbidding her husband from fighting Fatah unless it was in self-defence and confined to the PFLP's office premises. Um Fadi also highlighted how her husband abided by these principles ("they stayed *in that office*") even if it ended up costing him his life. Um Fadi related another incident that further underlined this point. She explained that her brothers, who were with Fatah, wanted to protect her husband and proposed to take him outside of the camp. However he refused and according to Um Fadi one of her brothers asked him: "What, the office is Jerusalem?" and he replied "This office will get me to Jerusalem, you can only get me out of it dead." This again highlighted his resolve to uphold PFLP principles, even if it meant his ultimate death. Similarly, Abu Mustapha Rashid not only abided by PFLP principles of not engaging in internal fighting, but he was killed in the indiscriminate bombing during an internal battle that he did not partake in. Rather, according to Um Fadi, he was trying to help others.

According to Um Fadi, her husband and her close friend and mentor, Abu Mustapha Rashid, died to uphold the principles of the PFLP, and by doing so they gave life to the PFLP. Um Fadi explained that "They were martyred for convictions and principles that *made* the PFLP. So I have to continue with the same principles that they died for even if the whole community wants to outcast me I don't care, because people gave their blood for this." For Um Fadi, the PFLP was "made" of principles; it was no longer "made" of people. Additionally, Um Fadi revealed that sacrifice gave life by creating a commitment in the minds of survivors to honor the ideals for which their comrades fell.[10] This point was highlighted by the song that Um Fadi mentioned, and that Abu Mustapha Rashid introduced her to in order to console her over the death of a young man. Um Fadi repeated a few of its lines: "It is not important if we are alive, it is not important if we die in the cry of war, if we find someone who carries the gun and continues the struggle." After looking up the song, I found that it ended with the following sentence: "If we find others [who continue the journey] then we did not die." It's clear that Um Fadi felt an obligation to continue with those same principles that the PFLP now stands for: otherwise her husband and friend would have died in vain. This was what she referred to as "a heavy load" at the beginning of her testimony.

Associating a faction with its stated ideology also separated it from the people currently in the faction. Um Fadi was not happy with the current state of affairs in the PFLP. She was critical of the leadership when they did not support her efforts to create economic opportunities for women in the camp through the sale of homemade products, even with a minimal sum. She voiced her discontent repeatedly throughout our discussion, pointing out that she was unable to help those in need. In the past, she explained, she used to help the sick, or if parents were about to take a child out of school due to lack of funds, she would collect enough money to prevent that. But now there is no money and she was secluding herself again at home. She asked me, "What should I do? Go and watch the sick? Especially when it is known that I am responsible for this. This is what is depressing me the most." The situation was making her uncomfortable with the current state of the faction, but for her to leave the PFLP was like letting down the people who had sacrificed their lives for it. She insisted that one must go on "regardless of the problems and obstacles" because those who sacrificed their lives died knowing that others will "continue the journey." Her sense of commitment and loyalty to the principles for which her husband and friends sacrificed their lives not only gave life to the PFLP, but also separated it as an entity from the current people and practices engulfed in it.

For Um Fadi, the PFLP was an entity that she learned about through its stated ideology. Ideology, in this sense, opened up a distance, a space of separation that made it possible to "learn about" and "enter" the PFLP apart from the relationships that brought her to it. She explained that upon her return from Palestine she became interested in learning more about the PFLP, which she did though reading its literature, including its conference proceedings. She added that Abu Mustapha Rashid was eager to help her, stressing that "the person who is inside something is not like the person who is about to enter" (*yalli dākhil al shī mish mitl yalli baddu yidkhul ʿalayh*). Here we get the image of the faction as a structure, as an entity (*shī*) that people enter. Additionally, a person's knowledge of the literature of the PFLP becomes a measure of the supposed depth of their membership. Other Palestinians also referred to this separation of the faction, which now exists at the level of ideas, from the people currently in it. In particular, it occurred most often with Fatah. It was common for Palestinians to say that "Fatah is not about Abu Mazen," "this is not the real Fatah," or "Fatah is not about those people." For many Palestinians "Fatah" no longer stood for its current leadership or its current members, but for past ideals for which their close friends or family members had fought.

Finally, what was particularly interesting about Um Fadi's case was that this apparent separation of the factions, which now existed at the ideational level, from their people also caused her to attempt to portray herself as being "outside" the PFLP, "about to enter" it upon her return from Palestine. Throughout our conversation Um Fadi was insistent on portraying her involvement with the PFLP as being the result of her own "conviction," which occurred "without pressure and after a long time." This was also emphasized by her initial mention of having an "independent personality" from her husband. Um Fadi was eager to explain to me that her involvement with the PFLP did not stem from her marriage to a PFLP member, but rather it was due to her own reflection and decision. Um Fadi's own portrayal of herself was linked to how the subject was seen to exist as an autonomous moral agent outside of power relations and society (Hindess 1996, 146–51; Mahmood 2005, 5–11). In this case "for an individual to be free, her actions must be the consequence of her "own will" rather than of custom, tradition, or social cohesion" (Mahmood 2005, 11). This stands in line with Um Fadi's attempted depiction of herself as choosing to join the PFLP out of "conviction" and not "out of pressure." This was again reflected in Um Fadi's description of the change she went through due to her visit to Palestine. She explained that she returned "with a full awareness/consciousness" (*waʿī kāmil*), which she contrasted with her attachment to the *thawra* prior to her trip, which stemmed from "the mood of the house" (*jaw al bayt*).

However, Um Fadi's self-positioning as being "outside" the PFLP, "about to enter it" two years after her husband's killing, was untenable by her own admissions. First, she had explained that she was privy to high-level discussions between her husband and the PFLP Chairman George Habash. This alone suggests the amount of information that Um Fadi had access to while her husband was alive. Second, her statement that she joined the PFLP due to her own "conviction" about its principles, and that this was not related to her association through marriage to a PFLP member, was also untenable. As explained earlier, what gave those principles their importance was precisely her husband's and Abu Mustapha Rashid's deaths. This was perfectly illustrated in Um Fadi's initial response when

I prompted her to describe her relationship with the PFLP. The critical part of her statement was:

> I told you the organization (*tanzim*), I respect it and I entered it out of conviction, without pressure and after a long time. And I don't forget that there are people who invested a lot in me, who helped me get the skills I have, who trained me, in the PFLP. People who were martyred. And this is what makes it hard. I feel it is a heavy load on me.

Um Fadi began her answer by talking of the *tanzim* and her respect for "it" and stressing that she "entered it" out of her own free will. Again the faction appears as a structure that a person "enters" "out of conviction" and not an ongoing and ever-changing relationship built out of association with other people. However, her second sentence betrays the image of factions as structures defined by their stated ideologies that was drawn in the first sentence. Here, she discussed her strong relationship with the *people* in the PFLP who were martyred, an obvious reference back to her husband and Abu Mustapha Rashid. Here her relationship with the PFLP was defined by her relationship to those close to her, who were killed upholding the PFLP principles. This showed how sacrifice gave life to the PFLP by associating it with ideals that people appeared to have died for. Through ideology the PFLP obtained a life of its own separating it not only from the people currently inside of it (its leadership and fellow PFLP members in Beddawi camp) but also from the people (Um Fadi's husband and Abu Mustapha Rashid) and the practices (their killing) that brought it into being.

There is no disputing that Um Fadi took her own decision to join the PFLP, but none of this happened while she was "outside" of the faction. There was no "outside" or "inside," but human relations. Nowhere did a person stand outside others and develop his/her own ideas. Of course a person could disagree with a certain political idea and stance, like Abu Ali did by hitting the bronze Lenin statue with his shoe, or his son Rabieh by handing over his gun when the PFLP decided to stand on the sidelines in a war that shattered his community, but none of their thoughts existed on their own, outside of the practice of interacting with others. Again, I am not arguing that Um Fadi had no ability to think on her own, or that she was predestined to join the PFLP simply by marrying a PFLP member. What I am saying is that Um Fadi was already entangled in the PFLP, which should be seen as a network of people, rather than a structure. She actually formed parts of it herself. We can only see her as being "outside" if we look at factions as structures existing separately from people. However, if we look at factions as people and practices then we can see how Um Fadi was already positioned within the PFLP web and that the line she "crossed" upon her return from Palestine, when she formally joined, was a line drawn internally, by specific practices that served to divide the world between the politically affiliated and the non-affiliated. Party ideology, as a form of knowledge, gave Um Fadi the appearance that she could stand "outside" the PFLP and grasp it in its entirety.

. . .

I end this discussion with one last example from Um Fadi's life that illustrates my argument that factions appeared to be defined by their stated ideologies while they were constituted by personal relations. In 1983, five years after the killing of her husband, and a few months after the killing of Abu Mustapha Rashid, Um Fadi's younger brother Ziad was kidnapped by Fatah al-Intifada for his perceived involvement with Fatah. Such kidnappings were dreaded and family members had only a few hours to try to secure the release of their loved ones before they would be transported inside Syrian territory. Once they crossed the border "God can't return them," as Um Fadi explained. I let Um Fadi recount the remainder of the story in her own words:

> One day they came to Ziad's house and took him. My mother was crying. I asked her: Who took him? She said I don't know; they just took him. And you should see my brother, he is so sweet. I lost my mind. I went outside barefoot, running, I went to the [Fatah al-]Intifada office, running, asking, where is my brother Ziad? They said not here, one of the guys said: you are asking about your brother? But they [Fatah] killed your husband! . . . I took him by his shirt and I pushed him onto the wall. [I told him:] 'I don't need someone like you to come and tell me such things and you know full well that my brothers had nothing to do with it, and if I knew who [killed my husband] I wouldn't wait for someone like you to talk to me like that.' I left. As I was going to the office of the Armed Struggle, I saw an ambulance go by and there was someone in it, I felt that it was Ziad. . . . I remembered that I knew one man who was with my father in the naval base, Abu Nash'at. He was with Fatah; he was from Jordan. They told me that he was with the Intifada now. . . .
>
> When he saw me, he stood up and said to me, Leila—he knew me from when I was a little girl—he said to me, what are you doing here? I told him, Abu Nash'at, they took my brother, and I want to bring him back now, I will not go back and tell my mother that I did not find my brother. I cannot. I prefer to die. I cannot imagine my mother like that. He wrote a letter and gave it to the guy driving me, he told him, take her to this place and let her see Ziad.

This story is powerful because it shows how ideology and personal relations interplay. Ziad (who at the time of research was a football coach in a secondary school in Tripoli) was taken because of his association with Fatah, for appearing to be a member of a structure defined by its ideology, by its political positioning, and in this case also characterized by the killing of Um Fadi's husband. However, what saved Ziad's life, beyond his sister's courage and quick thinking, was an old friendship between his long-deceased father and a comrade dating back more than twenty years. Um Fadi stressed the strength and longevity of the family's relation with Abu Nash'at by emphasizing that he called her "Leila" and not "Um Fadi," which indicated that he knew her prior to her marriage and to Fadi's birth. This example demonstrates both how factions, which were based on personal relations, appeared to be defined by their stated ideologies, and how that appearance was quite unstable and could quickly break down again when confronted with a personal relationship. That was precisely what Um Fadi did when she went to see Abu Nash'at in person. But this example also shows how powerful this appearance of separation could be when Palestinians engaged in internal fighting. Instances of violent factionalism were truly the hardest traumas for Palestinians to overcome, and this was precisely because they knew full well that people joined factions based on personal relations but would then be associated with a structure defined by its ideology and a certain political position, causing compatriots to fight each other.

FIGURE 13. Protest in Nahr el-Bared camp, June 2012. Photograph: Ismael Sheikh Hassan.

7

———

Conclusion

"The Guys Were Doing Something Great,
the Factions Destroyed It"

If the people want to live the factions need to die. If the factions want to
live the people need to die.

—AHMAD, YOUNGER GENERATION, SHATILA CAMP, DECEMBER 7, 2010

I know that the factions are killing me. I have a lot of ideas for the camp but
I can't execute them. If I propose them, people right away tell me that this
or that faction will step in my way.

—MUHAMMAD, YOUNGER GENERATION, NAHR EL-BARED CAMP,
NOVEMBER 12, 2011

The primary goal of this study has been to explore how unpopular and discredited
political factions are (re)produced on a day-to-day basis in the Palestinian refugee
camps of Lebanon, how they remain the center of political life in the face of widespread
condemnation. In answering these questions I had to question the ontological
nature of factions; I had to explore how factions, which are clearly made
of people, appear to take on a life of their own and can be invoked in the singular:
"Fatah did this" or "Hamas declared that."

What I found was that our understanding of the nature of factions changes
depending on which practices we focus on. By examining the personal narratives
of Palestinian refugees we saw how the initial contact with factions occurred out of
close, personal, and trusting relations. Palestinians encountered factions not
as party ideology but as people, people who were most often family members,
friends or neighbors. Space was instrumental in fostering these connections and
took various forms, including homes, classrooms, neighborhoods, and factional
centers. The strength and longevity of the relationship of a Palestinian to a faction
was a reflection of the closeness of the personal relations that were developed in
those spaces. As such, the relationship between a person and a faction is not a
relationship between a person and a structure, but a relationship between people:

135

it is about personal relations. Faction membership was not a reflection of a person's present position vis-à-vis a structure that she or he "enters" or "leaves"; rather it is a continuously unfolding story of human relations. In short, factions appeared as loose networks of people bound together with various degrees of trust and cohesion.

The centrality of personal relations in fostering and maintaining factional associations did not reflect a "backward" or "tribal" form of politics, where people were putting their analytical faculties on hold and blindly following those around them. Rather, Palestinians were constantly engaged in a critical analysis of the political situation and were often defiant of parental authority even when it was a family member who initially inspired them to partake in factional activities. Interpersonal trust played a crucial role in building personal/political relations in a world defined by constant war, displacement, and discrimination. While Palestinians may oppose a faction's *political stance* and openly voice their opposition, this did not mean that they would sever their ties with the *people* who had been their trusted friends for many years. This helped explain how Palestinian refugees made sense of the seeming contradiction of partaking in the reproduction of factions while openly critiquing them. Fatah, Hamas, Islamic Jihad, the PFLP, the DFLP, amongst others, were networks of people where ties were forged, experiences shared, skills gained, and knowledge transmitted. That was their first nature.

Factions, however, also appeared to have a second nature when we examined a different set of practices. By looking at practices of aid distribution, physical representation, and factional conflict, factions took the appearance of impersonal structures that existed separately and autonomously from the trusting personal relations that brought them into being. By relying on surveillance and monitoring techniques, and by being unaccountable to the Palestinian refugee population, aid distribution practices turned factions into impersonal structures that had power over people's lives. They now appeared as containers that encompassed their members with a top in control, and a bottom that lacked it. Factions also gained a life of their own through the creation of what appeared to be an "outside," a position from which we were made to believe that it was possible to see, critique, and study factions. It was this very illusion of being an "outside observer" that created the imagination that factions were bounded structures defined by their ideologies. However, ethnography makes this position untenable. Through a detailed examination of people's lives it became apparent that what appeared to be the "outside" was actually a position within the factions' network of relations.

By exploring the motives and methods of Palestinian refugees in joining factions as well as the subsequent evolution of that relationship, we realized that factions were loose networks of people coming together with varying degrees of trust and cohesion which changed with time and circumstances. Yet when we examined practices of aid distribution, physical representation, and factionalism, we concluded that factions appeared as immaterial and impersonal structures that controlled people's lives and fostered mistrust in the community. In other words, factions were formed through local *personal* and *trusting* relations, yet took on the appearance of *impersonal* structures that were *distrusted* by the community. Factions had a double nature.

What is the significance of exposing this double nature? Few people, whether Palestinian refugees or scholars, would probably disagree with the statement that factions are not actually edifices apart from the people that make them, but they nevertheless continue to treat them, speak about them, and study them as structures. What effect does that have and why is it important to point it out? I argue that when we treat or conceptualize factions as entities in their own right we create the belief that it is possible to remove them or change them. If we conceptualize factions as structures that exist apart from the people whom they encompass then it is only natural to believe that if they are unpopular then they should no longer be relevant, that they should "die." New popular or "grassroots" initiatives must then be able to change, replace, or unsettle the discredited factions. It is that very assumption that made me ask my initial question about how obviously unpopular and discredited political factions remained relevant. The question itself assumes a certain ontological nature of factions as self-contained entities. Yet as we have seen, factions have another nature: they are networks of people bound together by interpersonal relations that co-exist simultaneously with the heavy criticism of factions. This second nature makes these attempts to unsettle factions practically difficult, if not impossible, since factions do not exist separately from people. This impossibility creates in turn the illusion that the unpopular factions are powerful as attempts to unsettle them ultimately fail.

I illustrate this point through two examples: the 2012 protest movement that led to the annulment of the military permit system in Nahr el-Bared camp and the 2005 election of a "people's committee" in Shatila camp. Through these examples I show that in the current context of continued dissatisfaction towards factions Palestinians, as well as scholars, often put factions in opposition to "grassroots" or "independent" initiatives that attempt to better camp organization and life. When these initiatives fail, people and scholars are quick to point to "factions" as the spoilers. But factions, as we have seen, are made of people, people who are often part of these initiatives all along. And while these initiatives collapse for varied reasons, their failure or unsustainability is blamed on the factions. This act of denouncing the factions has two effects. One is to reify factions: by giving agency to factions we further their appearance of structure. And we also create the impression that *unpopular* factions have the power to destroy *popular* initiatives.

THE 2012 NAHR EL-BARED PROTEST MOVEMENT

On Friday June 15, 2012, a Lebanese army patrol accosted a young Palestinian man sitting on a motorcycle in Nahr el-Bared camp. An altercation ensued which quickly

FIGURE 14. Protest in Nahr el-Bared camp, June 2012. Photograph: Ismael Sheikh Hassan.

grew in size as more young Palestinian men converged on the scene and as the patrol called for reinforcements. Soon armored personal carriers were rolling down the camp's main street, using tear gas and shooting live ammunition. A fifteen-year-old water delivery boy named Ahmad Qassem was fatally shot in the head, and five other Palestinians were injured. Young men began throwing stones at the army, burning tires and building barricades. The army eventually retreated and the young men decided to remain in the streets and begin an open-ended sit-in. Three days later, at Ahmad's funeral, protesters stormed a barricade separating the funeral procession from the army. The army responded with live fire and a grocery store owner, Fuad Lubani, was fatally shot while standing at his home's doorstep, allegedly attempting to convince the protesters to move back. In a further act of provocation the army shot and injured two of his brothers and a cousin as they each, in turn, attempted to bring the bodies of their wounded relatives inside the family home.

The killings of Ahmad Qassem, and later Fuad Lubani, were the most immediate events that infuriated the protesters, but what drove the residents of Nahr el-Bared to rebel against the army was their treatment at the hands of the military apparatus for the past five years.[1] Residents repeatedly pointed out how they needed a permit to access their own homes (a process often used by the army to coerce residents to provide "information" about camp activities, somewhat as the army had attempted to do with me). Residents also found the conduct of soldiers at checkpoints to be particularly degrading. Protesters demanded the end of the military permit system, the return of confiscated land and homes, the expansion of the camp's cemetery, which could no longer accommodate new burials, and the release of those detained since the beginning of the events.

Many of the residents I spoke to about the initial days of the sit-in expressed both fear and defiance in the face of the army's response.[2] People were especially proud to state that Nahr el-Bared "was like Gaza," or "like Palestine," highlighting how through their resistance to the Lebanese army's repression they felt closer to their compatriots in Palestine who were seen as perpetual resisters. Nadia, the Talal family's daughter, who was fond of Turkish soap operas, told me how she ran faster than tanks as she looked for her brother during the initial clashes. Other residents described how women threw garbage bags from their windows and balconies onto the moving tanks and APCs; others explained how young men took their shirts off, publicly displaying their lack of fear at facing the army with nothing but their bare chests. Everyone's favorite story featured soldiers retreating in the face of stones or burning tires.

However, the Palestinian political leadership issued statements criticizing the sit-in and supporting the army. In a statement released in the first few days of unrest, they declared their deep relationship with the army and expressed their solidarity (Al-Jadeed TV 2012). The Palestinian Authority representative Azzam al-Ahmad declared to the media that "foreign elements" were trying to steer problems between the army and the residents of Nahr el-Bared (Ma'an News Agency 2012; Mroueh 2012). These statements infuriated the protesters, who feared that their leadership would not object if the army continued their violent repression. While the popular mobilization was clearly aimed at the Lebanese army's control over life in the camp, the protest also carried within it a second condemnation aimed at Palestinian political factions. The mother of the Talal family, Um Muhammad, explained to me how on the first day of unrest, several heads of factions attempted to approach the young men along with the army and stones were thrown at them, which amused her greatly. A common chant during the protests was "*hīrī hīrī hīrī, qiyāda shī bikharrī*" (loosely translated, "shitty leadership"). Young protesters appearing on YouTube videos distanced themselves from political factions (SolidarityPalestine 2012). Condemnations of the factions began to appear on blogs (Rami 2012).

Nevertheless, according to my interviewees, the factions were able to "take over" this budding opposition movement after the death of Fuad. They explained that the factions had been able to do so for three reasons. First was the issue of who would care for the families of the martyrs. The protesters did not have the financial resources needed to provide for the families who had lost a member and a breadwinner. Second, the need to negotiate with the army became more pressing after the killing of Fuad. The young protesters knew they could not protest endlessly without entering into discussion with the army. The best intermediary was considered to be the factions. Young protesters repeatedly explained to me that they felt it was wrong to speak to the army directly, as if it would dishonour the martyrs' sacrifices. They were also well aware that the army would not enter into direct negotiations with them. "At that time, the army is not going to talk to me, they will talk to the factions," said one young protester.

There was also a general sense that the political situation in Lebanon was too unstable, and everyone feared that the events in Nahr el-Bared would be wrongly linked to the Syrian uprising. Barely a month prior to the protests two prominent sheikhs, affiliated to the Syrian opposition, had been killed at a checkpoint by the Lebanese army. Demands for the withdrawal of the army from northern Lebanon grew louder at that time. Camp residents feared that local Lebanese leaders would use the camp mobilization as a way to further increase the pressure on the army towards their own ends. While everyone, including the protesters, wanted to protect the protest from Lebanese meddling, some felt that the situation was dangerous enough to warrant the intervention of more "experienced" parties, meaning the factions.[3]

Over the next month, the army refrained from entering the camp and the protesters continued their sit-in. It featured nightly events, such as dance and music performances, film screenings, political speeches, or just discussions between the different participants. Donations were collected locally and from the Diaspora to sustain the sit-in. The protesters also took it upon themselves to clean the streets of the residue of burned tires, a health hazard. Finally, in July the army released the detainees. A few weeks later it lifted the permit system and handed over confiscated land and properties. The protesters had achieved their goals, and this created much joy in the camp. However, many individuals were unhappy that this development was being portrayed as a victory for the factions. They were outraged that Palestinian political factions, who stood on the sidelines at the beginning of the protests, had managed to claim the fruits of this popular mobilization. Their credibility vis-à-vis the Lebanese government had increased and new security and coordination committees were now formed in conjunction with them (Dockery 2012).

Yet I contend that it was possible to have a different reading of how and when the factions' involvement began. Through my discussions with camp residents and by looking at pictures on Facebook and videos on YouTube, it was apparent that many of the people who participated in the initial events, even before Fuad's killing, were themselves part of the network of factions. For example, two of the Talal family's sons, Mahmud and Ahmad, attended several rallies. Ahmad was a self-identified Islamic Jihad member (chapter 3), while Mahmud kept a complex relationship with the DFLP (chapter 4). Similarly Rabieh (chapter 3)—who "left" the PFLP because of their non-involvement in the 2007 battle but had deep friendships with part of its youth group—and his father Abu Ali (chapter 4)—who hit the Lenin statue with his shoe—were part of the protests. Finally, Shadi (chapter 4), the ex-head of a PFLP NGO who was relieved of his services over a financial dispute, was also present early on and actually became one of the spokespersons for the young protesters. It seemed that factions had been part of the mobilization all along.

How can we explain this discrepancy in the accounts? Examining the moment when factions were said to have "taken over" helps us answer that question. From the narratives of camp residents, it appears that factions "took over" and "took credit" for the movement's successes once particular actions needed to be taken: the care for the martyrs' families, negotiating with the army, and analysing the political situation. These fall under three categories of practices, which I already investigated as causing the structural effect: the provision of care, the need for representation, and the apparent monopoly over political knowledge.

It seems then that our understanding of the factions' involvement in the protests depends on our conceptualization of factions. Looking at factions as a network of people we realize that factions had been part of the movement all along; they were never "outside" it. However, if we understand factions as entities with a life of their own, separate from the people, then their involvement appeared to occur only after Fuad's death. In other words, the participation of individuals who were part of the network factions did not seem to implicate the factions in the mobilization; it was the involvement of factions as entities in their own right that did. This point can be further highlighted by examining the involvement of the factions in the organizing committees of the protests.

Protesters I spoke to explained that factions became part of the organizing committees after Fuad's killing. However, this was again difficult to substantiate. Those same protesters added that the initial ad-hoc committees comprised a representative of the youth, of the popular committee, and of the inhabitants who lived close to the protesters' encampment. Since the popular committee was itself appointed by factions, it meant that faction members were already part of the organizing committees from the first day. However, the involvement of the popular committee members was not seen as involving the factions. For the protesters the involvement of the factions only began when certain individuals participated in the organizing committees as representatives of factions. In other words, factions only gained a presence once they were represented. It was not a person's involvement in the network of factions that involved the factions, but the factions' representation. In the latter case, the factions as bodies appeared to be involved instead of individuals.

There are therefore two ways to speak of this popular mobilization. We could say that at its beginning the 2012 protest movement was independent of factions and that the movement was actually against them; that ordinary people fought on their own against the army and against the factions that were in opposition to them. They sacrificed and finally won concessions from the army that the factions were later able to claim as "theirs." In other words, factions were able to reap the fruit of a popular mobilization that initially targeted them.

The second way we could write about these events would be to say that factions, seen as a network of people, were never outside this movement; they were present all along. They only appeared as entities in their own right once particular practices that cause the structural effect needed to be undertaken, such as the provision of care, the negotiation with the army and the need for political expertise. It was those practices that made the factions suddenly appear to be disconnected from the people who formed their very basis and who formed the protest movement. Like chameleons, they initially blended into the masses, only to appear later as actors in their own right. This does not mean that they were working "undercover," "plotting" their course of action and waiting for the right moment to appear and take over the protest movement. Their appearance and disappearance was a direct result of particular practices.

This was the power of the structural effect; it turned a network of people into a structure while hiding the actual social relations that form its very basis. The lifting of the permit system was no longer attributed to people, but to factions. Factions became something the media—and activists—could point to, while either crediting them with victory or accusing them of profiting from people's sacrifices. By appearing as structures the factions became the center of political life despite their widespread unpopularity. They were the ones with whom the army wanted to negotiate, they were the ones to whom funding was given, and they were the ones seen to have adequate political knowledge. In other words, the structural effect increased the occurrence of those very practices that caused it in the first place. It was a self-perpetuating mechanism, reproducing itself at each juncture.

This process can be further understood through the example of a popular election in Shatila camp in 2005, which, unlike the 2012 protest movement in Nahr el-Bared, has been examined by scholars. Through it we will see how the way we speak and/or write about factions and popular mobilizations affects the factions' abilities to morph into structures and gain relevance.

THE 2005 SHATILA ELECTION

In 2004 one of Shatila's main generators exploded and the camp went without electricity for eight months.[4] The faction-appointed Popular Committee was unable to remedy the situation. It was criticized as being inefficient and corrupt, and some residents even accused it of sabotage. In May 2005 as the electricity blackout was still ongoing, two Palestinian factions clashed in the alleys of Shatila and a man was killed by a stray bullet. Factions were not only seen as being unable to deal with the electricity crisis but were also seen as being a cause of insecurity in Shatila camp. Following this incident protests erupted that led to a public meeting in the camp's mosque attended by over two hundred people. The attendees decided to hold an election for a new eleven-member committee that was to be called the *Lajnat ahālī al-mukhayyam*, loosely translated "The Committee of the People of the Camp." I will refer to it as the *Ahali*. The Palestinian political factions that were present at that time in Shatila camp were part of what was called the "Alliance"

FIGURE 15. A saved news clipping from al-Safir newspaper, May 23, 2005: "80 percent participated in 'wedding-like' elections in Shatila." Photograph: Perla Issa.

(*Taḥāluf*) (Strindberg 2000, 60–76). Those factions were seen as being pro-Syrian. In 2005 the Syrian military left Lebanon following the assassination of then-Prime Minister Rafiq al-Hariri, which triggered massive demonstrations demanding the departure of Syrian troops. It was in that context that the Shatila elections were held. The Syrian military, which was seen as backing the *Tahaful* factions, had just left, and the PLO factions had not yet had time to establish themselves in the camp.

On May 22, 2005 approximately eight hundred people voted in Shatila's first election, about 30 percent of eligible voters (Kortam 2011, 202); organizers had hoped for a turnout of three hundred. According to contemporary newspaper articles, the event was joyful. "It's a wedding!" declared one of the organizers in Shatila camp (Alouwa 2005), emphasizing that the election was a great celebration. An elderly woman was quoted as saying: "I got out of bed in spite of my sickness [to vote], maybe now we will have representatives in the committees and we will have services and the corruption will end." An eleven-member committee was elected, and within a few months they resolved the electricity crisis in the camp and restored power. However, the committee did not remain active for very long, with several members resigning.

The literature on this election has presented it as an independent and grassroots initiative that was aimed against the factions. Kortam (2011, 202) explained that "the Palestinian population were fed up with their illegitimate leaders and needed a radical change" and Sayigh (2011, 59) added that the elected committee "would represent the camp's residents rather than the Resistance groups." Electoral rules stipulated that eligible candidates needed to be unaffiliated with any Palestinian political factions, a point the literature did not dispute (Abou-Zaki 2016, 65; Kortam 2011, 201; R. Sayigh 2011, 59) with the exception of Allan (2014, 129) who stated that her friends in Shatila observed that "of the thirty-two candidates who did register not one could claim political neutrality."

Discussing the demise of the elected committee, Kortam (2011, 203) mentioned that "six of the committee members withdrew their membership because they could no longer ignore the threats directed against them." Similarly, Abou-Zaki (2016, 69), Sayigh (2011, 59), and Allan (2014, 133) also mentioned that "political pressures" and "threats by pro-Syrian factions" forced members to resign. Kortam and Abou-Zaki added that the provision of water and electricity were commercialized in the camp. By repairing these services "the *Ahali* directly threatened an important financial resource of the local power brokers in the camp" (Abou-Zaki 2016, 70). Kortam (2011, 203) explains that the success of the *Ahali* "threatened the legitimacy of the Popular Committee" and that the "dominant political actors and factions wanted to prevent a new popular and dynamic force in the camp from changing the status quo and imposing a new balance of power."

From the literature it seemed that the story of the election was about a popular and grassroots initiative that was aimed against the corrupt factions who were ultimately able to bring it down as "their political and individual interests were at stake" (Kortam 2011, 203). However, by interviewing former members of the *Ahali* a more complex picture emerged, which put in doubt two claims that were repeated casually by scholars as well as by camp residents: the supposed independence of the elected candidates from factions and the factions' responsibility for the demise of the elected committee.

During the course of my work I met with seven former members of the elected committee and the vast majority, if not all, seemed to exhibit the type of complex relationships to factions that closely resembled the relationships that we explored in chapters 3 and 4, where people could not be neatly categorized as being "inside" or "outside" the factions. For example, when I first met Um Ali, the wife of Abu Ali, one of the elected members, she told me that eleven "independent candidates" were elected and that Abu Ali had received the most votes. However, as the discussion proceeded, complexities and nuances started to emerge. Um Ali told me that Abu Ali was actually "close to the PFLP." When I asked Abu Ali about his ties to the PFLP, he explained that really he had been a member of the DFLP but had left them. When I inquired into his reasons, he laughed and said, "It's a long story, a film." I then asked him if he was "independent," as the criteria for candidacy for the election required. Abu Ali answered that he was a "friend of the PFLP" but followed that assertion with a strong criticism of the factions.

Similarly, when Abu Steif, another elected member, saw me looking at the two pictures of Yasir Arafat hanging on the wall of his grocery store, he explained that he was officially a member of Fatah but that unofficially he had left them. His father had been an early member of Fatah before 1969 and as a child Abu Steif participated in the first training of the Fatah scouts (*ashbāl*, "lion cubs") in the early 1970s. He left Fatah in 2004 "for personal and not political reasons," but said "no matter where I go or come, for the last twenty years and for the next twenty years, people still tell me that I am Fatah." This scenario repeated itself with the other elected members who all claimed various types of relationships and histories to different factions including Hamas, Islamic Jihad, the PFLP and Fatah.

When I started to ask about the reasons for the demise of the *Ahali*, I found a lack of agreement between the former members, with two major points of contention. The first related to the resignation of three members, Abu Ali and Abu Steif as well as a third member who had since passed away. Abu Ali and Abu Steif explained that they had resigned out of personal conviction that work in the committee was no longer possible because of internal disputes. Abu Ali explained that problems started inside the committee. Only three or four people were working, not the eleven elected members; he had worked for a year and two months with no return, they were volunteering with no compensation, and it was starting to weigh on him both financially and physically. He then pointed to one incident in particular which finally led him to resign. He explained that he had heard that another elected member, Hajj Ismael, had gone to meet with Electricité Du Liban (EDL), the public Lebanese electricity company, with his brother, who happened to be the head of the faction-appointed Popular Committee. It seemed that Abu Ali had lost trust in one of his counterparts, who was the brother of the head of the *Tahaluf* Popular Committee that the *Ahali* was struggling against.

Abu Steif echoed Abu Ali by saying that the factions had not exerted pressure on him to quit. According to Abu Steif, the elected committee faced too many internal disputes on how to direct the work, disputes that related to different types of personalities and not to different factional affiliations. However other former members accused Abu Ali and Abu Steif of bowing to pressures from their respective factions, the PFLP and Fatah, who wanted them to quit, as the PLO was getting ready to form a popular committee of its own.[5] When I inquired into how they knew that the factions had requested that they quit and that they had indeed obeyed their factional leadership, I was told by one former member, Abu Ahmad, that he had himself witnessed a now-deceased PFLP official, who I will call Official Y, asking Abu Ali to quit. When I asked Abu Ali about this incident, he laughed, explaining that Official Y was a close friend of his and it was normal for him to discuss such an important decision with close friends. He proceeded to point out that the person accusing him of following orders, Abu Ahmad, was himself a member of Fatah who was part of the PLO Popular Committee at the time of my research.

Abu Ahmad, Abu Ali said, was used to obeying orders himself and thus might think Abu Ali did as well!

The second point of contention seemed to be related to the relationship of the *Ahali* with a French twinning committee from the municipality of Bagnolet, and in particular to a welcome reception that was being organized to greet a delegation visiting the camp. According to one version of the story told to me by two former members, Hajj Ismael and Abu Mustapha, the *Ahali* committee had made a group decision to hold the welcome reception in a hall in Shatila named *Majd al-Kurūm*, but at the very last minute the same PFLP Official Y convinced the other members to change the location of the reception to the People's Hall—a hall linked to the PFLP. Abu Mustapha even recalled that one day he was coming back from work and found Official Y waiting for him on the street in an attempt to convince him to move the reception. He added that this was being done even as the French delegation had already arrived at the edge of the camp and a small group of people had gone to accompany them to *Majd al-Kurūm*. How could they now change the location of the event? Hajj Ismael and Abu Mustapha refused and held the event in *Majd al-Kurūm*, but after this the rest of the members voted to freeze their memberships.

Abu Mustapha, who had gone to Cuba as a young student on a scholarship from the PFLP, explained that Official Y might have been able to influence him in other circumstances but not in this case, implying that when it came to the work of the *Ahali* committee, he acted as an "independent" who did not bow to pressures from factions. He then added that maybe Official Y had influence on others, implying that these others—but not him—might have caved to factional pressure. When I inquired about this incident with the other members I was told that this was their version of the story, but that what had actually happened was that Hajj Ismael and Abu Mustapha had met on their own with the French delegation and made their own decision to hold a reception for them. According to one member they had even decided to sign a partnership agreement with them without consulting the rest of the *Ahali* committee. This was why their memberships were frozen.

Looking at the demise of the *Ahali* committee, it seems hard to point fingers at the factions. How and even whether they had interfered was disputed. Those who did blame the factions mentioned two ways. One was to pressure "their people" to resign, and two was to cause divisions within the committee once that committee started to act as a representative for the camp. In both cases blame accrued to one person in particular, Official Y, a personal friend of one of the former members. How do we judge whether Abu Ali and Abu Steif quit because of their own personal conviction or under pressure from the factions seen as entities in and of themselves? How do we draw the line between personal opinions and factional political stances? Between a discussion among good friends or between faction members? These are important questions that stress how hard it is to treat factions as entities in their own right. These factions are first and foremost people who were part of the community, and not outside it.

Similarly, when I asked Hajj Ismael about his relationship with his brother who was the head of the *Tahaluf* Popular Committee, he explained that this was a source of constant pressure. He illustrated this point by saying that his brother would say that Shatila's wells were in good condition and did not need any rehabilitation, while Hajj Ismael would contradict him. He added that a lot of people used to criticize his brother in front of him, which was difficult for him. Hajj Ismael's predicament, that his own brother was part of the *Tahaluf* Popular Committee (and therefore part of the "enemy"), underscored how the Popular Committee and factions were comprised of individuals with whom other individuals may have personal and intimate relations.

These may be nuances, but they are important ones which scholars and others need to pay attention to when speaking and writing about such initiatives. In the current context of continued dissatisfaction with factions, Palestinian refugees, as well as scholars, have a strong desire for a change in Palestinian leadership. Therein lies the importance of the 2005 Shatila election, the first time that Diaspora Palestinians participated in an electoral exercise. This created much joy and excitement that I relived again and again as interviewees pulled from their closets and desks old binders and folders filled with newspaper clippings, electoral sheets, and various documents that they had proudly safeguarded for many years. This joy and enthusiasm about changing corrupt officials and again being at the helms of their own futures led many to claim that the election was an independent and grassroots initiative and that the candidates were unaffiliated to factions, as Um Ali told me and as the literature repeats. Yet everyone knows that factions, as people, are part of the initiatives all along, a claim that often arises later in the same conversation, for example, as Um Ali later told me, that Abu Ali is "close to the PFLP" or, as Allan mentions, that none of the candidates could claim political neutrality. Yet we repeat the claim of independence, which only serves to reify factions as distinct entities, creating the impression that they have boundaries and can therefore be removed from among the population, like a cancer that we can cut out.

The same false concept is at work when we blame the factions for the demise of the *Ahali*. Even Allan (2014, 133), who was aware that the elected candidates could not be labelled as "independents," blamed the demise of the *Ahali* on the factions, concluding that "threats by pro-Syrian factions compelled six committee members to withdraw." It is worthwhile to note that while she devoted eight pages to relate the circumstances of the election, she discussed the committee's breakdown in only one paragraph. Returning to the field to speak with participants, however, it seemed that again factions were chameleons; they appeared in people's everyday accusations and in academic writing, but disappeared when I started looking for them on the ground. Searching for how the factions destroyed the *Ahali* it was difficult to locate an answer. Abu Ali and Abu Steif blamed lack of commitment from other elected members; internal disputes; fatigue; and financial pressures. While pointing to "factions" Hajj Ismael, Abu Mustapha, and Abu Ahmad really put the blame on one specific individual, Official Y, doubting whether specific people acted according to their own will or someone else's, even when this someone else was a close friend or a relative. In this closeup view factions as entities disappear and are replaced by people, people with whom *Ahali* members and camp residents have various relationships. Yet our discourse and the literature gives them agency, blaming them for the complex failure of initiatives. This chameleon nature makes it seem that it is impossible to get rid of them. People might think that they are doing something without them, "independently," or even in opposition to them, only to discover that they had been present all along.

. . .

Palestinians are not unique in trying to change their political leadership while having intricate relations with those same parties they are trying to unsettle. As such the findings of this study about the factions' chameleon nature, as well as its lateral methodological approach, are not confined to it. While contexts change from one setting to another the reality is that what we commonly refer to as "political structures" are made of people, people who enter into different types of relationships with each other. What this study reveals is the importance of looking at these everyday relationships and practices while taking people's experiences with and perception of those "structures" seriously, in order to better understand the overall dynamics that may unintentionally give resilience to those very same "structures" that people are trying to unsettle.

I began this journey with one goal in mind: to find out how unpopular and discredited factions remained in charge. How did "empty buildings," mere shells, maintain their status as the center of political life in the face of widespread condemnation? What was their power? With time I realized that their source of power was my own formulation of that question. It was the "they." By making me believe that "they" were a discrete entity that I needed to struggle against, I was unknowingly strengthening "them." In my way of speaking, thinking, and acting I was reinforcing "their" appearance of structure. In other words, this study taught me that I too am part of the network of factions. This may seem like a depressing conclusion, as the prospect of change seems to be that much more elusive. But this study also points out that the factions' ability to blend into the masses and then appear as actors in their own right was not some intrinsic aspect of their being, but simply due to practices. This means that the appearance of structure was not predetermined. There was no inherent reason necessitating that factions, for example, distribute aid with little transparency, or that they commemorate annual anniversaries. These practices could always be otherwise, with significant implications for what factions are or could be. Put bluntly, different practices would create different imaginations. Armed with this new understanding a different journey begins. Knowing that we are on the inside rather than the outside, and that practices are at fault and not "factions," the new question becomes: can this novel perspective be used to destabilize the appearance of structure?

CHAPTER 1. INTRODUCTION

1. The term "lateral" is borrowed from Iris Jean-Klein (2003, 559), who studied the Palestinian political committees during the First Intifada in the West Bank through an immersion in the sociality of homes.

2. The concept of the state has always been elusive and difficult to define. The state has been described as a myth (Easton 1953, 111); an organ superimposed upon society (Marx 2010, 159); a tool of the bourgeoisie (Miliband 1973; Poulantzas 1975); an idea (Abrams 2006), an autonomous entity (Evans et al. 1985); a fetish (Taussig 1992); a mythical abstraction (Foucault 2006); an effect (Mitchell 1991); and a fantasy (Navaro-Yashin 2002). Additionally, scholars have often noted the strange nature of the state, which appears to be a unitary entity from a distance but which disappears when examined up close (Abrams 2006; Migdal 2001; Mountz 2004; Ringmar 1996).

3. Mitchell (1988, 44–48, 79, 92–94) argues that this occurs through a process he calls "enframing," which turns the world into a representation, what he refers to as "exhibition."

4. Ein el-Helwe camp is a Palestinian refugee camp in the south of Lebanon. It experiences periodic instances of factional violence and as such it is a recurrent feature of the Lebanese evening news (Nayel 2017).

5. Interview, Saida, December 3, 2011.

6. The PLO was established in 1964 by the Arab League and was taken over by the Palestinian Resistance Movement in 1969 (Schulz and Hammer 2003, 118–19).

7. For more detail on the Lebanese civil war and its intersection with the Palestinian resistance movement see Cobban 1986, 17–41.

8. At its peak the PLO had over 20,000 military and civilian personnel and an annual budget of over $200 million (Brynen 1995a, 36.

9. Due to the lack of coordination between the ISF and the Lebanese army, the military barracks stationed outside of Nahr el-Bared was not alerted when the ISF raided Fatah al-Islam's apartments in Tripoli, although both security apparatuses knew that members of Fatah al-Islam resided in Nahr el-Bared. See Kanj 2010, 189; Quilty 2007b.

10. In less than a week, the United States sent several transport planes carrying ammunition and weaponry (M.A. Khalidi and Riskedahl 2007, 33). The equipment provided was not the kind that would help the Lebanese army defend its borders from a foreign attack, such as anti-aircraft weapons, but weaponry designed for urban warfare, most likely for internal use, such as assault rifles, grenade launchers, sniper weapon systems, and bunker weapons (Schenker 2008). The United States also financed an $86 million project to train Internal Security Forces cadets in "the latest policing, law enforcement and community relations skills" (Galey 2010) making the US training program in Lebanon the fourth largest in the world (The White House 2013).

11. Stigmatized by Lebanese society as having caused the civil war (Haddad 2003, 85; Peteet 2005, 173–74), Palestinians served as a convenient scapegoat for any ill in Lebanon (Khalili 2005, 35; Sfeir 2010, 28–29). This was especially visible during the 2007 Nahr el-Bared conflict, as this was the only moment when unity in the Lebanese political spectrum was exhibited in a long period of internal and sometimes deadly divisions.

12. Interview, Nahr el-Bared camp, November 11, 2011.

13. The Lebanese government has stated that 226 militants were killed in the war and 215 were captured (Government of Lebanon 2008, 19).

14. Technically Nahr el-Bared consisted of two areas, what was commonly referred to as the "old camp" or simply the "camp"—the original camp officially under UNRWA's mandate since 1948—and the "new camp" or the "adjacent area"—the camp's extension over the years. In the remainder of this book I will refer to "Nahr el-Bared camp" as the combination of the old and new camp. If necessary I will speak directly of the new or old camp.

15. The documentary series *Chronicles of a Refugee* is available online at https://vimeo.com/channels/chroniclesenglish.

CHAPTER 2: "THE NEST OF THE CRAZY"

1. For further information on the legal restrictions for the purchase of land and apartments and the challenges faced after the 2007 war for the reconstruction of the new camp see Saghieh and Saghieh 2008, 20–29, 66–74.

2. A literal translation of *shibil* is a lion cub. These were the youngest members of Palestinian political factions who partook in basic military training. A *fidā'ī* is one who sacrifices his or her life for the cause. It was used to refer to the Palestinian guerilla fighters who became the symbol of the Palestinian resistance movement (Abufarha 2009, 7–8).

3. From September 1970 to July 1971 the Jordanian Army fought the armed Palestinian factions, leading to their disintegration in Jordan and their expulsion to Syria and Lebanon. Several refugee camps were turned to rubble and around three to five thousand Palestinians were killed (Cobban 1984, 49–52; Y. Sayigh 1997, 262–81).

4. Right-wing Christian militias besieged Tal al-Za'tar camp for two months and a large-scale massacre occurred where about four thousand Palestinians were killed, including

1,500 camp residents on the last day of the siege as the camp surrendered (Cobban 1984, 73; Y. Sayigh 1997, 400–1).

5. Force 17 was a Fatah commando unit, which expanded in the 1980s due to the significant availability of funds and Arafat's desire to create multiple security agencies that would secure his control over the military (Y. Sayigh 1997, 456–57).

6. Non-IDs are Palestinian refugees with no form of government-issued legal identification. According to the Lebanese state they do not exist. The children of non-IDs inherit their father's status and become non-IDs (Danish Refugee Council 2007).

7. From June 9 to June 15, 1982, a few hundred Palestinian and Lebanese fighters backed by PLO and Syrian artillery were able to hold off the Israeli Army at Khalda, a Lebanese town on the coast south of Beirut. This grace period of six days was essential to allow the PLO to prepare Beirut defenses (Y. Sayigh 1997, 527).

8. The PNC is the legislative body of the PLO; it acts like the PLO parliament in exile.

9. The PLA was set up in 1964 by the Arab League as the official military wing of the PLO. It was mainly stationed in Syria.

10. See the introductory chapter for more information.

11. The War of the Camps was a series of intense sieges and fierce bombings of several Palestinian camps in Lebanon from 1985 to 1987 (R. Sayigh 1994).

12. Palestine "from the water to the water" refers to historical Palestine, from the Mediterranean Sea to the Jordan River.

13. *Jam'iyah* (plural *jam'iyyāt*) is an informal savings association. Members of the association, linked by relations of trust, each contribute a fixed amount of money at fixed intervals and in turn receive a lump sum according to an agreed upon schedule. See Singerman 1995, 154–57.

14. At the time of my research the Lebanese national currency, the Lebanese Pound (LBP), was pegged to the US dollar at a rate of 1,500LBP per USD.

CHAPTER 3: "WE DRANK THE *JABHA* WITH OUR MOTHERS' MILK"

1. "Sons of dogs" is a widely used Arabic insult.

2. One resident listed them to me: PFLP, DFLP, Fatah, Fatah al-Intifada, Saiqa, Hamas, Islamic Jihad, PFLP-GC, Palestine Liberation Front (split in two, one with the PLO and one with the Alliance [*Tahaluf*]), Arab Liberation Front (also split into two, one with the PLO and one with the Alliance), the Struggle Front (*Jabhat al-Nidal*) (also split into two), and finally the People's Party (also split into two).

3. Palestinian People's Party.

4. Results from my interviews with newly-met Palestinians corroborated those results. Out of twenty-two interviews, seventeen Palestinian (eleven of the younger generation and six of the *thawra* generation) had contacts with factions, while only five Palestinian (four of the younger generation and one of the *thawra* generation) had no relations with factions.

5. Brynen (1990a, 1995b) also considered political patronage a major source of mobilization.

6. Results from my interviews with newly-met Palestinians corroborated those results. None spoke of party ideology, and only one out of twenty-two referred to financial reasons to explain his contact with a faction.

7. He explained that he had bought a bag of carrots for 2,000 LB. It was enough to make one and a half bottles of juice, which he could sell for 5,000 LB, making 3,000 LBP (2 USD) in the process. On the other hand, three corn-on-the-cobs cost him 1,000 LBP (0.67 USD), and he would sell each for 500 LBP (0.33 USD), allowing him to make 500 LBP (0.33 USD) for every three sales. At the beginning of his enterprise he had been popular, making a net profit of about 45,000 LBP (30 USD) a day, but soon after sales plummeted as the novelty of fresh carrot juice and corn-on-the-cob faded away, and he had to move on to his next attempt to make ends meet.

8. A local Palestinian who provided television satellite services to homes.

9. "*Jabha*," meaning "front," was the common Arabic diminutive for the PFLP.

10. Typically, parents named their first-born son after the name of the paternal grandfather; therefore anyone named Abu Ali would likely have both a father and an oldest son named Ali.

11. The Lebanese military intelligence bureau that controlled the camp from 1959 to 1969; see chapter 1.

12. Bakeries were communal at the time; women used to prepare their dough at home then go to the bakery to bake it.

13. Israeli artillery fire and commando raids in Lebanon were common in the early 1970s. They were intended to cause casualties, destroy guerilla bases, and coerce the Lebanese authorities to stem the rise of Palestinian militarism (Y. Sayigh 1997, 292).

14. Abu Ali was referring to the sixteen factions that had a seat on the popular committee of Nahr el-Bared camp.

15. *Fidāʾī* is a person who sacrifices himself for a cause. This was how Palestinians referred to freedom fighters.

16. The story actually repeated itself, as the troupe ended up associating themselves with another NGO but a few years later again left as a group once problems arose between the head of the troupe and the head of the NGO in Nahr el-Bared camp.

17. He was assassinated in 1972 by a car bomb planted by the Mossad, the national intelligence agency of Israel.

18. This information was obtained from Abu Fayez's son, whom I met in Beirut. It was corroborated by Um Muhammad.

19. *Hay al-Madāris* was an area in the old camp of Nahr el-Bared.

20. Shadi's relationship with the PFLP will be related in the next chapter.

21. This joke was mentioned to me early on in my fieldwork, and it was to be retold to me several times.

22. Factions had many organizations in the camps; some were legally registered with the Lebanese government as an NGO while others were not. For example, the DFLP had a legally registered NGO named Najdeh, which was active in relief, social care, health, education, cultural activities and vocational trainings. They also had the Ghad organization (focusing on youth) and Tadamon (focusing on women). For more information about the development of NGOs in Lebanon and the challenges they faced see Suleiman 1997.

23. At the time of my research, due to the demilitarization of Nahr el-Bared camp following the 2007 war, the factions could not employ paid guards for their offices as they did in other refugee camps in Lebanon.

24. The poverty line was set at 6 USD/person/day or 182.6 USD/person/month, which reflected the cost of minimal food and non-food livelihood requirements (Chaaban et al. 2010, 25). The extreme poverty line was set at 2.17 USD/person/day, equivalent to 66 USD/person/month, which reflected the cost of basic food needs (ibid).

CHAPTER 4: "WE ARE THE FACTIONS"

1. Najdeh is a DFLP-affiliated NGO which Mahmud had volunteered for in the past.

2. Chicken, potatoes, and a heap of onions all cooked together in the oven with a special homemade sweet red pepper sauce. The entire meal is then eaten with bread.

3. As seen in the previous chapter Fatah paid its students about 40 USD a month, amounting to 480 USD a year, while the DFLP paid 200 USD a year.

4. "Che Guevara Gaza" was the nom de guerre of a major PFLP figure in Gaza.

5. Sheikh Imam (1918–95) was a famous Egyptian singer known for his songs about social justice.

6. Up until that time, Palestinians in the north of Lebanon had to either pay for secondary schooling or stop their education.

7. The reconstruction of Nahr el-Bared camp was a complex joint endeavor involving UNRWA and the Nahr el-Bared Reconstruction Commission (NBRC). Analysis of this situation lies outside the scope of this study.

8. *Rajiin* was chosen instead of *ā'idīn* to stress that the demand for return to Nahr el-Bared camp should not be confused with the greater goal of return to Palestine.

9. Several Palestinian camps were destroyed during the Lebanese civil war (Tal al-Zaatar and Jisr al-Basha camps) and by Israeli aerial strikes (Nabatieh camp) and were never rebuilt.

10. For more information see Amnesty International 2008 and Human Rights Watch 2007a.

11. The shoe was considered the lowest and dirtiest part of the body and any association with it was considered insulting and degrading; see Kanaana 1995, 67. Abu Ali later connected his incident with Muntadhar al-Zaidi's action of throwing his show at the then-President of the United States George W. Bush. To Abu Ali "life is about taking a stand."

CHAPTER 5: "FACTIONS ARE LIKE SHOPS"

1. *Mana'ish* (*man'ūshi* in the singular) are traditional Arabic flatbreads topped with a variety of ingredients but most commonly with cheese, a mixture of thyme and oil, or ground meat with tomatoes and onions.

2. I put quotation marks around the expression "youth empowerment," as Ahmad felt frustrated rather than empowered by the program. He explained that the workshop leaders had asked the participants to select a project, which they would help them campaign for. The girls chose to work on schoolteacher violence against students in UNRWA schools while the boys chose to work on regaining access to the camp's football field, which had been appropriated by the Lebanese military. However, the workshop leaders ended up discouraging the boys from working on regaining their right to play football on the camp's field, arguing that it would be too confrontational to campaign against the army. While Ahmad agreed with that assessment he nevertheless thought that the workshop title needed

to be amended. In the end, boys and girls both worked on school violence, on the condition that they address all school violence: teachers against students as well as students against teachers

3. This estimate is based on the average monthly expenditure for Palestinian refugees living in camps in Lebanon; see Chaaban et al. 2010, 28.

4. At the time of my research calls to or from a cell phone in Lebanon cost 0.36 USD a minute (as much as two Nescafe one-cup bags per minute).

5. When Muhammad's first daughter was born the family obtained a similar A4 paper as the only form of identification for the newborn girl. Um Muhammad laughed on this occasion, saying that her granddaughter's ID was larger than the baby girl's own body, and that they could almost swaddle her in it.

6. It was customary for people to remove their shoes upon entering a home in an effort to keep the house clean. Camps' streets were notoriously dirty, since they lacked proper drainage.

7. Since their inception Palestinian political factions have been accused of just helping their own members; see R. Sayigh 2007, 169.

8. Jaber Suleiman (1997, 401) notes that over 80 percent of NGO funding is obtained from foreign sources.

9. Cash for Work programs are not unique to Palestinian refugee camps. They are implemented in many parts of the world, and a similar program exists in Jordan's Zaatari camp for Syrian refugees (Tobin and Otis 2016, 278).

CHAPTER 6: "FACTIONS ARE FORCED HUSBANDS"

1. The PPP is the renamed Palestine Communist Party.

2. This chant rhymes in Arabic: *Adāla! Ḥurriyya! Jabha Dimuqrāṭiyya!*

3. For example, Dajani (2006) calls for reforming the PLO in order to have legitimate representatives during the next round of negotiations. Nabulsi (2006) conducted interviews with Palestinian refugees in the Middle East, Europe, the Americas and Australia. She reports an overwhelming desire to reform the PLO to achieve proper representation. Barakat et al. (2013) debate different strategies to achieve democratic representation, from reforming the PLO to creating a new representative body.

4. Similarly Hasso (2005, xiv–xv) writes about the how the founders of the DFLP viewed "backwardness" as a significant problem and believed that the liberation of Palestine would only be successful once the party modernized the political attitudes and social values of the working class and peasantry.

5. A literal translation of *ashbāl* is lion cubs. These were the youngest members of Palestinian political factions who took part in basic military training.

6. In 1974 the PLO adopted the Ten-Point Program calling for the establishment of a Palestinian state on any liberated part of Palestine (Suleiman 2001, 93). The motion was supported by Fatah, the DFLP, and the Saiqa (Y. Sayigh 1997, 338; Gresh 1988, 179–88).

7. The PFLP, PFLP-GC, ALF, and PPSF opposed the Ten-Point Program and formed the "rejection front" (Y. Sayigh 1997, 344).

8. In 1978 tension between Fatah and the rejection front increased over the potential participation of the PLO in the peace negotiations between Egypt and Israel, which came on

the heels of Sadat's visit to the Israeli Knesset in Jerusalem. The violence was not confined to Beddawi camp, but fighting also occurred in Nahr el-Bared camp, Beirut, Damur, Tyre, and Sidon (Y. Sayigh 1997, 436).

9. Um Fadi here is referring to the 1983 battle between Fatah and Fatah al-Intifada in Nahr el-Bared camp.

10. Other research has been done into how sacrifice creates life. Writing about martyrdom in Palestine, Abufarha (2009, 14) points out that beginning with ancient mythology sacrifice has always been seen as that which creates life. He states that "in the Palestinian context the sacrificed Palestinian bodies in Palestine correlate alternative shapes to one another in a homologic relation; the dismembered body parts *creates* the new universe within which Palestine is *alive*" (author's emphasis). He goes on to argue, "the blood is water that nourishes the fields where streams would flow and birds would sing" and the "human flesh is soil where flowers bloom."

CHAPTER 7: CONCLUSION

1. Khaled Yousef, another Palestinian protester, was killed in Ein el-Hilweh camp in the south of Lebanon during a protest in solidarity with Nahr el-Bared.

2. I visited Nahr el-Bared camp about a month after the protests started. I conducted seven in-depth interviews as well as about twenty informal conversations.

3. My own interactions with the protesters did not substantiate this view. For example, as I was sitting one evening in the protesters' encampment, a middle-aged man introduced himself to me. I had never met him before. He explained that this movement needs "real men" and "*rujūlī*" (manliness). A young boy, probably no more than fourteen years old, replied back that what was needed was "*ḥikmi*"(meaning wisdom). The middle-aged man then replied, "Go to UNRWA if you want *ḥikmi*," playing on the double meaning of *ḥikmi* in colloquial Arabic: both wisdom and medical care.

4. I relate the story of the election by piecing it together from seven in-depth interviews with former elected members conducted in 2010 and 2019. All names have been anonymized.

5. As mentioned earlier, Shatila at the time had a popular committee controlled by the *Tahaluf*, and after the withdrawal of the Syrian troops from Lebanon, the PLO was getting ready to establish its own popular committee in the camp.

Abbas, Mahmoud, Hussein Shaaban, Basem Sirhan and Ali Hassan. 1997. "The Socio-Economic Conditions of the Palestinians in Lebanon." *Journal of Refugee Studies* 10 (3): 378–96.

Abou-Zaki, Hala. 2012. "Rapports à l'Espace et au Politique en Mutation chez les Réfugiés Palestiniens des Camps, dans le Liban d'Après-Guerre, 1990–: Le Cas du Camps de Chatila." Conference: "Palestine—National et Subjectivités: Interrogations sur le Cas Palestinien." École des Hautes Études en Sciences Sociales, Paris, France.

———. 2013. "Revisiting Politics in Spaces 'Beyond the Center': The Shatila Palestinian Refugee Camp in Lebanon." In *Local Politics and Contemporary Transformations in the Arab World*, edited by Malika Bouziane, Cilja Harders, and Anja Hoffmann, 178–95. Basingstoke: Palgrave Macmillan.

———. 2016. "Repenser le politique dans le camp de Chatila: L'experience des Ahali." *A contrario* 2 (23): 57–75.

Abrams, Philip. 2006. "Notes on the Difficulty of Studying the State." In *The Anthropology of the State: A Reader*, edited by Aradhana Sharma and Akhil Gupta, 112–30. Oxford: Blackwell Publishing.

Abu-Amr, Ziad. 1994. *Islamic Fundamentaliam in the West Bank and Gaza: Muslim Brotherhood and Islamic Jihad*. Indianapolis: Indiana University Press.

Abu-Lughod, Lila. 1991. "Writing Against Culture." In *Recapturing Anthropology: Working in the Present*, edited by Richard G. Fox, 137–62. Santa Fe, New Mexico: School of American Research Press.

Abufarha, Nasser. 2009. *The Making of a Human Bomb: An Ethnography of Palestinian Resistance*. Durham, NC: Duke University Press.

Al-Haj, Majid. 2004. *Immigration and Ethnic Formation in a Deeply Divided Society: The Case of the 1990s Immigrants From the Former Soviet Union in Israel*. Leiden: Brill.

Al-Husseini, Jalal, and Riccardo Bocco. 2011. "Dynamics of Humanitarian Aid, Local and Regional Politics: The Palestine Refugees as a Case-Study." In *Palestinian Refugees:*

Identity, Space and Place in the Levant, edited by Are Knudsen and Sari Hanafi, 128–46. London: Routledge.

Al-Jadeed TV. 2012. "Delegation of Palestinian Political Factions and the Army Met Today to Discuss the Events of Nahr el-Bared." June 17, 2012. Accessed June 17, 2012. http://www.aljadeed.tv/MenuAr/news/DetailNews/DetailNews.html?id=21688.

Al-Natour, Suheil. 1997. "The Legal Status of Palestinians in Lebanon." *Journal of Refugee Studies*, 10 (3): 360–77.

Allan, Diana. 2014. *Refugees of the Revolution: Experiences of Palestinian Exile*. Stanford, CA: Stanford University Press.

Alouwa, Saada. 2005. "80% Participated in the 'Wedding-Like' Elections in Shatila." *al-Safir*, May 23, 2005.

Amnesty International. 2008. "Lebanon—Amnesty International Report 2008: Human Rights in the Lebanese Republic." Beirut: Amnesty International. Accessed March 3, 2013. http://www.amnesty.org/en/region/lebanon/report-2008.

Asad, Talal. 2004. "Where Are the Margins of the State?" In *Anthropology in the Margins of the State*, edited by Veena Das and Deborah Poole, 279–88. Santa Fe, NM: School of American Research Press.

Barakat, Rana, et al. 2013. "An Open Debate on Palestinian Representation." al-Shabaka: The Palestinian Policy Network. Accessed November 18, 2013. http://al-shabaka.org/round table/politics/open-debate-palestinian-representation.

Bathist, Hani M. 2007a. "Army: Fatah al-Islam in Standoff at Nahr al-Bared." *The Daily Star [Online]*. March 19, 2007. Accessed March 3, 2013. http://www.dailystar.com.lb /News/Local-News/Mar/19/Army-Fatah-al-Islam-in-standoff-at-Nahr-al-Bared .ashx#axzz2G8W4lXQv.

———. 2007b. "Calm Returns to Nahr al-Bared after Gunfight." *The Daily Star [Online]*. May 5, 2007. Accessed March 3, 2013. http://www.dailystar.com.lb/News/Politics/May/05 /Calm-returns-to-Nahr-al-Bared-after-gunfight.ashx#axzz2G8W4lXQv.

Baumgarten, Helga. 2005. "The Three Faces/Phases of Palestinian Nationalism, 1948–2005." *Journal of Palestine Studies*, 34 (4): 25–48.

Bevir, Mark. 2006. "How Narratives Explain." In *Interpretation And Method: Empirical Research Methods And The Interpretive Turn*, edited by Dvora Yanow and Peregrine Schwartz-Shea, 218–90. Armonk, NY: M.E. Sharpe.

Bill, James A., and Robert Springborg. 2000. *Politics of the Middle East*. New York: Addison Wesley Longman.

Broning, Michael. 2013. *Political Parties in Palestine: Leadership and Thought*. New York: Palgrave Macmillan.

Brynen, Rex. 1990a. "The Politics of Exile: The Palestinians in Lebanon." *Journal of Refugee Studies*, 3. 3. 204–27.

———. 1990b. *Sanctuary and Survival: The PLO in Lebanon*. Boulder, CO: Westview Press.

———. 1995a. "The Dynamics of Palestinian Elite Formation." *Journal of Palestine Studies* 24 (3): 31–43.

———. 1995b. "The Neopatrimonial Dimension of Palestinian Politics." *Journal of Palestine Studies* 25 (1): 23–36.

Chaaban, Jad, et al. 2010. "Socio-Economic Survey of Palestinian Refugees in Lebanon." Beirut: American University of Beirut. https://www.unrwa.org/userfiles/2011012074253.pdf.

Clapham, Christopher. 2004. *Third World Politics: An Introduction*. London: Routledge.

Cobban, Helena. 1984. *The Palestinian Liberation Organization: People, Power and Politics*. Cambridge, UK: Cambridge University Press.

Cubert, Harold. 1997. *The PFLP's Changing Role in the Middle East*. London: Frank Cass & Co.

Dajani, Omar M. 2006. "Preparing for the Inevitable Negotiation." *Journal of Palestine Studies* 35 (3): 39–45.

Danish Refugee Council. 2007. "Survey Report on the Situation of Non-ID Palestinian Refugees in Lebanon." Beirut: Danish Refugee Council.

Das, Veena. 2004. "The Signature of the State: The Paradox of Illegibility." In *Anthropology in the Margins of the State*, edited by Veena Das and Deborah Poole, 225–52. Santa Fe, NM: School of American Research Press.

———, and Deborah Poole. 2004. "State and Its Margins: Comparative Ethnographies." In *Anthropology in the Margins of the State*, edited by Veena Das and Deborah Poole, 3–33. Santa Fe, NM: School of American Research Press.

Dockery, Stephen. 2012. "Nahr al-Bared Permit System To Be Scrapped." *The Daily Star [Online]*, July 12, 2012. Accessed March 1, 2014. http://www.dailystar.com.lb/News/Lebanon-News/2012/Jul-12/180264-nahr-al-bared-permit-system-to-be-scrapped.ashx#axzz2uP8zLFDS.

Easton, David. 1953. *The Political System: An Inquiry into the State of Political Science*. New York, NY: Alfred A. Knopf.

Elghossain, Anthony. 2008. "Nahr al-Bared Victory Launched Suleiman to Baabda." *The Daily Star [Online]*, May 26, 2008. Accessed March 20, 2011. http://www.dailystar.com.lb/News/Politics/May/26/Nahr-al-Bared-victory-launched-Suleiman-to-Baabda.ashx#axzz2Fl3GcRjg.

Evans, Peter, Dietrich Rueschemeyer, and Theda Skocpol. 1985. *Bringing the State Back In*. Cambridge: Cambridge University Press.

FAFO. 2007. "Characteristics of Displaced Palestinian Refugees from the Nahr el-Bared Refugee Camp: Results from the August 2007 Survey of 999 Families." Beirut: FAFO.

Ferguson, James, and Akhil Gupta. 2002. "Spatializing States: Toward an Ethnography of Neoliberal Governmentality." *American Ethnologist* 29 (4): 981–1002.

Fontana, Andrea, and James Frey. 2005. "The Interview: From Neutral Stance to Political Involvement." In *The Sage Handbook of Qualitative Research*, edited by in Norman Denzin and Yvonna Lincoln, 695–727. California: Sage Publications.

Foucault, Michel. 1977. *Discipline and Punish: The Birth of the Prison*. London: Penguin.

Foucault, Michel. 1991. *Discipline and Punish: The Birth of the Prison*. London: Penguin.

Foucault, Michel. 2006. "Governmentality." In *The Anthropology of the State: A Reader*, edited by Aradhana Sharma and Akhil Gupta, 131–43. Oxford: Blackwell.

Frisch, Hillel. 2009. "The Death of the PLO." *Middle Eastern Studies* 45 (2): 243–61.

Fuller, C.J., and John Harris. 2001. "For an Anthropology of the Modern Indian State." In *In The Everyday State and Society in Modern India*, edited by C.J. Fuller and Veronique Benei, 1–30. London: Hurst and Company.

Galey, Patrick. 2010. "Over 70 ISF Officers Graduate from US-sponsored Policing Academy." *The Daily Star [Online]*, March 19, 2010. Accessed March 20, 2011. http://www.dailystar.com.lb/News/Politics/Mar/19/Over-70-ISF-officers-graduate-from-US-sponsored-policing-academy.ashx#axzz2MVdT12dA.

Gerlach, Luther P., and Virginia M. Hine. 1970. *People, Power, Change: Movements of Social Transformation*. Indianapolis, IN: Bobbs-Merrill.

Ghanem, As'ad. 2010. *Palestinian Politics after Arafat: A Failed National Movement*. Indianapolis: Indiana University Press.

Ghazal, Rym. 2007. "Three Palestinians Killed in Protest outside Nahr al-Bared." *The Daily Star [Online]*, June 30, 2007. Accessed March 3, 2013. http://www.dailystar.com .lb/News/Politics/Jun/30/Three-Palestinians-killed-in-protest-outside-Nahr-al-Bared .ashx#axzz10QQt8Xxw.

Government of Lebanon. 2008. "A Common Challenge, A Shared Responsibility: The International Donor Conference for the Recovery and Reconstruction of the Nahr al-Bared Palestinian Refugee Camp and Conflict-Affected Areas of North Lebanon." Beirut: Government of Lebanon.

Gresh, Alain. 1988. *The PLO, the Struggle Within: Towards an Independent Palestinian State*. London: Zed Books.

Gunning, Jeroen. 2008. *Hamas in Politics: Democracy, Religion, Violence*. New York: Columbia University Press.

Gupta, Akhil. 1995. "Blurred Boundaries: The Discourse of Corruption, the Culture of Politics, and the Imagined State." *American Ethnologist* 22 (2): 375–402.

———. 2001. "Governing Population: The Integrated Child Development Services Program in India." In *States of Imagination: Ethnographic Explorations of the Postcolonial State*, edited by Thomas Blom Hansen and Finn Stepputat, 65–96. Durham, NC: Duke University Press.

———. 2005. "Narratives of Corruption: Anthropological and Fictional Accounts of the Indian State." *Ethnography* 6 (5): 5–34.

Gupta, Dipak K., and Kusum Mundra. 2005. "Suicide Bombing as a Strategic Weapon: An Empirical Investigation of Hamas and Islamic Jihad." *Terrorism and Political Violence* 17 (4): 573–98.

Haddad, Simon. 2003. *The Palestinian Impasse in Lebanon: The Politics of Refugee Integration*. Brighton: Sussex Academic Press.

———. 2010. "Fatah al-Islam in Lebanon: Anatomy of a Terrorist Organization." *Studies in Conflict and Terrorism* 33 (6): 548–69.

Hammersley, Martyn, and Paul Atkinson. 1983. *Ethnography: Principles in Practice*. London: Routledge.

Hansen, Thomas Blom. 2001. "Governance and Myths of State in Mumbai." In *The Everyday State and Society in Modern India*, edited by C.J. Fuller and Veronique Benei, 31–67. London: Hurst and Company.

———, and Finn Stepputat. 2001. "Introduction: States of Imagination." In *States of Imagination: Ethnographic Explorations of the Postcolonial State*, edited by Thomas Blom Hansen and Finn Stepputat, 1–38. Durham, NC: Duke University Press.

Hasso, Frances. 2005. *Resistance, Repression, and Gender Politics in Occupied Palestine and Jordan*. Syracuse, NY: Syracuse University Press.

Hilal, Jamil. 1995. "The PLO: Crisis in Legitimacy." *Race & Class* 37 (2): 1–18.

———. 2010. "The Polarization of the Palestinian Political Field." *Journal of Palestine Studies* 39 (3): 24–39.

Hindess, Barry. 1996. *Discourses of Power: From Hobbes to Foucault*. Oxford: Blackwell.

Hoigilt, Jacob. 2016. "Fatah from Below: The Clash of Generations in Palestine." *British Journal of Middle Eastern Studies* 43 (3): 456–71.

Hroub, Khaled. 2006. *Hamas: A Beginner's Guide*. New York: Pluto Press.

Human Rights Watch. 2007a. "Lebanon: Investigate Army Shooting of Palestinian Demonstrators." July 3, 2007. Accessed March 3, 2013. http://www.hrw.org/news/2007/07/03/lebanon-investigate-army-shooting-palestinian-demonstrators.

Human Rights Watch. 2007b. "Lebanon: End Abuse of Palestinians Fleeing Refugee Camp." June 12, 2007. Accessed March 3, 2013. http://www.hrw.org/news/2007/06/12/lebanon-end-abuse-palestinians-fleeing-refugee-camp.

Human Rights Watch. 2007c. "Lebanon: Fighting at Refugee Camp Kills Civilians: Lebanese Army and Fatah al-Islam Must Protect Civilians in Nahr al-Bared. May 22, 2007. Accessed March 3, 2013. http://www.hrw.org/news/2007/05/22/lebanon-fighting-refugee-camp-kills-civilians.

International Crisis Group. 2009. "Nurturing Instability: Lebanon's Palestinian Refugee Camps." *Middle East Report 84*. Brussels: International Crisis Group.

———. 2012. "Lebanon's Palestinian Dilemma: The Struggle over Nahr al-Bared." *Middle East Report 117*. Brussels: International Crisis Group.

IRIN. 2007. "Lebanon: Rebuilding Camp will be UNRWA's "Largest Humanitarian Project." November 14, 2007. Accessed March 7, 2012. http://www.irinnews.org/printreport.aspx?reportid=75296.

Ismail, Salwa. 2006. *Political Life in Cairo's New Quarters : Encountering the Everyday State*. Minneapolis: University of Minnesota Press.

Israeli, Raphael. 2008. *Palestinians between Nationalism and Islam*. London: Vallentine Mitchell.

Jalloul, Faysal. 1994. Naqd al-silaḥ al-falasṭīnī. Burj al-Barajna: Āhlan w thawratan w mukhayaman. Beirut: Dar al-Jadid.

Jean-Klein, Iris. 2003. "Into Committees, Out of the House? Familiar Forms in the Organization of Palestinian Committee Activism During the First Intifada." *American Ethnologist* 30 (4): 556–77.

Jensen, Michael Irving. 2009. *The Political Ideology of Hamas: A Grassroots Perspective*. Translated by Sally Laird. London: I.B. Tauris.

Kanaana, Sharif. 1995. "Palestinian Humor during the Gulf War." *Journal of Folklore Research* 32 (1): 65–75.

Kanaaneh, Moslih. 1997. "The 'Anthropologicality' of Indigenous Anthropology." *Dialectical Anthropology* 22: 1–21.

Kanj, Jamal Krayem. 2010. *Children of Catastrophe: Journey from a Refugee Camp to America*. Reading, UK: Garnet.

Khalidi, Muhammad Ali, and Diane Riskedahl. 2007. "The Road to Nahr al Barid: Lebanese Political Discourse and Palestinian Civil Rights." *Middle East Research and Information Project* 244: 26–33.

Khalidi, Rashid. 1986. *Under Siege: P.L.O. Decisionmaking During the 1982 War*. New York: Columbia University Press.

———. 2006. *The Iron Cage: The Story of the Palestinian Struggle for Statehood*. Boston: Beacon Press.

———. 2007. "The Palestinians and 1948: The Underlying Causes of Failure." In *The War for Palestine*, edited by Eugene L. Rogan and Avi Shlaim, 12–36. Cambridge: Cambridge University Press.

Khalidi, Walid. 1992. *All That Remains: The Palestinian Villages Occupied and Depopulated by Israel in 1948*. Beirut: Institute for Palestine Studies.

Khalili, Laleh. 2004. "Grass-Roots Commemorations: Remembering the Land in the Camps of Lebanon." *Journal of Palestine Studies* 34 (1): 6–22.

———. 2005. "A Landscape of Uncertainty: Palestinians in Lebanon." *Middle East Report* 236: 34–39.

———. 2007. *Heroes and Martyrs of Palestine: The Politics of National Commemoration.* Cambridge, UK: Cambridge University Press.

Knudsen, Are. 2005. "Islamism in the Diaspora: Palestinian Refugees in Lebanon." *Journal of Refugee Studies* 18 (2): 216–34.

———. 2011. "Nahr el-Bared: The Political Fall-out of a Refugee Disaster." In *Palestinian Refugees: Identity, Space and Place in the Levant*, edited by Are Knudsen and Sari Hanafi, 97–110. London: Routledge.

Kortam, Manal. 2011. "Politics, Patronage and Popular Committees in the Shatila Refugee Camp, Lebanon." In *Palestinian Refugees: Identity, Space and Place in the Levant*, edited by Are Knudsen and Sari Hanafi, 193–204. London: Routledge.

Kuttab, Daoud. 2011. "Wanted: New Palestinian Political Parties." *Huffington Post*, April 21, 2011.

Ma'an News Agency. 2012. "Official: Palestinian Refugees in Lebanon Not Taking Sides." June 25, 2012. Accessed June 27, 2012. http://www.maannews.net/eng/ViewDetails.aspx?ID=498230.

Mahmood, Saba. 2005. *Politics of Piety: The Islamic Revival and the Feminist Subject.* Princeton, NJ: Princeton University Press.

Marx, Karl. 2010. "Critique of the Gotha Programme." In *Marx Today: Selected Works and Recent Debates*, edited by John F. Sitton, 145–62. New York, NY: Palgrave Macmillan.

Masalha, Nur. 2012. *The Palestine Nakba: Decolonising History, Narrating The Subaltern, Reclaiming Memory.* London: Zed Books.

Maynard-Moody, Steven, and Michael Musheno. 2006. "Stories for Research." In *Interpretation And Method: Empirical Research Methods And The Interpretive Turn*, edited by Dvora Yanow and Peregrine Schwartz-Shea, 316–30. Armonk, NY: M.E. Sharpe, Inc.

Maynes, Mary Jo, Jennifer Pierce, and Barbara Laslett. 2008. *Telling Stories: The Use of Personal Narratives in the Social Sciences and History.* Ithaca, NY: Cornell University Press.

McAdam, Doug. 1982. *Political Process and the Development of Black Insurgency, 1930–1970.* Chicago: University of Chicago Press.

Migdal, Joel. 2001. *State in Society: Studying How States and Societies Transform and Constitute One Another.* Cambridge: Cambridge University Press.

Miliband, Ralph. 1973. *The State in Capitalist Society: The Analysis of the Western System Of Power.* London: Quartet Books.

Milton-Edwards, Beverley. 1992. "The Concept of Jihad and the Palestinian Islamic Movement: A Comparison of Ideas and Techniques." *British Journal of Middle Eastern Studie,* 18 (1): 48–53.

———, and Stephen Farrell. 2010. *Hamas: The Islamic Resistance Movement.* Cambridge, UK: Polity.

Mitchell, Timothy. 1988. *Colonising Egypt.* Cambridge, UK: Cambridge University Press.

———. 1990. "Everyday Metaphors of Power." *Theory and Society* 19 (5): 545–77.

———. 1991. "The Limits of the State: Beyond Statist Approaches and their Critics." *American Political Science Review* 85 (1): 77–96.

———. 2002. *Rule of Experts: Egypt, Techno-Politics, Modernity.* Berkeley: Univerisity of California Press.

Moughrabi, Fouad. 1983. "The Palestinians After Lebanon." *Arab Studies Quarterly* 5 (3): 211–19.

Mountz, Alison. 2004. "Embodying the Nation-State: Canada's Response to Human Smuggling." *Political Geography* 23: 323–45.

Mroueh, Wassim. 2012. "Palestinian Official: Foreign Powers Inciting Clashes in Lebanon Camps." *Daily Star [Online]*, June 22, 2012. Accessed March 1, 2014. http://www.dailystar .com.lb/News/Middle-East/2012/Jun-22/177733-palestinian-official-foreign-powers -inciting-clashes-in-lebanon-camps.ashx#axzz1yVPoi3XP.

Nabulsi, Karma. 2006. "Palestinians Register: Laying Foundations and Setting Directions." Oxford, UK: Nuffield College, University of Oxford.

Nahrelbared. 2007. *Majzarat ta'arad laha al-'a'idun 'ila mukhayam Nahr el-Bared [The Returnees to Nahr el-Bared are Massacred]*. Accessed February 20, 2013. http://www .youtube.com/watch?v=GtnLKLwz1Po.

Navaro-Yashin, Yael. 2002. *Faces of the State: Secularism and Public Life in Turkey*. Princeton, NJ: Princeton University Press.

Nayel, Mohamad-Ali. 2017. "Ain al-Hilweh Camp: The Physical and Administrative Walls Surrounding Palestinian Refugees in Lebanon." *The Funambulist* 12: 38–43.

Ortner, Sherry B. 1995. "Resistance and the Problem of Ethnographic Refusal." *Comparative Studies in Society and History* 37, no. 1 (January): 173–93.

Pachirat, Timothy. 2011. *Every Twelve Seconds: Industrialized Slaughter and the Politics of Sight*. New Haven, CT: Yale University Press.

Pader, Ellen. 2006. "Seeing with an Ethnographic Sensibility: Explorations Beneath the Surface of Public Policies." In *Interpretation And Method: Empirical Research Methods And The Interpretive Turn*, edited by Dvora Yanow and Peregrine Schwartz-Shea, 161–75. Armonk, NY: M.E. Sharpe.

Pappe, Ilan. 2006. *The Ethnic Cleansing of Palestine*. Oxford, UK: Oneworld.

Peteet, Julie. 1987. "Socio-Political Integration and Conflict Resolution in the Palestinian Camps in Lebanon." *Journal of Palestine Studies* 16 (2): 29–44.

———. 1991. *Gender in Crisis: Women and the Palestinian Resistance Movement*. New York: Columbia University Press.

———. 1995. "'They Took our Milk and Blood': Palestinian Women and War." *Cultural Survival* 19 (1): 50–53.

———. 2005. *Landscape of Hope and Despair: Palestinian Refugee Camps*. Philadelphia: University of Pennsylvania Press.

Poulantzas, Nicos. 1975. *Political Power and Social Classes*. London: Verso.

Qawas, Nafez, and Mohammed Zaatari. 2007. "PLO Backs Army Entry into Nahr al-Bared." *The Daily Star [Online]*, May 24, 2007. Accessed March 7, 2012. http://www.dailystar .com.lb/News/Politics/May/24/PLO-backs-army-entry-into-Nahr-al-Bared.ashx#axzz 10QQt8Xxw.

Quilty, Jim. 2007b. "The Collateral Damage of Lebanese Sovereignty." *Middle East Research and Information Project Online*, June 18. Accessed February 23, 2021. https://merip.org /2007/06/the-collateral-damage-of-lebanese-sovereignty.

———. 2008. "Lebanon's Brush with Civil War." *Middle East Research and Information Project Online*, May 20. Accessed February 23, 2021. https://merip.org/2008/05/lebanons -brush-with-civil-war.

Ramadan, Adam. 2009. "Destroying Nahr el-Bared: Sovereignty and Urbicide in the Space of Exception." *Political Geography* 28 (3): 153–63.

———. 2010. "In the Ruins of Nahr al-Barid: Understanding the Meaning of the Camp." *Journal of Palestine Studies* 40 (1): 49–62.

Rami. 2012. "Al-'amal al-waṭani al-falasṭīnī fī lubnān: quwat al-sha'ib, bū'is al-qiyāda [National Palestinian Work in Lebanon: The Strength of the People, the Weakness of the Leadership)]." *Nahr el Bared—News from the North Lebanon Palestinian Camp*, July 7, 2012. Accessed February 27, 2014. http://albared.wordpress.com/2012/07/01.

Rempel, Terry. 2010. "UNRWA and the Palestine Refugees: A Genealogy of Participatory Development." *Refugee Survey Quarterly* 28 (2–3): 412–37.

Ringmar, Erik. 1996. "On the Ontological Status of the State." *European Journal of International Relations* 2 (4): 439–66.

Rosenfeld, Maya. 2004. *Confronting the Occupation: Work, Education, and Political Activism of Palestinian Families in a Refugee Camp*. Stanford: Stanford University Press.

Rougier, Bernard. 2007. *Everyday Jihad: The Rise of Militant Islam among Palestinians in Lebanon*. Cambridge, MA: Harvard University Press.

Roy, Sara. 2011. *Hamas and Civil Society in Gaza: Engaging the Islamist Social Sector*. Princeton: Princeton University Press.

Sabella, Bernard. 2001. "La socialisation politique des jeunes Palestinians: Positions des Adolescents et de leur parents en matiere de politique et de societe." *Monde Arabe: Maghreb Machrek* 171–172: 42–51.

Saghieh, Nizar, and Rana Saghieh. 2008. "Legal Assessment of Housing, Land and Property Ownership, Rights, Transfers, and Property Law related to Palestinian Refugees in Lebanon.". Beirut: Norwegian Refugee Council.

Sayigh, Rosemary. 1994. *Too Many Enemies: The Palestinian Experience in Lebanon*. London: Zed.

———. 2001. "Palestinian Refugees in Lebanon: Implantation, Transfer or Return?" *Middle East Policy* 8 (1): 94–105.

———. 2007. *The Palestinians: From Peasants to Revolutionaries*. London: Zed.

———. 2011. "Palestinian Camp Refugee Identificatios: A New Look at the 'Local' and the 'National.'" In *Palestinian Refugees: Identity, Space and Place in the Levant*, edited by Are Knudsen and Sari Hanafi, 50–64. London: Routledge.

———. 2012. "Palestinian Refugee Identity/ies: Generation, Region, Class." In *Palestinian Refugees: Different Generations, But One Identity*, 13–28. Birzeit, Palestine: Birzeit University.

Sayigh, Yezid. 1997. *Armed Struggle and the Search for State: The Palestinian National Movement 1949–1993*. Oxford, UK: Clarendon.

Schanzer, Jonathan. 2008. *Hamas vs. Fatah: The Struggle for Palestine*. New York: Palgrave Macmillan.

Schatz, Edward, ed. 2009. *Political Ethnography: What Immersion Contributes to the Study of Power*. Chicago: University of Chicago Press.

Schenker, David. 2008. "The Future of U.S. Military Aid to Lebanon." *PolicyWatch 1407*. Washington, DC: The Washington Institute. Accessed December 31, 2012. http://www.washingtoninstitute.org/policy-analysis/view/the-future-of-u.s.-military-aid-to-lebanon.

Schulz, Helena Lindholm and Hammer, Juliane. 2003. *The Palestinian Diaspora: Formation of Identities and Politics of Homeland*. London: Routledge.

Sfeir, Jihane. 2010. "Palestinians In Lebanon: The Birth of the 'Enemy Within.'" In *Manifestations of Identity: The Lived Reality of Palestinian Refugees in Lebanon*, edited by Muhammad Ali Khalidi, 13–34. Beirut: Institut Francais du Proche-Orient and The Institute For Palestine Studies.

Sharma, Aradhana, and Akhil Gupta. 2006. "Introduction: Rethinking Theories of the State in an Age of Globalization." In *The Anthropology of the State: A Reader*, edited by Aradhana Sharma and Akhil Gupta, 1–48. Oxford: Blackwell Publishing.

Shehata, Samer. 2006. "Ethnography, Identity, And The Production Of Knowledge." In *Interpretation And Method: Empirical Research Methods And The Interpretive Turn*, edited by Dvora Yanow and Peregrine Schwartz-Shea, 244–63. Armonk, NY: M.E. Sharpe.

Sheikh Hassan, Ismael, and Sari Hanafi. 2010. "(In)Security and Reconstruction in Post-Conflict Nahr al-Barid Refuge Camp." *Journal of Palestine Studies* 40 (1): 27–48.

Singerman, Diane. 1995. *Avenues of Participation: Family, Politics and Networks in Urban Quarters of Cairo*. Princeton, NJ: Princeton University Press.

SolidarityPalestine. 2012. *AlBared—Demands of Demonstrators*. June 17, 2012. Accessed February 27, 2014. http://www.youtube.com/watch?v=FpwVLoLQBKo.

Soss, Joe. 2006. "Talking Our Way to Meaningful Explanations: A Practice-Centered View of Interviewing for Interpretive Research." In *Interpretation And Method: Empirical Research Methods And The Interpretive Turn*, edited by Dvora Yanow and Peregrine Schwartz-Shea, 127–49. Armonk, NY: M.E. Sharpe.

Strindberg, Anders. 2000. "The Damascus-Based Alliance of Palestinian Forces: A Primer." *Journal of Palestine Studies* 29 (3): 60–76.

Sukarieh, Mayssoun, and Stuart Tannock. 2013. "On the Problem of Over-researched Communities: The Case of the Shatila Palestinian Refugee Camp in Lebanon." *Sociology* 47 (3): 494–508.

Suleiman, Jaber. 1997. "Palestinians in Lebanon and the Role of Non-Governmental Organizations." *Journal of Refugee Studies* 10 (3): 397–410.

———. 1999. "The Current Political, Organizational, and Security Situation in the Palestinian Refugee Camps of Lebanon." *Journal of Palestine Studies* 29 (1): 66–80.

———. 2001. "The Palestinian Liberation Organization: From the Right of Return to Bantustan." In *Palestinian Refugees: The Right of Return*, edited by Naseer Aruri, 87–104. London: Pluto.

———. 2006. "Marginalised Community: The Case of Palestinian Refugees in Lebanon." Brighton: University of Sussex—Development Research Centre on Migration, Globalisation and Poverty.

Svoboda, Eva, Veronique Barbelet, and Irina Mosel. 2018. "Holding the Keys: Humanitarian Access and Local Organizations." *Humanitarian Policy Group Report*. Accessed February 23, 2021. https://www.odi.org/publications/11023-holding-keys-humanitarian-access-and-local-organisations.

Taarnby, Michael, and Lars Hallundbaek. 2008. "Fatah al-Islam: Anthropological Perspectives on Jihadi Culture." Working Paper. Madrid: Real Instituto Elcano. http://www.realinstitutoelcano.org/wps/portal/rielcano_eng/Content?WCM_GLOBAL_CONTEXT=/elcano/elcano_in/zonas_in/dt6-2008.

Taraki, Lisa, ed. 2006. *Living Palestine: Family Survival, Resistance, and Mobility Under Occupation*. Syracuse, NY: Syracuse University Press.

Taussig, Michael. 1992. "Maleficium: State Fetishism." In *The Nervous System*, 111–40. New York, NY: Routledge.

The Daily Star. 2006. "Camp Shootout kills Palestinian Security Officer" *The Daily Star [Online]*, November 25, 2006. Accessed March 3, 2012. http://www.dailystar.com.lb/News/Local -News/Nov/25/Camp-shootout-kills-Palestinian-security-officer.ashx#axzz2 MVdT12dA.

———. 2007. "Army Keeps Cordon Around Refugee Camp Near Tripoli After Clashes." *The Daily Star [Online]*, March 21, 2007. http://www.dailystar.com.lb/News/Local -News/Mar/21/Army-keeps-cordon-around-refugee-camp-near-Tripoli-after-clashes .ashx#axzz2G8W4lXQv.

The White House. 2013. "Fact Sheet: U.S. Security Assistance to Lebanon." Washington, DC: The White House. Accessed November 3, 2013. http://wh.gov/l2hwS.

Tobin, Sarah, and Madeline Otis. 2016. "NGO Governance and Syrian Refugee 'Subjects' in Jordan." *Middle East Research and Information Project* 278. Accessed February 23, 2021. https://merip.org/2016/04/ngo-governance-and-syrian-refugee-subjects-in-jordan.

Usher, Graham. 2006. "The Democratic Resistance: Hamas, Fatah, and the Palestinian Elections." *Journal of Palestine Studies* 35 (3): 20–36.

Wedeen, Lisa. 1999. *Ambiguities of Domination: Politics, Rhetoric and Symbols in Contemporary Syria*. Chicago: University of Chicago Press.

———. 2010. "Reflections on Ethnographic Work in Political Science." *Annual Review of Political Science* 13: 255–72.

Worth, Mary Hawke. 2006. "Contending Conceptions of Science and Politics: Methodology and the Constitution of the Political." In *Interpretation And Method: Empirical Research Methods And The Interpretive Turn*, edited by Dvora Yanow and Peregrine Schwartz-Shea, 27–49. Armonk, NY: M.E. Sharpe.

INDEX

Page references in *italics* indicate photographs.

167

Founded in 1893,
UNIVERSITY OF CALIFORNIA PRESS
publishes bold, progressive books and journals
on topics in the arts, humanities, social sciences,
and natural sciences—with a focus on social
justice issues—that inspire thought and action
among readers worldwide.

The UC PRESS FOUNDATION
raises funds to uphold the press's vital role
as an independent, nonprofit publisher, and
receives philanthropic support from a wide
range of individuals and institutions—and from
committed readers like you. To learn more, visit
ucpress.edu/supportus.